Mary Ann —
Thank you.

Fred

The Justice Diary

This compelling collection of interviews and case studies reveals the gap between just responses to crime and the outcomes of criminal justice proceedings. They are at once unsettling and inspiring.

— **Dale DeWild**, Professor of Sociology (ret.), Central College in Pella, Iowa

Van Liew gives voice to parents and youth, prosecutors and public defenders, judges and everyday citizens, raising critical questions about due process, race, class, and punishment. Threaded throughout the stories, he offers a better compass using the foundational concepts of restorative justice.

— **Nancy Berns**, Professor of Sociology, Drake University,
and author of *Closure: The Rush to End Grief and What It Costs Us*

Through the intimate insights of this diary we glimpse the many faces of those caught up in our current justice system: victims, offenders, justice professionals, and community members.
Van Liew's vignettes of people seeking transformation give us all grounds for hope.

— **T. Richard Snyder**, PhD, Chair of the Restorative Justice Institute
of Maine and author of *The Protestant Ethic and the Spirit of Punishment*

The Justice Diary

An Inquiry into Justice in America

FRED VAN LIEW

The Justice Diary: An Inquiry into Justice in America
Copyright © 2015 Fred Van Liew
Kikus Press, Des Moines

Aside from brief passages in a published review, no part of this book may be reproduced or transmitted in any form or by any means, electronic or mechanical, including all technologies known or later developed, without written permission from the publisher.

Some names and locations have been changed to protect privacy.

Cover photo: Roman Bonnefoy, "Affichage sauvage rue de l'Arbalète à Paris," www.romanceor.net. Used with permission.
Cover and page design: Trio Bookworks

For speaking engagements, consulting, and other inquiries, contact Fred Van Liew at fvanliew@gmail.com.

Library of Congress Control Number: 2015905484

ISBN, print: 978-0-9962679-0-8
ISBN, ebook: 978-0-9962679-1-5

Printed in the United States of America

Contents

Foreword

Howard Zehr

Reading this collection of essays (and it's hard to put this down, once started), I have to admit to some envy. Fred Van Liew is living one of my dreams: wandering the country, listening, observing, conversing with all sorts of people. Admittedly, though, Fred has the personality for it, and I, as an introvert, probably don't.

In a textbook I've used when teaching research classes, the authors differentiate between two metaphors for the knowledge-seeker (researcher)—miner and traveler. The miner sees knowledge as something buried in people, who are "subjects," so the researcher is the expert who digs it up, recognizes its value, and puts it to use. Subjects and their knowledge are considered unrefined raw material to be used by the researcher, who must not contaminate it and who is an objective expert, personally affected by the exchange little if at all.

Travelers, on the other hand, are on a journey through the land with a story to tell upon return. As wanderers, they enter into conversations and explore the territory, returning with a story that is the result of these interactions. They are personally affected by this experience and view the people they interact with as equals and co-creators of knowledge. I have encouraged my students to be travelers rather than miners.

According to the authors of the research text, the Latin meaning of "conversation" is "wandering together with." In this set of reflections, or diary entries, Fred is clearly a traveler; he is having "conversations with." He embodies a key value of restorative justice, of which he is a proponent: the importance of respectful listening and dialogue.

As a former prosecutor, Fred is in a unique insider/outsider position. He knows the system from the inside, and, when he drops in on justice officials or court, has credibility as a result. Yet, because he is no longer in this role and, more importantly, because of his willingness to listen and learn, he is trusted by outsiders as well.

One of Fred's observations about the crisis in the American justice system is that it lacks curiosity and imagination. This is exactly what Fred brings to his journey and to these reflections, and this is why his essays are so insightful.

Something is clearly wrong with our justice system. A chorus of academic analyses is emerging, and these are important. But in *The Justice Diary* Fred puts his finger on the crux of things by listening to real people and sharing their experiences through his own reflections. This is his report on "wandering with"—on how it has affected him, and what it suggests for us as a society.

Howard Zehr is Co-Director of the Zehr Institute for Restorative
Justice and Distinguished Professor of Restorative Justice
at the Center for Justice & Peacebuilding,
Eastern Mennonite University

Author's Note

This book is, as the title suggests, a diary of sorts. It is a record of a year, plus a few months, during which I attempted to look at my world through a justice lens. In doing so, injustices in our country, many of which I had ignored or paid little attention to, were brought into greater focus. It documents my travels, within my hometown and throughout the country, which introduced me to individuals deeply affected by "the system" as well as those deeply concerned with the harm it can do, and oftentimes does, to people and their communities.

The Justice Diary recounts conversations It had with police officers, lawyers, court personnel, ministers, professors, restorative justice advocates, community organizers, educators, victims of racial bias and racial profiling, ex-offenders, and other ordinary people. It recounts my observations of the business of justice, as a citizen spectator at court appearances, hearings, and trials in courthouses from Manhattan and Mississippi to Iowa and New Mexico. And at times, it recounts experiences I had while serving as a prosecutor for more than two decades.

Actually, I was a prosecutor twice. For two years in the mid-'80s and from 1991 until my retirement in the fall of 2010. I never thought I would be a prosecutor. Nothing I had ever read or seen suggested I should be one. From an early age I assumed I would be a criminal defense attorney, like Clarence Darrow or Perry Mason. But it happened. For nearly twenty years I was a bureau chief in the criminal bureau of the Polk County Attorney's Office in Des Moines, Iowa. Among other tasks, I made charging decisions and assigned cases. I had been an attorney since 1984, but it wasn't until I became a bureau chief and discovered firsthand the weight of responding to criminal wrongdoing that I experienced what it was like to be a cog in a machine. Each day was a day of reviewing arrest warrant requests and new criminal charges, and observing overcrowded courtrooms, mass guilty pleas, guilty pleas taken at the jail for the sake of expediency, and probation and parole revocation hearings in which the burdensome and oftentimes unrealistic expectations placed on offenders resulted in failure and a return to jail or prison. I knew something was wrong, but I couldn't describe the illness or articulate a cure.

I considered quitting only a few months into the job, but before I could, I received a letter. It was from a friend of mine, a minister. We had worked together on homeless issues a few years earlier when I was a Legal Aid attorney. He wrote that I needed to find out about something called "restorative justice." He said it might make a difference, that restorative justice had the potential to make sense of a senseless system. He gave me enough information so that I could start looking into it. I found out soon enough that restorative justice had been around since the '70s and that Howard Zehr, the founder of the restorative justice movement in the United States, had written a provocative book titled *Changing Lenses*. I ordered a copy, read it on a Sunday, and was changed. What I learned was that in the United States we look at criminal wrongdoing through the wrong lens, a punishment lens. Zehr suggested that we should, instead, use a reparative lens and that we should respond to criminal wrongdoing by bringing victims and offenders together in dialogue. The benefit, he said, was that stories of harm and loss could be told and remedies could be discussed and agreed to.

I took Zehr's vision to heart, and for nearly twenty years attempted as best I could to be a restorative justice prosecutor, to the extent that the traditional system would allow. There was no road map, but there was some progress, and many people—victims and offenders—benefited by being given the opportunity to engage in conversations that addressed their real needs. Some of the entries in this book tell the stories of some of the transformations that came about.

I think it's important for the reader to know that much of what is contained in these pages first appeared online in the *Justice Diary* blog. Beginning in January 2013, I blogged regularly for a little over a year, when at home and when on the road, sometimes while in a local library or coffee shop, but just as often while sitting on the tailgate of my pickup truck or in my tent late at night. I blogged because that gave me a good way to capture and reflect on the injustices, big and small, that came into my field of vision. Many of the posts chosen for the book offer a glimpse of ordinary people's experiences with the system—through the eyes of a former prosecutor looking at it through a justice lens.

Blogging as a genre is generally informal in style. It's a style I'm well suited for, having never been particularly adept at writing research papers. As a result, the selections made for this book, although revised and edited, are also informal. Each is independent and self-contained. They stand on their own. Although I hope most readers choose to start at the beginning and read through to the end, it's not absolutely necessary. Opening this book at any page will give the reader a snapshot of where I was, who I met, and what my thoughts were about justice, and injustice, on a particular day.

Our country, as a result of increased media attention given to the failed war on drugs, to the scourge of mass incarceration, and to the appalling number of wrongful convictions, is becoming much more intolerant of a criminal justice system that is antiquated and nonresponsive to the real needs of the people, victims and offenders (who, often, have been victims themselves) alike. In the aftermath of the deaths of Michael Brown in Ferguson, Eric Garner in New York City, Walter Scott in North Charleston, Freddie Gray in

Baltimore, and countless others, we can no longer pretend that all police, prosecutors, and judges always do their work competently and ethically. It is my hope that this book will, in some small way, add to the growing cry for justice in this country and prompt its readers to take more time to look at their world through a restorative lens.

About the Quotation in the Cover Art

Gandhi's words symbolize one of the central problems of our criminal justice system: its focus on punishment. But blindness—that is, the condition of having partial or entire vision loss—is often used as a synonym for ignorance. This is a cruel irony, since people with disabilities are overrepresented in our justice system and also frequently victims of violence. So I am reminded that powerful metaphors can have unintended consequences, even as I interpret Gandhi's message to be strictly about the cyclical nature of violence and revenge.

Acknowledgments

*I would like to thank my mother, who taught me about injustice,
Michael McBride, who taught me about social justice,
and Howard Zehr, who taught me about restorative justice.
A special thanks to Ann Delgehausen, my editor,
who cared enough to make me work hard.*

The Justice Diary

Atonement

Members of the Temple B'nai Jeshurun woke on a Saturday morning to find neo-Nazi graffiti scrawled on the side of their synagogue. There were no suspects, but there was anger and outrage.

At one level, the incident was a galvanizing experience, bringing together the broader religious community in a way never witnessed in Des Moines. At another, however, it brought forth shadows normally hidden within many good and well-intentioned people; some cried out for a justice like that sought by vigilantes and lynch mobs.

Two weeks later an eighteen-year-old male and a seventeen-year-old girl—boyfriend and girlfriend—were charged with felony criminal mischief. I held on to the case rather than assigning it to a felony prosecutor. And I called Steven Fink, the rabbi at Temple B'nai Jeshurun, asking how he was doing, and how members of the temple were doing. He told me he was angry, that others were angry and afraid. I asked if he had ever heard of restorative justice and then described its potential for healing. I asked if he would consider meeting with the young offenders.

He said my description of restorative justice made sense to him, and that it was consistent with his tradition, but in this instance he thought that neither he nor temple members would consider meeting the offenders. I thanked him for his time, gave him my number, and encouraged him to call if he had questions. He did, a week later to the day.

Rabbi Fink told me there had been much discussion following our phone conversation. He said there were some temple members who saw the wisdom of a meeting and others who said a meeting would be used to minimize the harm done and would result in the offenders receiving just a slap on the wrist. But in the end, a consensus was reached that the temple should go forward with a meeting, even in the face of uncertainty and possible revictimization.

It was agreed that an evening meeting would take place at the synagogue. The people representing the interests of the temple at large would be the rabbi, two Holocaust survivors who had gone into hiding following the graffiti desecration of the synagogue, a former member of the Israeli army, and three temple elders. The young offenders would be accompanied by their attorneys, I would be present in my role as prosecutor, and an experienced mediator would facilitate the conversation.

The evening came. We found ourselves seated around a large conference table at the synagogue. Low lighting and centerpieces made of candles and flowers set a tone appropriate for the seriousness of the gathering. Following the requisite introductions, an explanation of the process, and the signing of a confidentiality agreement, the stories began.

They flowed out—hesitatingly at first, and then in a rush, with tears, anger, and fear. Old memories were resurrected. Details of childhood nights in concentration camps rose to the surface. Stories were told of the struggle to survive, to grow up, to make a life, to raise a family despite the scars and the nightmares. This night, for everyone present, there was no escaping what had happened fifty years earlier, in a foreign land, to those who had died and to those who had survived.

The offenders had stories of their own. The young man, eighteen years old but looking only twelve, had run away from home two years earlier. He'd been abused physically and emotionally by his stepfather. He suffered from hearing loss and a speech defect. He was taunted at school. He made his way to Alabama. Members of the Aryan Nation admitted him to their school, where for months he was indoctrinated in the ways of bigotry and hate.

His education completed, he left the school and made his way back to Iowa, where he hoped to recruit and nurture his own community of neo-Nazis. His success was limited: his only recruit was the girl who fell under the spell of his vision. The two came up with a plan to spread their message and draw attention to their cause. The synagogue was a logical target.

The gulf between the experiences of the synagogue members and the teenagers was wide. But over the course of the evening, as people exchanged stories, the gulf narrowed. Self-awareness gave way to awareness of others. For the young man, pictures of Jews from photo albums he had studied at the Aryan Nation school were replaced by faces of wisdom and suffering.

The temple members, slowly at first, came to see the offenders for what they were—lost, abused, and frightened children. Early calls to "throw the book" at the two gave way to compassionate understanding that there must be a better way.

One of the Holocaust survivors asked the young man what he wanted from the temple members. He replied that he wanted forgiveness. Rabbi Fink, who had been silent for much of the evening, spoke. He said that in his tradition, the tradition of Abraham, Isaac, and Jacob, forgiveness had to be earned and, in this instance, nothing had been done to earn it. He spoke of atonement and its importance to the Jewish community. He said that if the two were to atone for their transgressions, then—and only then—forgiveness would be possible.

And so it was in the context of atonement that the victims and the offenders came together in an effort to construct a plan to make it possible for forgiveness to be earned. The temple members wanted the two to succeed: to earn their way out of the guilt that had overtaken them that evening.

Following a dialogue befitting the tradition the synagogue honored, the victims and the offenders decided together that the two teenagers would each perform 200 hours of service—100 under the supervision of the temple's custodian and 100 with Rabbi Fink, meeting weekly to study Jewish and Holocaust history. Also, the temple would help the young man find a hearing specialist, the young man would have his Nazi tattoos removed, and both teenagers would obtain job-seeking skills, psychological assessments, and their GEDs.

A second meeting would be held in six months. If the two had atoned in the manner agreed to, forgiveness would be given, and the temple, through Rabbi Fink, would recommend that the criminal charges be dismissed.

In the best biblical tradition, it all came to pass. The young man and young woman worked hard, exceeding the expectations of the custodian and Rabbi Fink. They gained confidence in themselves as the result of their physical and intellectual labors, and from establishing new relationships. They passed their high school equivalency exams, secured employment, got married, and had a child. The rabbi and the custodian were invited to their wedding, which the custodian was able to attend. The temple gave the young couple a wedding gift. Five years later, at a gathering of restorative justice practitioners, supporters, and police, Rabbi Fink held back tears while speaking of the two young offenders who had become his friends.

* * *

I take classes at Eastern Mennonite University. With their new technology I'm linked with restorative justice practitioners from around the world. Practitioners from other countries often ask why it is that the United States has the highest incarceration rate in the world. They ask how our communities might engage in a dialogue with justice system professionals to look objectively at what works and what doesn't. They ask whose role it is to commence a dialogue and sustain it. They wonder when the "us versus them" attitude pervading our present system will give way to an attitude that says "we're all in this together"—that we can no longer afford to fill our jails and prisons, creating an underclass in our society with little chance of succeeding and contributing to the greater good. Shouldn't we be asking these questions in our communities?

Juvenile Justice—Is There a Better Way?

It's 3 in the morning, and I can't sleep. I'm thinking of my grandson. I'm thinking of his innocence, of his newly emerging smile, of his incredible blue eyes that light up so delightfully when he is attended to. And I'm thinking of the conversation I had one afternoon recently with a distraught mother.

She called to tell me the story of her son, a bright and engaging seventeen-year-old: A boy with so much promise, like my grandson. A nearly straight-A student who has already earned more than a year of college credit. A boy who had never had the slightest brush with the law—until recently.

She wanted to tell me, all in one breath it seemed, what her son had done and how he'd been treated. Her boy hadn't murdered anyone, hadn't burglarized the home of an elderly couple, hadn't assaulted and robbed someone. But he had done something wrong. While employed part-time at a local store, he had wrongly processed some credit card applications. The store has an incentive program for initiating credit card applications, and the boy received at least $100 he wasn't entitled to.

After his actions were discovered, store security descended upon him. He was removed from his work station and taken to a small room inside the store. For nearly two hours, while one security worker guarded the only possible exit, a second employee interrogated the boy. They told him to turn off his cell phone. They did not inform him that he could remain silent or contact his parents. One employee told the boy that he'd been caught red-handed and needed to confess or the police would be called.

Wanting to get out of the room and get home, the boy finally signed a confession and a second document indicating that he agreed to pay the store a civil penalty. But that wasn't the end of it. The police were called.

No one asked the boy for his side of the story. The so-called evidence obtained by store security was all the police needed to charge him. The police didn't call the boy's parents. Instead, they put him in handcuffs and took him into custody, leading him through the store in plain view before placing him in the back of a patrol car. He sat there until a police wagon arrived to take him to the Polk County IA Juvenile Detention Center, where he was turned over to different authorities.

The detention center is a state-of-the-art facility for which Polk County residents deserve to be proud. If you go to the Polk County website you'll find that the center "will provide safe and secure detention care for juveniles who require custody pending disposition and placement."

For parents who've never had a child taken to the center it's important to know the means by which juveniles held at the facility are prevented from leaving the premises: locked doors, fences, other mechanical fixtures, and staff security.

Apparently, this boy, this model student who'd never been in trouble but who made a mistake, required custody in a safe and secure detention facility behind locked doors that would keep him from escaping.

And what about the law? If you look at Chapter 232 of the Iowa Code, you will find that a child accused of committing a delinquent act shall not be placed in detention unless one of the following circumstances is present: "(1) There is a substantial probability that the child will run away or otherwise be unavailable for subsequent court appearance. (2) There is a serious risk that the child if released may commit an act that would inflict serious bodily harm on the child or on another. (3) There is a serious risk that the child if released may commit serious damage to the property of others."

I wonder what law the police were following when they transported the honor student in handcuffs to a detention center.

Putting the law aside, and even putting aside the impact on this boy, what is the cost to taxpayers when the detention center is utilized? According to the director of community and family services, it costs Polk County $440 a day to detain a child—totaling nearly $4 million in fiscal year 2011–2012.

So what became of this boy?

Fortunately, detention center staff called his parents and he was released to them. Two weeks later, the boy and his parents met with a juvenile court officer who treated them with respect. The officer said he'd made several inquiries of the store to obtain information about the boy's actions because the police report did not sufficiently support the filing of a delinquency petition.

Although the family was informed they could fight the allegations, the boy said he just wanted "to get it over with." He entered into an agreement requiring him to meet periodically with a juvenile court officer, perform community service, and commit no more crimes.

Later, I asked the boy's mother how he was really doing. She replied that things were different. He had shut down. He didn't want to talk, and he'd lost interest in pursuing his college dreams.

According to the director of community and family services, it costs Polk County $440 a day to detain a child—totaling nearly $4 million in fiscal year 2011–2012.

Then she questioned me: How could this have been handled differently? Wasn't there a better way? How many other boys have been treated this way? What about the boys who are not honor students? What about the boys of color? Her boy had accepted responsibility for his actions, but what about the store? What about the police? What should she tell her son?

I asked myself: What should I tell my grandson about justice when he is seventeen? Perhaps justice will look different by then. Perhaps as a society we will have learned to be less retributive. Maybe the American trail-'em-nail-'em-jail 'em brand of justice will have given way to a more restorative one in which apologies are more important than confessions, and restitution is more important than incarceration.

A long-time Department of Corrections official once told me that roughly 40 percent of criminal wrongdoers are "self-correcting." What he meant was that more than one-third of those who have an initial contact with the justice system never need to have contact with it again—that first brush with the law is all that's necessary. Let the wrongdoer go and you will never see him or her again. The embarrassment and shame are both the punishment and the cure.

What if the store security staff had chosen not to interrogate the boy but instead called his parents and held a restorative meeting?

What if the boy had been given a second chance and what was owed to the store was taken out of his future wages? If for some reason the police had to be involved, what if they'd called the parents and helped the boy and his parents work with store officials to devise an accountability plan?

What if it had been decided that more punishment was needed? What if it had been left to the parents to decide the what, when, and where of it? What concerned parent would not be up to that task?

We Need to Repair, Not Throw Away

My first grandchild was born three months ago. I turned sixty last week. Neither retirement nor raising five children has prepared me to be a sexagenarian grandpa. These milestones remind me of how I felt when I first noticed my graying hair at the age of forty. But it's different this time. What they say is true: You really do begin to care less about yourself and more about the next generation and the one after that. You begin to see toddlers not as spillers of milk but as future saviors of our planet. You begin to see teenagers not for the trouble they cause but for the hidden promise that exists within them.

But these new perspectives are in conflict with society's tendency to throw away rather than repair. Michelle Alexander, author of *The New Jim Crow: Mass Incarceration in the Age of Colorblindness*, jars us with a shocking statistic: In less than thirty years, the prison population in the United States exploded from around 300,000 to more than 2 million, with drug convictions accounting for the majority of the increase. As a result, the United States has the highest incarceration rate in the world—eight times that of Germany, for example. Even those of us who see the tragedy in these numbers feel powerless to do anything for the lost souls who are frequently paroled to lives of marginalization and despair, unable to find meaningful and productive work to support their families and their communities.

But what about the kids? What about those yet to turn eighteen who make mistakes? Is it too late for them?

There was a time when our experts and researchers were convinced that even the most troubled children could be rehabilitated. Unfortunately, that era gave way to the rhetoric of politicians who railed that we have to be tough on crime, no matter the age of the offender. Public money was shifted from support for families and effective programs to more law enforcement, more lawyers, more judges, and more detention facilities.

Perhaps the tide is turning.

The *Des Moines Register* reported recently that juvenile arrests are declining in Iowa, fewer youth are committing crimes, and the number of youth in the juvenile system is down. The numbers in part reflect a new philosophy of keeping youth out of the juvenile justice system as long as possible because the deeper kids get into the system, particularly low-risk kids, the more likely it is that they will be damaged.

Last month, in *Miller v. Alabama*, a landmark decision concerning juveniles and cruel and unusual punishment, the U.S. Supreme Court cited evidence about "children's diminished culpability and heightened capacity for change."

Writing for the majority, and quoting from previous cases, Justice Elena Kagan stated: "'[Y]outh is more than a chronological fact.' . . . It is a time of immaturity, irresponsibility, 'impetuousness[,] and recklessness.' . . . It is a moment and 'condition of life when a person may be most susceptible to influence and to psychological damage.'". . . Justice Kagan further commented that "our history is replete with laws and judicial recognition that children cannot be viewed simply as miniature adults."

So what's been happening in Polk County with our juvenile justice system?

According to the Des Moines Police Department, juvenile arrests declined from 2,178 in 2006 to 1,133 in 2010, a 48 percent decrease over five years. During the same time frame, Polk County court records show that delinquency petitions—the documents filed by prosecutors to get kids into court—declined from 717 in 2006 to 355 in 2010, a 50 percent decrease over five years.

Clearly, the decline in prosecutor filings was consistent with the decline in police arrests.

What about 2011? Des Moines arrests went up slightly, from 1,133 to 1,176, a statistically insignificant 3 percent. However, prosecutor filings increased from 355 to 868 in 2011, a whopping 145 percent increase.

What happened? Why the sudden reversal by the Polk County attorney, despite research that shows damage can be done by putting kids further into the system? What does the county attorney think of the philosophy of keeping youth out of the juvenile justice system as long as possible?

Though statewide statistics don't appear to suggest it, perhaps there is a new philosophy developing among prosecutors that runs counter to the most recent research findings.

* * *

In my semiretirement I work with individuals and groups interested in restorative justice, a philosophy that says that crime is fundamentally a violation of people and relationships. These violations create obligations and responsibilities. Proponents of restorative justice say our retributive system of punishment and incarceration should move toward a more restorative approach, one that seeks to heal and put right the wrongs.

In April I attended a meeting at the Cumberland County Courthouse in Portland, Maine. The courtroom was packed with prosecutors, defense attorneys, juvenile court officers, and mediators—all present to hear about restorative justice. I had visited Portland on three prior occasions to train a group from a local Unitarian church that was starting its own community-based restorative justice program.

At the April meeting, Elizabeth Chapman, leader of the church initiative, told how the congregation had voted a year earlier to create a restorative justice center. The center would be a vehicle to help keep kids out of the formal justice system if possible.

The chief juvenile prosecutor in the Cumberland County district attorney's office followed Chapman. She said the local juvenile system supports keeping youth out of court and that the program offered by the church offers the necessary accountability without burdening the court system or stigmatizing young people.

These children and grandchildren are everyone's responsibility. If we forget that, they will soon be the adults who fill our overcrowded prisons.

So is there a new philosophy among prosecutors? Is what is happening in Polk County an aberration?

William Stuntz, a former prosecutor and Harvard Law School professor, articulated the ills of our current justice system in *The Collapse of American Criminal Justice*. He concludes: "The criminals we incarcerate are not some alien enemy. Nor, for that matter, are the police and prosecutors who seek to fight crime in those criminals' neighborhoods. Neither side of this divide is 'them.' Both sides are us. Democracy and justice alike depend on getting that most basic principle of human relations right."

* * *

I was a prosecutor until a few years ago, and I often advised the Department of Human Services in child welfare cases. I was reminded daily of the importance of grandparents in the lives of children in the care and custody of DHS. Grandparents are less about timeouts and more about taking time.

Perhaps the Polk County attorney's office should hire some grand-parents to bring a fresh perspective to juvenile justice—a perspective that would look beyond court filings and get-tough approaches, and focus on the reality that these children and grandchildren are every-one's responsibility.

If we forget that, they will soon be the adults who fill our over-crowded prisons. What then will be the financial cost? More impor-tant, what will be the cost to human potential and human dignity?

Keeping an Eye on Justice

Have you ever wondered how our justice system works? You might think you know from watching *Law and Order*, *Boston Legal*, or *The Practice*, or from following a murder trial covered by the news. But if you really want to know what justice looks like for defendants, vic-tims, and witnesses, spend a morning or afternoon at the courthouse on Fifth and Mulberry in downtown Des Moines. For every case that draws media attention, there are hundreds of others important only to those involved. Walk into any criminal or juvenile courtroom and you will get an education on what the police stop people for and which crimes judges consider serious enough for sending offenders to jail or prison. You will observe defense attorneys who zealously advocate for their clients and attorneys who don't. If you are fortu-nate, you will see prosecutors who have a sense of the spirit of the law as well as the letter of the law.

Recently, I received a call from a friend who knew that I volunteer with A Mid-Iowa Organizing Strategy (AMOS, a community orga-nizing group comprised of nearly thirty area churches advocating for social justice). AMOS's justice research team was starting a Court Watch program modeled after similar efforts around the country. He asked if I would observe a juvenile hearing at the courthouse the next day. A judge would be considering whether a sixteen-year-old girl would be released to her mother or spend Christmas at the detention center. In August, police stopped the girl for public intoxication and, because she made some poor decisions since then, she was placed in detention on November 30. My friend said the judge who presided over the previous hearing had treated the girl's mother poorly.

The next day I met the mother at the courthouse. We sat outside the courtroom for thirty minutes until being advised that the hearing had been moved to the third floor. We arrived just in time to see her daughter being led down the corridor wearing prison-like garb, her hands clasped together and wrists secured by leather restraints connected with a heavy-gauge chain. We followed her into the courtroom and found a seat in the back. The judge entered, introduced himself, and explained that he was filling in for the judge originally assigned the case. The prosecutor said she was filling in for another prosecutor. The defense attorney, having just met the girl outside the courtroom, said he was filling in for another public defender. It seemed the only person who knew anything about the case was the juvenile court officer who had been supervising the girl.

Although this was supposed to be a hearing, it didn't appear there would be testimony. The lawyers, juvenile court officer, and judge talked among themselves, but neither the girl nor her mother were called as witnesses. The only question was whether a "shelter bed" was available for the girl as an alternative to the locked detention center. When it became clear that the girl would not return home, I nudged the defense attorney and whispered that surely the mother had a right to say something. He reluctantly informed the judge that the mother wanted to speak. She rose and tearfully pleaded for her daughter to be released to her care. She then asked if she could give the judge an affidavit she had prepared. The judge received it, said he would put it in the court file, but that he didn't have time to read it as he only had five minutes. The saving grace for this girl was that while calls were being made to find a bed, the judge did read the affidavit and appeared to be moved. In the affidavit, copies of which were given to others in the courtroom, the mother referred to the previous court appearance:

> I am still in shock over what occurred at court. . . . I
> remember the judge informed me that I needed to show

participation in some type of services in order to regain my daughter. I did not know, no one throughout these years has even suggested, that I did something worthy of losing my daughter. . . . I may have simply caught the judge on a bad day. . . . It is my sincere hope that other young persons and their families are not treated the way I was in court on a hearing where every outward indication was that this was a court designed to aid my daughter.

The judge talked with the girl and accepted her commitment to participate in a day treatment program. He spoke with the mother again, who assured him she would contact authorities if her daughter failed to follow through. The judge entered an order releasing the girl to her mother.

Court watchers around the country are having an impact. They are asking how our justice systems can become more transparent. They are asserting that justice system professionals should be subject to scrutiny in the way other public servants are. They believe the general public should take a more active role in monitoring the decisions and performances of those entrusted with the business of justice in our communities.

The Justice Machine in New Mexico

Yesterday's drive from Liberal was a straight shot to Tucumcari. Highway 54 passed through flat land and the oil and gas fields of far western Oklahoma and Texas. I was surprised to see the fields give way at times to the white wind turbines I see in western and northwestern Iowa. Passing through Hooker, Oklahoma, I saw a sign announcing the "Texas County Juvenile Detention Center." I made a U-turn and drove east on a gravel road, arriving at a single story brown building with a barbed wire–enclosed basketball court. I parked, walked to the entrance, and pushed the security button, hoping to strike up a conversation. A middle-aged woman introduced herself as the director of the center. She opened the door slightly, wanting to know what I needed. I explained that I was retired, had been a juvenile prosecutor, and that I wanted to talk with someone about the center and about the juveniles detained there. She invited me in and offered a chair. She again asked what I wanted. I told her I was curious about how different jurisdictions deal with juveniles who end up in the system. I then asked how many beds were in the facility. She said six. I asked what the young people were in for. A lot of things, she said. I asked about the average length of stay. She said she couldn't say. I asked to what extent drugs were a problem. She again couldn't say. I asked a few more questions and the responses were just as vague. I finally gave up, thanked her, and excused myself. I walked to my truck and sat for a while, reviewing the road map. A patrol car pulled up with a deputy at the wheel. I asked if there was a problem and he said he was wondering what I was up to. I told him what I had told the director, and I asked if there was a problem. He sheepishly replied that the people inside were suspicious of me. I offered my driver's license. He declined and suggested I drive to the park and finish my business. I drove off, listening to an NPR interview with three officials from the California Department of Corrections. Their responses to callers were eerily similar to those of the director—hesitant, defensive, and non-responsive.

From Hooker I continued south on 54, passing through Texhoma and stopping for lunch in Stratford. Outside a Subway I tried striking up a conversation with a young Latino man, inquiring if I could ask him a few questions. I said I wasn't a police officer or someone he might not want to talk with. He was friendly but when I asked about the local police, the court system, and how young people are treated, he looked around with a hint of fear in his eyes and said he couldn't say anything. I thanked the young man for his time and continued on to Tucumcari, an uneventful drive through miles of open space, punctuated at times with islands of cattle stations that enclosed more cows than I have ever seen.

* * *

Over lunch, attorney David James of the New Mexico Public Defender Department spoke about what it means to represent the underdog against the state and its superior resources. He said most of his clients are poor and people of color, and in New Mexico, the farther south you go the harsher the justice imposed. His caseload is comprised primarily of felony property crimes. "Commercial burglary" is particularly discouraging because it is frequently the charge when someone who has been convicted of shoplifting and told not to return does return to the same store and is arrested a second time. David said the New Mexico legislature created the offense after strong lobbying by Walmart. And he reminded me that those at the bottom of our social ladder are treated far more harshly than those higher up and in a position to steal millions of dollars.

* * *

I spent yesterday afternoon at the county courthouse in Santa Fe. It's the courthouse used for domestic and family matters and for felony criminal cases. After passing through security, I wandered about the first floor looking for a trial. It appeared that people liked to take Friday afternoons off. After ascending the stairway to the second floor, I proceeded down one long hallway and then another, arriving at a door ajar. I entered into the rear of a large courtroom. A low gate separated about eighty spectators from two groups of lawyers, a judge seated on an elevated bench, court personnel, and a couple of armed deputies. To the right of the judge was a large television screen. On it were thirty men in prison clothing seated in rows.

I sat down in the first row behind the barrier, close enough to one group of attorneys so I could tap the nearest lawyer, a woman, on the shoulder. I asked if she was a defense attorney. She smiled and said she was a prosecutor and that the defense attorneys were seated at the large table across the way. She added that most of the defense attorneys were with the public defender office. The contrast between the suit-and-tie prosecutors and the jeans-wearing public defenders was striking. The prosecutor explained that felony pretrial conferences were taking place and that the defendants we could see on the monitor were in a room at the county jail some distance away. I sat back and watched. For two hours the orange-clad defendants, one after another, left their seats and moved to a table where they sat alone, staring into a camera. This occurred each time the judge in the courtroom called out a name and a number, also prompting a prosecutor and a defense attorney to leave their tables and stacks of files and approach a podium together. The lawyers spoke with the judge about what discovery had been done and still needed to be done, and whether the case would proceed to trial or result in a guilty plea. All but one of the court personnel, and all but one of the fifteen or so attorneys, appeared to be white. Every one of the defendants appeared to be Latino. Likewise, nearly every one of the spectators was brown skinned.

As the afternoon went on, the machinery of justice did its job well. Defendant after defendant took his seat before the camera, sometimes asking questions of his lawyers and sometimes volunteering information about a job awaiting him if he could just be released. Every defendant was a "pretrial detainee" being held in jail awaiting trial, unable to come up with enough money to post the set bond. I don't know what the fee is in New Mexico, but in most jurisdictions a defendant must give a bondsperson 10 percent of the total bond set by the judge. The bondsperson keeps all of the defendant's money, sometimes several thousands of dollars.

It's important to remember that each defendant is presumed innocent. Yet they remain in jail, awaiting trial, separated from their families, unable to pay their bills, and unable to participate in a meaningful way in their defense. Our system, so concerned that they might flee or miss a court date, incarcerates them, aggravating their already precarious situations.

One of the ironies is that most of them will be released at a later date, having entered a guilty plea or having been convicted at trial. They will have "served their time."

Is Justice Blind?

After observing the felony pretrial conferences at the Santa Fe courthouse, I made my way to a second courtroom. I opened the door slightly and could see that a trial was in progress. I entered, found a seat in the back, and adjusted my focus to a different kind of proceeding. Unlike the courtroom down the hall, this one had a jury box. Each of the twelve seats was taken, suggesting a criminal trial. No witnesses were being questioned. Instead, a distinguished-looking white man in his sixties was addressing the jury.

I had walked in on the closing arguments of the trial, and this attorney represented the defendant. Solemnly, he reminded the jurors of their responsibility to hold the prosecutor to his burden to prove, beyond a reasonable doubt, that the defendant was under the influence of alcohol when his vehicle was stopped a few months earlier. While making his argument the attorney pointed to his client, another distinguished-looking white man in his sixties, and insisted the jury presume the man innocent unless the prosecutor met his considerable burden.

I'd arrived too late to learn the important facts of the case, but not too late to witness a justice different from that taking place down the hall. There, public defenders represented the incarcerated men. Here, it appeared a fair amount of money had been paid to secure the best legal counsel to represent the accused drunk driver. There, the defendants were being held in jail, unable to make bail. Here, as I learned after the trial, the defendant lived out of state and had the resources to post bail and lead a normal life until making the trip to Santa Fe for his day in court.

Following the trial I spoke with the prosecutor. A bright young man, he was two years out of a Maine law school. In contrast to the three-piece tailored suit worn by the defense attorney, the young prosecutor wore a sport jacket and slacks that looked like they came off the rack at JCPenney.

Do differences in age, stature, influence, and clothing have an impact on jurors when they deliberate? What if the two attorneys were in opposite roles? What if the prosecutor was the elected county attorney, well respected in the Santa Fe community, whereas the attorney for the defendant was a public defender who had recently moved to the state?

I'm reminded of my first jury trial as a prosecutor, in 1984. The defendant, charged with a residential burglary, wore expensive clothes and gold chains around his neck. His attorney was at least ten years older than me, taught at a local college, and was as dapper as his client. My suit was from a second-hand store. Even though I presented evidence that the defendant had a heroin addiction and didn't have income sufficient to support his addiction let alone pay his bills, the jury found him not guilty.

When it was permissible, I telephoned three women who had been jurors. Each said that despite the logic that the defendant was stealing in order to support his addiction and himself, they had concluded that no one who could afford such nice clothing, expensive jewelry, and hire a high-priced lawyer would commit burglaries. What the jurors didn't know was the defendant had committed a string of burglaries that allowed him to purchase the clothing and jewelry. They also didn't know that the defense attorney was in private practice but had been appointed to represent his client who earlier said he didn't have the resources to hire a lawyer.

Why Isn't Justice Simpler?

The two-day drive home was uneventful. The unusually warm days suggested an early spring and its accompanying optimism. But occasionally I drifted back to observations and conversations that suggested a justice that is not blind, a justice that has a dark side: The prosecutor who told me that in Santa Fe justice goes lightly on the casual marijuana user because pot is the drug of choice of so many of the community's artists. The seasoned community organizer who shared that the farther south you go in New Mexico the tougher the law gets. The public defender in Albuquerque who spoke of corruption throughout the justice system. The two courtrooms where I observed one justice for the brown skinned and the poor, and another for the white and the well-to-do.

While driving, I shared some of these thoughts with Juliann, my middle child. Juliann, a graduate student in public health, has traveled widely—Europe, South America, India, and Africa. She has witnessed more inequities than most. But she hasn't become insensitive to injustice. She asked rhetorically: Why isn't justice simpler? Why don't we just ask whether or not someone has been hurt? Why don't we approach justice like the five-year-old who knows right from wrong instinctively? I told her that I couldn't easily answer her questions but that for thousands of years humankind has struggled with these questions and has attempted to construct systems to respond to wrongdoing within the community.

I told her about listening to Max Dimont's *Jews, God and History* on the drive through Kansas. Dimont writes about how the Jews, four centuries before the time of Jesus, designed a legal system based on the dignity of humanity and individual equality before the law. According to Dimont, individuals accused of crimes were considered innocent until proven guilty, had the right to confront their accusers, were allowed to testify on their own behalf, were not subject to double jeopardy, and could appeal convictions. Juliann said this sounded familiar. I went on to tell her that Mosaic law established the principle that people could do anything not specifically denied to them. Instead of saying, "Do such and such a thing," the laws typically said, "Don't do this or that." Even where Mosaic law made a positive statement, it was often either an amendment to a negative commandment or else hemmed in by a negative admonition, saying, in effect, "When you do this, then don't do that." By fencing in only the negative, Mosaic law left an open field for positive action, allowing people greater flexibility. As long as they did not do anything specifically prohibited, they could do anything they wanted to do.

Juliann said that when she was growing up she had the idea that this was how our justice system worked, but lately she wasn't so sure.

Follow-Up to "Keeping an Eye on Justice"

What a difference a month makes—and a newspaper article. In "Court Watching" I wrote about a hearing involving a sixteen-year-old girl detained for twenty days on a public intoxication charge. The girl and her mother had been treated poorly at a previous hearing. At the hearing I attended, a substitute judge released the girl to her mother over the Christmas holiday, requiring her to return to court in January. The mood at that December hearing was one of indifference. It wasn't until the judge read a statement prepared by the mother that the focus changed from the lawyers and their cell phones to the family before the court.

The mood in that same courtroom during the January hearing, held this past Friday, was markedly different. The *Des Moines Register* had published my account of the earlier hearing. There had been a great deal of talk in the courthouse about the article. At the December hearing I was treated rudely by the court attendant. Last Friday she was all smiles. In December the prosecutor barely spoke and seemed to care little about what was going on. Last Friday she was prepared, spoke competently, and was all smiles as well. I could go on. Suffice it to say everyone at Friday's hearing was on their A game. The girl's attorney, who had not attended the previous hearing, spent several minutes with her prior to the start of Friday's hearing, and the judge who had filled in at the last hearing had been assigned permanently to the girl's case—an odd and unexpected turn of events, according to the girl's attorney.

How much did my newspaper article influence this case? It's hard to say. Whether or not the outcome would have been different, it did appear that the level of respect for the family had risen considerably. More importantly, the young girl had been home for the past month rather than locked up. She spent Christmas with her family. She was participating in a day treatment program and doing well. Her relationship with her mother was greatly improved. She was in street clothes rather than jail clothes. She looked confident.

There will be another hearing in a month. The judge suggested that if the girl continued to participate in treatment and things went well at home, he would likely give the girl a consent decree, which means that she would not have a record because of the offense.

The practice of court watching is in its infancy in Des Moines. Thirty volunteers have been trained, and another thirty will be trained this week. There is some tension. The community wants to know how its justice system works. Those inside the system are looking out and are nervous.

A Noble Experiment

The *Register* published an editorial yesterday called "Court Watch Program Puts Citizen Eyes on Courts." It's created quite a stir. A friend of mine was at the courthouse this morning and was descended upon by a prosecutor and a defense attorney who were concerned about who my friend was talking with on his cell phone. He got the impression that they thought his call was about court watching. Following a previous *Des Moines Register* article on court watching, another attorney was approached by a judge who stated things had gone too far.

I've heard about similar confrontations and concerns. You have to wonder what people are afraid of. You would think they would welcome the public into the courthouse to observe how the justice system operates. If these professionals were confident in their roles and proud of what they do, they would want people to see their work and come away from their experiences with a greater faith in the system. If there are bad eggs in the basket, you would think the competent and respectful professionals would want them found out. But there is talk that court watchers are going after certain judges or prosecutors or other lawyers. Rumors are that court watchers are radicals or subversives—that they have an ax to grind.

If those who pass such judgments would attend a Court Watch training, they would find something entirely different. If they had attended the Court Watch training last night at Bethel African Methodist Episcopal Church, they would have come away feeling comfortable about those taking the time to be trained and volunteering to sit quietly in the back of courtrooms observing, taking notes, and generally engaging in a noble activity. Of those trained last night there was a retired teacher with a master's degree in education, a woman with a PhD in environmental science, a middle school teacher, a pastor of twenty years, a business instructor, a retired social worker, a retired woman with a master's degree in fine arts who is active in the NAACP, a social worker with an undergraduate degree from Grinnell College and a master's degree from the University of Iowa, a retired attorney, a freshman studying political science at

Simpson College, a teacher with a master's degree in behavioral disorders, a longtime state employee with degrees in psychology and organizational development, and a pastor with a doctorate of ministry. What these volunteers have in common is a deep concern for kids and their futures, a desire for kids who engage in wrongdoing to

If there are bad eggs in the basket, you would think the competent and respectful professionals would want them found out.

be held accountable and for the consequences imposed to be reasonable, and a desire for consequences that do more good than harm. What these conscientious people want is a justice system that looks at the big picture and the long run, and not a justice system that is a machine grinding people down. Only time will tell what will come of this. But it is a noble experiment.

First Day on the Job

Today was my first day at the Iowa State Capitol as a lobbyist for the Center for Restorative Justice Practices, of which I am the director. I had planned to get there after lunch, in time for a Senate Judiciary Committee meeting scheduled for 3:00. I found a free parking spot near the capitol, arriving early enough to wander around and get acclimated—bathrooms first, then the law library. In between, Marty Ryan, a lobbyist, told me about a little-known freebie— computers with Internet access lining a hidden side aisle.

I introduced myself to the librarian, who seemed glad to see someone. I told her I hadn't been in the library for years, since 1984.

I was just out of law school then, working for the attorney general's office and assigned to the Environmental Law Division. I had one client, the Conservation Commission. One of my tasks was to write title opinions. The commission would often purchase land parcels or receive them as gifts. Prior to the closing, I would have to make sure that the State was receiving a clean title. I knew nothing about this work, having never taken a real estate transactions course in law school. So I would sneak over to the law library from my office at the Hoover Building and teach myself to write title opinions by using an ancient book called *Marshall's Iowa Title Opinions and Standards.* I actually learned something and, in a perverse way, came to like the work. Having studied history, I found that title abstracts are a particular kind of history book. You find all kinds of juicy things in it—lawsuits, divorces, deaths, adoptions, marriages, floods, pestilences—the stuff of life.

After my orientation to the library, I visited the offices of the clerks of the House and Senate, grabbing whatever written material I could find about the 2013 session—membership, current leadership, session timetables, seating charts, committee assignments, phone lists, etc. I even found the big candy bowl in the back of the House chamber. Being late in the day, it was nearly empty.

Are we making the best decisions about how

to spend tax dollars? Shouldn't more money

be spent on effective mental health treatment

so that fewer dollars are spent on prison beds?

I made it to Capitol Room 22 just in time to hear a presentation by Dr. Harbans Deol, a psychiatrist for the Department of Corrections. It didn't take long to see that Dr. Deol's mission was to convince the Judiciary Committee, and everyone else in the room, how mentally ill most of Iowa's prison population is. Here are just a few of Dr. Deol's facts:

- 2,500 inmates in Iowa's prisons have a "severe mental illness";
- 90 to 95 percent of these inmates will be returned to the "community";

- the 2,500 inmates constitute 30 percent of the overall prison population;
- another 21 percent have "other mental illnesses";
- severe depression is a major problem, and in any given week 30 to 40 inmates are on a suicide watch;
- the Iowa prison population is an aging one, with the incidence of dementia getting higher each year;
- 50 percent of female inmates and 30 percent of male inmates have a "substance use disorder";
- looking on the bright side: for many people who enter the prison system with mental health issues, if they were treated properly, they would not be criminals.

What does this tell us about our justice system? Are we making the best decisions about how to spend tax dollars? Shouldn't more money be spent on effective mental health treatment so that fewer dollars are spent on prison beds?

Our Need to Forgive

None of us have to look far to see the pain caused and the harm done by a failure to forgive. I would guess most families have at least one relationship in need of forgiveness.

I see it everywhere. A woman I know and her only sister had a falling out a decade ago and still don't speak. A former colleague and his brother exchanged harsh words at a family gathering years ago and now have nothing to do with each other. I see it in the workplace. Recently I facilitated a meeting with two employees of a medical group who had a disagreement during their first year of working together. The initial hurt snowballed until communication became nonexistent. I see it in schools; kids want to forgive and be forgiven but have neither the words nor the skills to do so. I see it in victim–offender meetings; a young burglar wants forgiveness but doesn't know how to ask for it. I see it in families; the terminal illness of a parent brings to the surface unresolved issues that will go unresolved unless apology and forgiveness are exchanged.

Several years ago I read Simon Wiesenthal's *The Sunflower: On the Possibilities and Limits of Forgiveness*. While imprisoned in a concentration camp, Wiesenthal was sent to the bedside of a dying Nazi soldier. Haunted by his crimes, the soldier wanted to confess to, and obtain absolution from, a Jew. Faced with a choice between compassion and justice, silence and truth, Wiesenthal said nothing. Years later he wondered if he had done the right thing. In *The Sunflower*, Wiesenthal not only addresses his own dilemma but asks the question of others: What would you do? He asks theologians, political leaders, writers, jurists, psychiatrists, human rights activists, Holocaust survivors, and victims of genocide in Bosnia, Cambodia, China, and Tibet. Their responses are a reminder that Wiesenthal's questions are not limited to events of war.

A couple of months ago I spoke to a therapist friend about forgiveness and gave him my copy of *The Sunflower*. He said he would read it. Recently, he told me that not only had he read it but he quotes from it frequently. He said he is working with an elderly woman and her daughter who have had forgiveness issues going back forty years. He's met with them three times and has been using *The Sunflower* as a common source of reference. He told me that at their last meeting, mother and daughter cried together and touched each other for the first time in years.

In our society's talk of punishment and accountability for criminal offenders, I wonder if the human need to forgive and be forgiven has been ignored.

I'm working with a church in Maine that has established a community mediation center that is informed by restorative justice. They are moved by the possibilities of a transformative approach that focuses on harm and healing and makes possible expressions of remorse and forgiveness. It speaks to them at a deep level.

Who Would Ask the Questions?

Ten people showed up to court watch yesterday morning—two court watchers for each of the five juvenile courtrooms. First-timers were partnered with those who had experience. Yesterday confirmed that partnering court watchers makes a lot of sense. Partners compare notes, help each other complete the observation forms, and process what they observe after each hearing. Partnering also increases the visibility of court watchers.

My partner and I were assigned to a courtroom with one of the newer juvenile judges. Throughout the hearing the professionals appeared competent and well prepared, and they treated us with respect. It's important, however, to look beneath the surface. It's to be expected that the justice professionals will be on their best behavior when court watchers are present. But we need to ask ourselves whether the cases should have made it to the courtroom in the first place. In the two cases we observed, should formal charges have been filed? Both juveniles were male and minority—Latino and African American. Both were ninth graders, fourteen and fifteen years old, respectively. Neither had a prior record, neither was charged with a felony, and neither had committed a crime of violence. Could their cases have been handled informally?

It will be interesting to see what consequences the judge imposes and whether or not the supervision and services ordered could have been provided informally, without the need for court involvement.

At the hearing involving the African American boy there was a gentleman seated in front of me. While the prosecutor was reading the charges filed against the boy, I tapped the man on the shoulder and asked if he was a relative. He said he was the boy's stepfather. I asked if he thought the boy had been treated fairly throughout the process—from arrest to court. He said he didn't think so. He didn't believe his stepson was guilty, and he had repeatedly told the boy's attorney that. He believed the case should have gone to trial. At the hearing the boy did not actually plead guilty. Instead, he stipulated that there was sufficient evidence in the police reports for him to be found guilty. This is a commonly used procedure that allows a defendant to be found guilty without a guilty plea and without a trial. After the hearing the stepfather asked if we could talk again. I gave him my business card. He said he would call.

Was race a factor in either of these cases? Did it make a difference that both boys were represented by a public defender? The attorney for the Latino boy met him for the first time only minutes before the hearing. Did the boys have representation by zealous advocates? Without court watchers, would anyone be asking these questions?

Restorative Justice in Our Schools

On Saturday thirty people met at Grace United Methodist Church. They spent the day in training, taking the first steps toward becoming school peacemakers. School mediation, like court watching, is part of an AMOS initiative to enlist community volunteers to help address the ills of our juvenile justice system. It's hoped that volunteer mediators can engage students in conversations around bullying, fighting, abuses of social media, truancy, and other areas where kids need to be able to talk and be listened to.

On my drive to the church I reflected on a truancy mediation I facilitated at a local high school. When I entered the small conference room, Anna, her mother, and a school social worker were already seated. I knew little of the facts, other than that Anna, a ninth grader, had missed several days of school since the beginning of the school year. This looked like a typical case, although I've learned that truancy is often the tip of the iceberg. Kids miss school when they are overwhelmed. This was true with Anna. After the social worker reviewed Anna's attendance history, we began to peel back the onion.

As an eighth grader, Anna was a good student. She rarely missed school, had good grades, and wanted to succeed. This year was different. Anna was hospitalized in December, severely depressed. She had met a boy a month earlier and had become pregnant within weeks. In March, less than a month before her truancy mediation, she turned fifteen. She no longer lived at home because of a fight between her boyfriend and her stepfather. Instead, she lived with her boyfriend and her boyfriend's father. When asked to characterize her boyfriend—seventeen, a dropout and unemployed—Anna said that he wasn't much help. Anna knew she had to stay in school but, because of her absenteeism, she was attending an alternative school two hours a day, four days a week. It was likely that when the semester ended she would not have earned any credits for the school year. She was already in a deep hole.

We talked with Anna about her options. Would she be interested in living with another family? Would she agree to let the system help her? Anna started to cry. She wanted help but didn't know where to turn. She loved her mother but knew her mother was overwhelmed and couldn't help her. Anna agreed to let the social worker contact the local human services office. Another meeting was scheduled. Anna was promised that a public health nurse would be there and so would a lawyer who would look after her legal interests. Anna broke down and confided that she was so depressed she thought she might harm herself. She agreed to allow the social worker to take her to the hospital.

Leaving the school, I reflected on the role of volunteer mediators. Should restorative justice be integrated within the system or should it be community-based? How would Anna have been served if her case had been referred to a church group or a nonprofit? How would the referral have been made? Would it have been handled expeditiously? Would the right people have been at the table? Would immediate action have been taken to protect Anna and her unborn child? What about the system? Is it true that systems co-opt just as power corrupts? Is it true that a good person, informed by his or her faith, ethics, or compassion, is rendered ineffective or impotent to effect change when employed within the justice system?

I'm cautiously optimistic that well-trained community mediators can meet the challenges that come with being outsiders.

Cruel and Unusual Punishment

I was at the State Capitol again today. It was "Insurance Day." You could get all the pens and yellow stickies, pizza and chocolate chip cookies you wanted. Kathy Stachon, a Senate staffer who provides assistance to lobbyists, introduced me to some key people and then sat me down with her iPad and the Iowa legislature's website. She showed me how to add clients, check on committee assignments and study bills, look up the debate schedule, and make a declaration that states the lobbyist's opinion on the bill, which, according to Kathy, allows a lobbyist to participate in subcommittee meetings on that bill. This means you can sit with the legislators who are discussing proposed legislation and participate in the conversation.

After meeting with Kathy I went to the law library and looked up the study bills for the Senate and House Judiciary Committees. Out of the twenty-five listed, I made eleven declarations. One of them, Senate Study Bill 1111, was about "the possession of alcohol by certain minors and juvenile court jurisdiction." A second one, Senate Study Bill 1099, was about "county attorney duties when representing the Department of Human Services in juvenile court." I chaired a DHS study group a year and a half ago looking at similar legislation. Two other study bills particularly caught my eye: House Study Bill 33 and Senate Study Bill 1089—both about "the sentencing of minors convicted of murder in the first degree."

Why is this legislation being considered now, in 2013? This past June the U.S. Supreme Court in *Miller v. Alabama* held that mandatory life without parole for those under the age of 18 at the time of their crimes violates the Eighth Amendment's prohibition of cruel and unusual punishment. One of the boys in the *Miller* case was 14 at the time of the murder he was eventually convicted of. He had been high on drugs and alcohol when he committed the crime. His stepfather had physically abused him. His alcoholic and drug-addicted mother had neglected him. He had been in and out of foster care. He had tried to kill himself four times since the age of 5. Justice Elena Kagan, author of the majority opinion, wrote that even though the boy deserved a severe punishment, the sentencing judge "needed to examine all these circumstances before concluding that life without any possibility of parole was the appropriate penalty." Justice Kagan added that "by making youth (and all that accompanies it) irrelevant to imposition of that harshest prison sentence, such a scheme poses too great a risk of disproportionate punishment," and that sentencing judges are required "to take into account how children are different, and how those differences counsel against irrevocably sentencing them to a lifetime in prison."

Miller was a huge decision. What it said was that a state can't legislate that every juvenile convicted of first-degree murder shall be sentenced to life in prison without the possibility of parole.

After the *Miller* decision, Iowa governor Terry Branstad commuted the life sentences of thirty-eight juveniles, reducing their terms to sixty years. Gordie Allen, a Drake University Law professor representing two Iowa women sentenced to life as juveniles, called Branstad's action an "overreach" and said that "the governor misunderstood the court ruling that says sentences should be determined case by case."

So why should we care about HSB 33 and SSB 1089? Because the House version provides that a person convicted of murder in the first degree "who was under the age of eighteen at the time the offense was committed shall be eligible for parole after serving a minimum term of confinement of sixty years." The Senate version sets the minimum term of confinement at forty-five years.

If the House version becomes law, a juvenile convicted of murder at the age of sixteen must stay in prison at least until the age of seventy-six. Isn't this the "cruel and unusual punishment" that the Supreme Court in *Miller* said is unconstitutional?

Rosa Parks Remembered

Rosa Parks would have been one hundred years old on Monday. In 1955, Parks refused to give up her seat to make way for a white customer. That moment sparked the Montgomery Bus Boycott, lasting 381 days. By the end, black residents could ride the buses as equals with white residents. Parks' act and the subsequent boycott fueled the Civil Rights Movement. But long before Parks refused to obey bus driver James Blake's order, she was sensitized to racial injustice. In recalling her childhood and her long walks to the local all-black elementary school, she said: "I'd see the bus pass every day. But to me, that was a way of life. We had no choice but to accept what was the custom. The bus was among the first ways I realized there was a black world and a white world." In reflecting on that day in 1955,

Parks said: "Many times I had problems with bus drivers, but this was the first time that people in Montgomery took enough notice of this incident to cooperate with each other and remain off the bus, and that attracted the attention of the entire city, first of all, other places, the country and it just spread."

In April 2012, President Obama visited the Henry Ford Museum and sat on the now famous Rosa Parks bus. He reflected on the experience: "I just sat in there for a moment and pondered the courage and tenacity that is part of our very recent history, but is also part of that long line of folks who sometimes are nameless, oftentimes didn't make the history books, but who constantly insisted on their dignity, their share of the American dream."

The Civil Rights Movement of the 1960s brought about sweeping changes and altered American history. Michelle Alexander, in *The New Jim Crow: Mass Incarceration in the Age of Colorblindness*, argues, however, that a new racial caste system has arisen in the United States, and that a major social movement is necessary to dismantle it. Alexander documents the exploding prison population in this country, which has increased from 300,000 in the early 1980s to over 2.3 million. Alexander says that "if Martin Luther King Jr. is right that the arc of history is long, but it bends toward justice, a new movement will arise; and if civil rights organizations fail to keep up with the times, they will be pushed to the side as another generation of advocates comes to the fore. Hopefully the new generation will be led by those who best know the brutality of the new caste system."

* * *

This morning court watchers met at Plymouth Church to share recent experiences at the Polk County Courthouse. Afterward, I spoke with an older woman who was silent during the meeting. She told me we can't lose focus and we must look closely at what is happening within our justice system. She said we've become lazy and complacent as a nation and must wake up to harm that is happening to so many who come into contact with the system.

This evening I had coffee with a writer for the *Des Moines Register*. We talked about *The New Jim Crow*, the prevalent get-tough-on-crime attitude, and the growing marginalization of both juveniles and adults who are caught up in the system. As we parted, he looked at me and said "This country needs a social movement."

How Quickly Life Changes

I received a call today from a man wanting to tell me about his wife. He said she'd been in a terrible accident. It happened at night on a two-lane country highway. She was heading home from a social gathering and came upon two cars stopped in the road. There had been an accident caused by a drunk driver. The man told me his wife crossed over to the left side of the road so she could pass. She didn't know the driver of the vehicle that had been rear-ended had exited and was standing in the highway. He was struck by her passing car. The caller was silent for a moment, and then he told me his wife was in jail. She had been charged with vehicular homicide, a felony. Her blood alcohol concentration had been tested at .085—.005 over the legal limit. She was being held on a $50,000 bond. The maximum sentence for vehicular homicide is twenty-five years in prison.

The caller continued to speak—about his wife, her family, his family, their financial situation, the uncertainty. My mind scanned the months to come. What would justice look life for this woman, her husband, the man who had been killed, those who survived him? The criminal case would run its course. There might be a trial, a conviction, or an acquittal. There might be a guilty plea to a lesser charge. But after the files of the court, the prosecutor, and the defense attorney are all closed and archived, the suffering will continue. The victims will be many—two families forever changed.

Last March I received a similar call. On the line was a woman with a Middle Eastern accent. She told me she was from Iraq. She said her best friend, also from Iraq, had just lost her son, who had just turned eighteen. He had been at the mall the evening before with a companion. They were driving home in the dark, his friend at the wheel, when the car started to sputter. They pulled off the interstate, onto the shoulder. The driver stayed in the car, but the passenger, the son, got out of the car and stood next to it. At nearly the same moment, an older man, both a husband and a father, awoke behind the wheel of his car just in time to see the parked car ahead of him. He swerved right to avoid a collision. For a split second his headlights shone on the young man. Nothing could be done.

I told the caller I would meet with the mother. I did the next day, and the journey began. The first thing I learned was that her husband, the boy's father, had left for Baghdad two days earlier to make arrangements for the boy's wedding, planned for the next year. The father didn't know yet of his son's death. I spent two hours in their small West Des Moines apartment looking at family and school photos with the mother and with her only living child, a beautiful ten-year-old boy. It was the first of many visits—sometimes to talk about legal matters, sometimes to talk about what might have been. There were tears at that first meeting, but not grief. Grief came soon enough—and remains.

The wrongful death action has been settled and the estate closed, but there is no resolution for this family that left Baghdad two years ago to start a new life. At one point there were discussions of a possible meeting—the boy's family with the driver and his family. The mother thought this might bring her some peace. Inquiries were made. There was suspicion because of the legal entanglements, but a meeting was a real possibility. The door was shut, however, when the driver died of cancer. The boy's mother grieved over his loss as well. The legal files have been closed and archived. But the victims are many. Two families are forever changed.

Where Was the Teaching Moment?

I court watched Thursday with Art and Bev. Both retired, Art had been a corporate attorney, and Bev a social worker. They trained to be court watchers because they are concerned about kids. We sat in on a disposition hearing in a delinquency case. Before the start, Art and Bev spoke with the judge, the prosecutor, and the defense attorney. All three were cordial and patient with questions. After the conversations, a young boy entered the courtroom with his mother. Both were African American. A few weeks earlier, the boy had entered a plea of guilty to assault with injury. Thursday's hearing was for the judge to inform him of his sentence. It was the prosecutor's recommendation that the boy receive a consent decree. If granted, the boy wouldn't have a record. The judge followed the recommendation and told the boy that if everything went well, there was a good chance he would not be on probation for long. The boy was praised for his behavior in recent months. At the conclusion, he was told he would be responsible for restitution, if any. The juvenile court officer then spoke and informed the court that she had never received a victim impact statement requesting compensation of any kind.

After the hearing I introduced myself to the boy and his mother, explained the reasons for the AMOS Court Watch program, and asked the mother what she thought of the process. She was direct and quick to the point. She said her son should never have been in court. It was a waste of time and a waste of money. She said the incident involving her son had happened almost a year ago. He was in sixth grade and eleven years old at the time. He had no prior involvement with the police or the juvenile justice system. The incident involved a BB gun. She said it was a "game gone bad." After the incident nothing happened. No one from the school said anything, and there was no communication from the parents of the other boy involved. It wasn't until three months later that she heard her son was going to be charged. By the time of the sentencing hearing, seven months had passed since the family's initial contact with the system.

After my conversation in the hallway I returned to the courtroom. The boy's attorney was talking with Art and Bev. She told them she also practiced in Dallas County and that if the incident had happened there a charge would never have been filed.

So why was this boy in court? Why wasn't he allowed to enter into an informal adjustment? He would have been supervised by a juvenile court officer, and services would have been provided if any were needed. Why wasn't there a restorative justice response? Why didn't the system arrange a meeting with the two boys most affected by the incident? Why wasn't there an opportunity for this boy to apologize? Where was the teaching moment?

Setting People Up to Fail

A few weeks ago I was asked to visit a woman who was being held in the Polk County Jail. I was told it was her first experience with incarceration and there were concerns she might not be doing well. The woman had been at a rally against corporate agriculture, attempting to draw attention to corporate greed, and she had been arrested for trespass. Rather than being taken to jail, she was issued a citation by the police and advised to appear in court at a later date.

On a Sunday evening I arrived at the jail. After passing through security, I was led through secured doorways and down concrete corridors until reaching a guard station, where I was assigned to a meeting room. I was given a seat at a small plastic table. A few minutes later the door opened and a young woman came in. We introduced ourselves and then she told her story. She said she showed up for her hearing, took a seat in the back of the courtroom, and waited for her name to be called. When her time came she walked to the front and stood before the judge. She was advised of the charge against her and asked how she would plead. She said guilty. There was no conversation about the incident, or her concerns about exporting American agriculture to third-world countries, or her motivation for drawing public attention to the harm caused. She was not asked to justify her philosophy of civil disobedience. The judge merely accepted her plea and imposed a sentence.

The young woman then told me the judge had said to her that she would be on probation for a year and pay a probation fee, and that she would have to perform fifty hours of community service, take a class, pay a fee for the class, and pay court costs. The young woman told the judge she couldn't do that. She said she helped run a soup kitchen as a volunteer. The judge's response was to direct her to the probation office elsewhere in the courthouse. She found the office and described her situation just as she had to the judge. The probation officer said he couldn't put her on probation if she couldn't complete the terms. She was sent back to the judge, who sent her back to the probation officer. On her return to the probation officer, she was told that because she could not sign the probation agreement in good faith, she was in violation of her probation. She was then taken to the Polk County Jail.

The young woman grew silent, wiped her eyes, hung her head for a minute or so, and then looked up at me. She said that there were other people there at the jail like her. People with little or no prior criminal history who have committed minor offenses, who really haven't hurt anyone. She stopped, and then started again. "You know," she said, "they just set us up to fail."

The next morning she appeared before a judge at the Polk County Jail and was given a thirty-day sentence. Someday she will have to pay for her jail stay—seventy dollars for each day.

A Failure of Imagination

I read a story recently that was written by a young man nearing the end of the second year of an extended visit to Germany. It wasn't the usual travelogue, nor was it the tale of a transplanted American immersing himself in a new culture. He wrote about the value of living in a foreign land and understanding little of what was going on around him, little of the language or the politics or the problems of the day, little of the public concerns. While this might sound like the typical "ugly American," traveling abroad and clueless, what the writer described was a process of uprooting in order to free one-self. He wrote that living in Germany had liberated his imagination, allowing him to approach people and events without confining or labeling them.

* * *

Just after sunrise this morning I was walking on the beach in Puerto Morelos, Mexico. The only sound was the crashing surf. Halfway between the long dock and the old lighthouse though, I heard a hint of bagpipes. I walked on, and the sweet Scottish sound increased. Soon the source presented itself. Twenty yards off the beach was a bear of a man serenading himself and the sea breeze. I approached him discretely, with only the intention of thanking him for his morning song. But a conversation was struck up. I learned that he was David from Saskatchewan, a farmer and a retired geologist. He and his wife spend a month every year in this small fishing village thirty minutes from Cancun. Every morning he plays his father's hundred-year-old bagpipes. He told me with pride that he's played them faithfully for over fifty years, to honor his father and to honor his own spirit.

It's not difficult to trace the cause of the dysfunction of our criminal justice system to a failure of imagination.

I left David to his morning ritual and continued my walk toward the lighthouse. It struck me that what David was engaged in requires an act of imagination, a leap from what is expected to something that elevates. I considered others I had met on this brief trip to the land of the Mayans. Eddie, the masseuse who had the courage to immigrate from Nigeria. Daphne and Miki, the lesbian couple who help run the Alma Libre bookstore on the main street. Andria, in her early twenties, who is applying her Cordon Bleu education to the recently opened La Casa del Farito. Adrian, a young man from Southern California who leads snorkeling tours during the high season and works on his English and his Spanish in the process. Christy, who left everything behind in Utah to manage the Cabana Puerto Morelos, where we are staying. And the retired woman from Vancouver who left Toronto a year ago with her husband to follow her ninety-two-year-old mother to British Columbia and start a new life. What they all have in common is imagination—the ability to see that the prescriptions of others do not necessarily apply to them, a recognition that what has been is not what has to be.

And then, for some odd reason, I thought about the criminal justice system and its lack of imagination. About how systems, like some people, have a tendency to stagnate, rely on old ways, resist change, become entrenched. Of course this is not a new recognition. Much has been written about businesses that fail for these very reasons. But little is said about our criminal justice system and its inability to attract those with imagination who might elevate it from its present malaise. It's not difficult to trace the cause of the dysfunction of our criminal justice system to a failure of imagination.

A Conversation with Warren Buffett

I had a long talk with Warren Buffett the other day, the kind you have with figures who are important in your life even though you've never met. When I was a Little Leaguer I used to talk with Mickey Mantle about hitting left-handed pitches. And when my kids were little I used to talk with Dr. Spock about my kids' behavior. Now that I'm closer to needing nursing home care than child care, I talk with Warren Buffett.

This time I wanted to talk with him about our criminal justice system. I've often wondered what the system would look like if it were run like a business. What if taxpayers gave their money to Berkshire Hathaway to manage police officers, prosecutors, and judges? It's interesting to consider what kind of justice we would have if those responsible for the outcomes were answerable to shareholders. I wanted to know what Mr. Buffett thought about the justice system as an investment and whether his fund managers would invest in it over the long run.

When I posed these questions he said he never invests in a business he can't understand and that from what he'd read about our country's exploding prison population, he had concluded that the justice system is unlike any enterprise he had ever been involved with. We turned our attention to the prisons opening in Mitchelville and Fort Madison, Iowa. I told him the *Register* had reported that the Iowa Department of Corrections hoped to raise spending from $367 million a year to $415 million a year over the next two years to pay for the two new prisons, nine other facilities, numerous community corrections offices, and staff in eight judicial districts. That immediately got his attention. He told me he has several absolutes when it comes to investing. Rule Number 1 is never lose money. Rule Number 2 is never forget Rule Number 1. He said it sounded to him like Iowa taxpayers are losing money when it comes to paying to lock people up. But he wanted to know more. You see, Mr. Buffett asks questions incessantly. He wanted to know how many people are incarcerated in Iowa, how many others are on probation or parole, how much it costs annually to incarcerate one person, and what the outcomes might be if that same amount were spent in other ways. I told him that Iowa prisons hold nearly 8,300 inmates, an additional 30,000 offenders are supervised in community corrections programs, and the average annual cost per Iowa inmate is nearly $35,000. By comparison full-time tuition, fees, room, board, and books at Iowa State University is half that—so two students could get a free college degree for every inmate we incarcerate.

Mr. Buffett then wanted to know what the research shows about the effectiveness of incarceration. I told him the United States incarcerates 2.3 million people in prisons and jails—a 500 percent increase over the past thirty years—and there is increasing evidence that large-scale incarceration is not the most effective means of achieving public safety. I said, according to the Sentencing Project, changes in sentencing law and policy, not increases in crime rates, explain most of the growth of the national prison population.

I could see Mr. Buffett's mental machinery at work as he crunched the numbers and calculated the effect on the national economy. With his customary restraint he said surely most of these people are violent offenders and need to be incarcerated. I suggested we go online and look at the Iowa Board of Parole's 2011 report to Governor Branstad. We found a page that showed the months served by inmates for the most common offenses—2,417 inmates to be exact. Of those paroled in 2010, 768 had committed property crimes, 862 had committed drug offenses, 651 were paroled for other nonviolent offenses, and 136 had committed crimes against persons. Mr. Buffett pulled out his calculator and determined that the total cost to taxpayers to incarcerate just the 768 released after serving time for property crimes was more than $56 million. He paused, and then asked if it really makes sense to put nonviolent offenders behind bars at such great expense? He suggested it might be better to treat the drug problem as a public health problem rather than a crime problem.

We then returned to the question that initiated our conversation: Is the criminal justice system worth investing in? Mr. Buffett said he wasn't sure but that he's very concerned about kids—concerned enough that he'd be willing to invest money in the juvenile justice system. Then the questions started: How many children are incarcerated in Iowa? How many others are somewhere else in the juvenile system? How much would it cost annually to incarcerate one child in a detention center? How might the money be better spent?

Who Should Initiate Dialogue with the System?

There is a fundamental incompatibility between the principles of restorative justice and how our government-run justice systems define and administer justice. I'm discovering that there is a significant challenge in discovering how to dialogue with the system in a way that fosters collaboration rather than confrontation. A question for which there is no apparent answer is how do those outside the system, those who have a deep concern for how justice should be administered in their communities, engage with justice system professionals?

* * *

I had lunch recently with a law professor who had previously been a public defender. I quizzed him about actions that criminal defense attorneys might take in attempting to change laws that unnecessarily damage offenders.

A case in point: In Iowa, offenders can receive a deferred judgment if they have a clean or nearly clean record and a statute does not otherwise prohibit it. A deferred judgment means there will be no conviction of record. For example, someone who pleads guilty to shoplifting and receives a deferred judgment can say that he has not been convicted of a crime. This is a big deal, particularly when jobs are so difficult to find and any blemish can be fatal to attempting to secure meaningful employment. However, with the public's easy access to criminal histories, the value of the deferred judgment has diminished considerably. Now, although a deferred judgment is still expunged from an individual's court record, it is not expunged from the state criminal history database. Anyone can purchase the criminal history of anyone else for less than $20. This is done all the time, particularly by potential employers. The consequences are obvious.

I asked the law professor why it is that attorneys don't try to change the law so that only prosecutors, law enforcement, and judges can know that someone has received a deferred judgment. I knew what the answer would be—that lawyers are only concerned about the individual case and not the big picture. Indeed, that was his answer. So I followed up by asking how the community could engage in a discussion to look at these issues; surely it's in the best interest of the community that we not create an underclass with our criminal offender labeling. Again the law professor had no satisfactory answer, commenting only that someone should take it up as a cause. Finally, I asked why Iowa's two law schools wouldn't take an active role in commencing a dialogue on this and related issues. At this point the law professor excused himself, saying he needed to get to his next class.

The Good Fortune to Be a Lawyer

I was in Chicago recently and spent the better part of two days at the Cook County Criminal Courthouse, adjacent to the Cook County Jail. I had hoped to visit the jail, the largest in the country, but discovered that visitation is by invitation only. You either have to have a reservation or be on an inmate's list of favorites. The jail has held its share of famous criminals, such as Al Capone, Richard Speck, and John Wayne Gacy. Many more average folk have slept in its cells. On an average day the population approaches 10,000. I'd wanted to visit the jail primarily because of its notoriety but also because I am a longtime admirer of the famous Chicago lawyer Clarence Darrow. Having had many clients who knew the jail well, Darrow is remembered for a speech he delivered there in 1902. Always the advocate for the poor and the despised, Darrow told a packed house:

There are more people who go to jail in hard times than in good times—few people comparatively go to jail except when they are hard up. They go to jail because they have no other place to go. They may not know why, but it is true all the same. People are not more wicked in hard times. That is not the reason. The fact is true all over the world that in hard times more people go to jail than in good times, and in winter more people go to jail than in summer. Of course it is pretty hard times for people who go to jail at any time. The people who go to jail are almost always poor people—people who have no other place to live first and last. When times are hard then you find large numbers of people who go to jail who would not otherwise be in jail.

But as I said, without a reservation I wasn't able to get a look inside the Cook County Jail, so I visited the courthouse instead. My first stop was a courtroom on the fifth floor. I peeked in the door and saw that a jury trial was going on. I took a seat in the back, one of the few available, and found that I had arrived in the middle of the State's case against a young black man on trial for first-degree murder. The courtroom was packed, with friends and relatives of the accused on one side and friends and relatives of the victim on the other. I sensed that every spectator, no matter which side they were on, had suffered a significant loss.

After listening to the testimony of the State's gunshot residue expert I left quietly and made my way down to the fourth floor in search of another trial. A courtroom on the west end was in use. I peeked in and found a proceeding markedly different from the previous one. The courtroom was packed but entirely with white people. With everyone dressed like lawyers, it looked like a bar association meeting. I again took a seat in the back, just in time to hear the State's attorney give his closing argument in a case in which another Chicago attorney was charged with taking contraband into a penal institution. While volunteering with a free legal service for indigent suspects, Sladjana Vuckovic had allowed a prisoner she was visiting to use her cell phone. The contraband was the cell phone, and the penal institution was a conference room in a precinct station. If convicted, she was looking at a maximum of fifteen years in prison.

You can learn a lot by listening to closing arguments. From Ms. Vuckovic's lawyer I learned that the former U.S. Attorney for the northern District of Illinois had testified for the defendant. He had told the jury that he didn't know it was against the law to allow a suspect to use a cell phone and, in fact, two years earlier he had visited a nephew in jail and had allowed him to make calls to relatives. A retired police officer with extensive experience in training other police officers about jail procedures and protocols had also testified. He also told the jury that he was unaware that a cell phone could be considered contraband.

Apparently, the jury believed the former U.S. Attorney, the former police officer, and Ms. Vuckovic; it deliberated less than an hour and acquitted her. A short time later, in front of the courthouse, I listened to Ms. Vuckovic speak to reporters about her experience. She said: "I was just able to witness how the criminal justice system works, and I am one of the lucky ones. I mean, it's like a factory in here that leads to the prison industrial complex. It's unbelievable what I've witnessed in the past year and a half, firsthand—to be one, a defendant, in the system."

You have to wonder how the 10,000 inmates in the Cook County Jail on any given day feel about the system, most of whom do not have the good fortune to be a lawyer.

Seeds of Justice

I'm giving a sermon Sunday at First Parish Church in Portland, Maine. It's a daunting task. Unitarians have a long and rich history when it comes to social justice issues, dating back to the early abolitionists and suffragettes. They are now at the forefront of today's pressing social justice issues, speaking out on racial, reproductive, immigration, environmental, and LGBTQ justice. What can I possibly add? But I've been thinking about what a feminist friend reminded me of recently—that all politics is personal. Can't the same be said about justice?

Although our first sense of justice might be instilled in us by parents or grandparents, or by our teachers or ministers, it may be that our sense of justice also has roots in events in our lives that we come to see later as pivotal. Maybe this is something worth talking about.

I was reading about Daniel Ellsberg recently. Long before he released the Pentagon Papers and was subsequently charged with espionage, Ellsberg lived a favored life, studying to be a concert pianist. He later received a PhD in economics from Harvard, which led to positions at the Pentagon and the State Department. It was while working as an analyst with the Rand Corporation that he began to understand the deceit being perpetrated by our government on the American people in relation to the way the United States was conducting the Vietnam War. The tipping point came while he was listening to a speech given by a draft resister who was awaiting a criminal sentencing that would send him to prison. It was then that Ellsberg truly understood that we were engaged in an unjust war and that he had a moral responsibility to do something about it.

Oscar Romero had a similar epiphany. His appointment as archbishop of El Salvador was welcomed by the Salvadoran government, but many feared that his conservative reputation would negatively affect liberation theology's commitment to the poor. Romero's life course was altered dramatically, however, when his good friend Rutilio Grande, a progressive Jesuit priest, was murdered. Grande's death, the direct result of his efforts to create self-reliance groups among the poor, had a profound effect on Romero, who later said, "When I looked at Rutilio lying there dead I thought, 'if they killed him for doing what he did, then I too have to walk the same path.'" In response to Grande's murder, Romero began to speak out against poverty, social injustice, torture, and assassinations. Ultimately, Romero was murdered, while celebrating Mass, one day after giving a sermon in which he called on Salvadoran soldiers to stop carrying out their government's campaign of repression and violation of human rights.

We are indebted to Daniel Ellsberg, Oscar Romero, and others who have taken great risks to do the right thing. We are also indebted to the pivotal events in their lives that planted seeds that later gave rise to their heightened sense of justice, out of which action became a necessity. Haven't we each been influenced by people and events that make us sensitive to the pain of others and, at the right time and place, compel us to respond?

I have a therapist friend who is fond of talking about "seeds of intuition"—those moments or encounters that at the time of their occurrence cause us to be vaguely aware, perhaps even as children, that what is happening now may have implications far into the future. These seeds of intuition or insight suggest that we each carry a prophetic instinct that provides us with the capacity to envision or anticipate our future life course.

Only after many years did I come to recognize the seeds of justice planted in me. My first awareness of justice and its counterpart, injustice, came from reading the autobiography of Clarence Darrow when I was ten. Darrow was the early twentieth-century lawyer known as "the attorney for the damned." It was Darrow who convinced me at an early age that being a lawyer for those without a voice could be one of the highest callings in our society. My second education in justice came two years later. My father had left my mother when I was nine, and on the day of my eighth grade graduation the authorities came and took me and my four siblings away from our mother. The system did nothing over the next several years to reunite us. Looking back, I can see the genesis of my own sense of justice. It can be found in the injustice of poverty, in the injustice inflicted by systems that are neglectful and often meanspirited, and in the injustices often perpetrated by a society that is quick to divide "us" from "them."

Perhaps on Sunday I can have a conversation with the Unitarians about seeds of justice.

Sitting with Kids in Pain

I gave a sermon this morning. Following coffee, I met with twenty church members to explore what restorative justice might look like for them. This exploration is not new for a core group at the church. Since the summer of 2011 I've had the pleasure of meeting with eight to ten church members three times, training them to facilitate conversations with juveniles who had committed offenses or who were in conflict.

As I prepared for this afternoon's meeting I recalled a visit to Portland, Maine, last April. There was a meeting at the Cumberland County Courthouse in a courtroom packed with prosecutors, defense attorneys, juvenile court officers, and mediators. They had gathered to hear about restorative justice. The leader of the initiative at this Unitarian church told how the congregation had voted a year earlier to create a restorative justice center. It would be a vehicle to help the neighborhood where the church is located and to help keep kids out of the formal justice system if at all possible. Then the chief juvenile prosecutor in the district attorney's office spoke, saying that the local juvenile system supports keeping young people out of court. She added that the restorative justice program offered by the church had the necessary accountability in place to prevent burdening the court system or stigmatizing the youth.

Nearly a year has passed. The hope that the juvenile justice system would be a steady source of referrals to the church's restorative justice center has not been realized. Old habits are hard to break, and believing that there is a better way to do justice does not necessarily make it so. There are critical players in every system who have to buy into the paradigm shift. The old way of doing business endures until those in positions of authority make it a priority to change the course of the ship. That may yet happen in Cumberland County. Perhaps new judges will come along, or new prosecutors or new juvenile court officers. Perhaps pressure will come from outside the system. But in the meantime, the committed restorative justice practitioners at First Parish Church are not deterred.

They continue to reach out, to make connections. They are presently establishing a relationship with a neighboring high school that, whether it fully realizes it or not, has a tremendous need for community peacemakers to come into the school. To date, the restorative justice volunteers have facilitated four conversations involving students in conflicts, and they are encouraged by their efforts and the results.

At this afternoon's meeting everyone acknowledged the need for the church to be a resource for schools. Kids in conflict need compassionate adults to sit with them and with their conflict without passing judgment. Kids need to be involved in processes that are healing and that provide a model to follow when future harms are caused. One of the participants, a teacher, spoke about how important it is to sit with kids in pain. The youngest member of the group spoke about his desire to help lessen some of the pain and suffering in the world. Parents spoke of how their children have been damaged by overworked or stressed-out school staff members. Near the end, a former teacher adamantly expressed her belief that restorative justice needs to be in every school in a meaningful way.

> *Kids need to be involved in processes that are*
>
> *healing and that provide a model to follow*
>
> *when future harms are caused.*

When the people finished their conversation there was a sense of hope, for young people and for themselves. One participant said he really wanted this to be a part of his life. Another spoke of restorative justice offering her a new direction. A third said she had been thinking that she might resume her teaching career and that working with kids who are hurting and in conflict would be more beneficial for the kids and more meaningful for her.

* * *

This evening I took a walk through downtown Portland. It was snowing, and the temperature was well below freezing. As I approached an intersection I saw a teenage boy seated on the sidewalk. He was shivering. We had a conversation. He said he had been homeless since November after being kicked out by his alcoholic father. He had never known his mother. He said he spent his nights at the local youth shelter and his days on the street looking for work, which he rarely found. He said he dropped out of school because he didn't fit in. While we were talking, two other teenagers approached. They stayed nights in the same shelter. Both had been kicked out of their homes, and neither was in school. I asked the girl, a sixteen-year-old, why she wasn't in school. She said no one liked her there so she finally quit to ease the pain of isolation. We spoke awhile longer, and then they went their way. I had to wonder whether their lives would be different if there had been a restorative justice volunteer in their schools.

The Veil of Ignorance

Kim Coit is a lawyer, businessman, author, community volunteer, and deep thinker about justice. We had coffee this afternoon, and he spoke at length about his desire, as he approaches seventy, to write about his vision for justice for future generations. I asked why he had this interest at this stage of his life, and his answer was simple—he wants to reflect on what he wishes he had known at the beginning of his journey and that, belatedly, he knows now. He says he looks around at his generation and is keenly aware, with regret, of what it did not do. It did not fix poverty. It did not reverse the environmental damage it had done. It didn't fix our government. It didn't end racism.

As his swan song, Kim wants to offer his fix for the world. He says the most important part of the fix is justice. If the world were just, there might not be any wars, there might not be poverty, there might not be children who are hungry or old people who are cold. Kim says it all comes down to creating a just world. He wants to target high school seniors and college freshmen in order to reach a core group that has not made definite academic plans and might consider studying and working in the field of justice. He wants to increase the number of college graduates who look at the world through a lens of justice.

Kim has been most influenced by John Rawls, a Harvard philosopher. Kim supports Rawls' "veil of ignorance" theory, which is a method of determining the morality of a certain issue based upon the following thought experiment.

Decision makers should know nothing about their own abilities, tastes, and position within the social order of society. The veil of ignorance blocks off this knowledge, so that it's impossible to know what burdens and benefits of social cooperation would result once the veil is lifted. With this knowledge blocked, decisions would be based on equitable principles that would determine the distribution of rights, positions, and resources in their society.

Rawls' thought experiment dictates that decision makers should be ignorant of their place in society, their class position, or their social status. Likewise, they should not know their fortune in the distribution of natural assets, abilities, intelligence, and strength. The idea is to render moot personal considerations that are morally irrelevant to the justice or injustice of principles meant to allocate the benefits of social cooperation. In an imaginary society, one might or might not be intelligent, rich, or born into a preferred class. Since one may occupy any position in the society, the veil of ignorance forces the decision makers to consider society from the perspective of all members, those fortunate and those less fortunate.

This is deep stuff at almost midnight. I'll think about it more tomorrow, and I may even go to the source, Professor Rawls himself. For the sake of future college freshmen and those of their generation, I hope that Kim will be able to communicate and apply Rawls' "veil of ignorance" so it can become a useful tool for our future justice practitioners and policy makers.

The Need for Social Entrepreneurs

I drove from Portland to Rockland this morning to meet Dick Snyder at the Brass Compass Cafe. Just down the street from the Farnsworth Art Museum and its world-famous collection of Andrew Wyeth originals, the Brass Compass is not much bigger than a phone booth—at least from the outside. Inside, however, the locals pack in around tiny tables to satisfy their rocky coast appetites. Dick and I found a corner spot near the back wall, each ordering a Maine-style breakfast just before the lunch crowd converged.

Wearing a weathered fleece vest over a blue work shirt, Dick is seventy-six but looks a decade younger. There is little about him that suggests that for years he was a professor of theology and ethics at Union Theological Seminary in New York City. In 2001 Dick left academia and retired to Maine, but his passion for justice followed. As a result of innumerable conversations about the punishment mentality of our culture, he convinced some key locals that ware-housing offenders just doesn't work, and with their help he founded the Restorative Justice Project of the Midcoast in 2005. It is now a model not just for Maine but for the country, and it advocates for fundamental changes in how we do justice in our schools and in the community at large.

In the spring of 2012 Dick took his passion for justice one step further and founded the Restorative Justice Institute of Maine, which endeavors to bring about a widespread cultural and systemic change in how the people of Maine approach wrongdoing. It was this initiative that took me to Rockland. I wanted to know: How are things going? What is the focus of the Institute's efforts? What are the points of resistance ? Does he really think that significant sys-temic change is possible? How do outsiders affect the institutional mind-set of the dominant justice system? Dick said that it is too early to answer these questions fully, but that the Institute has been advocating for restorative justice at the state and local levels and in schools. He said that in the near future it will start to develop and cultivate a network of restorative justice projects in all regions of the state. In the long run, he hopes that an approach that combines prevention, restitution, and rehabilitation will become mainstream, causing Maine's criminal justice system to become more effective and less costly, address victims' needs adequately, reduce recidivism, and make Maine communities safer.

Our conversation turned to the challenge of educating the general public on the need for the change this restorative justice vision calls for. We talked about how justice system players need to be convinced that by adopting and implementing restorative justice processes, it's possible to streamline the system and divert nonviolent offenders from the formal system without sacrificing public safety. We talked about how longtime restorative justice advocates and practitioners need to establish a dialogue with the business community and fiscal conservatives and enlist their support. And we talked about the importance of attracting creative thinkers to the restorative justice cause, infusing the movement with the same social entrepreneurial spirit that has successfully energized other global causes in recent years.

As we shook hands and prepared to leave, I suggested to Dick that he convene a summit of gray-haired restorative justice thinkers and practitioners to strategize and develop a restorative justice vision for the next generation. He promised to get back to me.

Records Sealing Day

It was "Juvenile Records Sealing Day" at the Drake Law School Legal Clinic today. Brent Pattison, director of the Center for Children's Rights, hoped for a big turnout. Law students were prepared to advise anyone eighteen or older who had a juvenile record how their records might be sealed. By early afternoon a dozen had been helped.

Most people think juvenile records are private and not available to the public or that if they are not private, they go away when a child turns eighteen. Neither is true. When a child is found guilty of or pleads guilty to an offense, he or she is formally labeled a "delinquent" and a record is made of the delinquent act. In Iowa the record is available to the general public on the state's website and remains there even after the child becomes an adult. This is a big problem. It can make getting a good job difficult, cause problems when looking for housing, and prevent high school graduates from getting into their schools of choice. Teenagers turned adults can do something about this, but they have to know what. Iowa law allows for a juvenile record to be sealed if more than two years have passed since the juvenile case was closed and the offender is at least eighteen. But the former offender must know to petition the court, seeking to have a judge order the record sealed, which often requires hiring an attorney.

That's why what Professor Pattison and his law students did today was such a good thing. But Pattison says free clinics like today's should be made unnecessary. To that end, Drake students have drafted legislation that would make the sealing process automatic. Known as SSB 1215, the legislation is making its way through the process. A senate subcommittee will soon consider it. The bill provides that the court schedule a hearing two years after the date of the last official action in a juvenile delinquency case, or after the date the child becomes eighteen years of age, whichever is later. The bill would then allow a judge to order the records sealed if there is no objection from the county attorney. There is more to the bill than that, and it doesn't apply to every case, but it's a start. It's a recognition that although juveniles should be held accountable for their delinquent acts, the consequences imposed on them as teenagers should not continue to haunt them as adults.

When the System Fails a Child

Today I witnessed an injustice so grave that I'm sickened by it. The injustice was perpetrated by the system—not the one we call the "criminal justice system," nor the one we call the "juvenile justice system," but the machine, the bureaucracy we call the "child welfare system." It was perpetrated by the Iowa legislature, which is charged with protecting our children—the system designed to respond to allegations of child abuse and child neglect.

This system sometimes takes a child or children into its custody. We are asked to trust that those children within its custody will no longer be abused or neglected. We are led to believe that this system, and those employed by it, will make decisions in the best interests of those children. This is not always the case. I can share only a few details because there remains a glimmer of hope that the right thing will still be done. I cannot disclose the names because those who are guilty of negligence of duty, or deceit, or mean-spiritedness may continue their harmful ways out of spite. What I can say is that this is the story of a little boy who has lived most of his five years with his maternal grandparents and who knows them as the only loving parents he has ever had. He was taken from his mother as an infant. She had serious problems and was unable to parent at that time. The boy was placed with the mother's parents, and he thrived with them for the next four years. Nothing in the record suggests otherwise.

I have in front of me a stack of affidavits nearly an inch thick praising the grandparents for the devotion and care they demonstrated in raising the boy. Statement after statement attests to how the grandparents and the child interacted at church; on the playground; in the neighborhood; on grandpa's lap, where the child was read to; and next to grandma at the piano, where she played and the boy sang. But somewhere along the way the child's guardian ad litem (GAL), the attorney appointed to represent the interests of the boy throughout the lengthy court process, took a disliking to the grandparents. Perhaps it was because they were so protective. Perhaps because they wouldn't jump when asked. The reason for this animosity is unclear. What is known is that this GAL's "overreaching and disdain" toward the grandparents, as described by their lawyer, led to the boy being removed and placed with paternal relatives who live halfway across the state and who had not met the boy until he was nearly four years old. It should be noted that the only reason ever given by the state for wanting this boy separated from his grandparents was a fear that they would allow the boy's mother to come too close. This is absurd, as it was the grandparents who first alerted authorities to the parental shortcomings and first involved the State in the welfare of the boy. Complicating matters, there are allegations that the GAL deliberately misled the court on more than one occasion.

Today's new injustice took place at a meeting with supervisors at the highest level. It was a meeting to inform the grandparents of the government's decision on who would be allowed to adopt the boy. The grandparents were told that they had not been "selected." No reasons were given: No explanation of the criteria used in the selection process. No facts offered to support the distant relatives as the better custodians and future parents. No answers to questions about whether the government took into account that the boy is now "acting out," when he never did before. No answers to questions about whether the government was concerned that the boy now needs counseling, when that was never necessary before.

What I saw today was grandparents who were providing their grandson with all the love he will ever need as a child. I saw grandparents who were given no answers by a system that ripped a child from the only home he has ever known.

A Name to Remember

Colton Morman is a name to remember. He's a junior at Drake University. We met this afternoon to talk about court watching. Drake professor Nancy Berns had asked if I would train a group of honors students to be court watchers. Two weeks ago we held a two-session training with nearly thirty students. Colton missed the second session because of a snowstorm. He called the next day to see if we could meet so he could catch up. I could tell he was serious about it. Today I found out why.

Colton is a unique young man with a unique history. He's African American, raised by white grandparents in rural Dallas County. He looks big-city but he's a farm boy. We reviewed what he had learned at the first class about the juvenile justice system. We then spent time with the form that court watchers use when observing hearings at the courthouse. Colton asked good questions. He's a quick study, and he has a mature sense of what justice ought to look like. He believes that if just one child benefits from having average citizens in a juvenile courtroom, then the Court Watch program is worth it.

At the end of our session I asked Colton what he planned to do with his political science degree. He didn't hesitate: He intends to go to law school. This came as no surprise. I could imagine him as an excellent advocate for those without a voice. I asked whether, having grown up in rural Iowa, he'd ever been the victim of racial prejudice. He didn't hesitate: He said that during his first years he was the only black person in his community and in the school he attended. He didn't think of himself as black, and no one ever drew attention to it. It wasn't until a bus ride home from school that he was awakened to racism. He was a sixth grader, sitting near the back of the bus, when a boy who had been his friend the year before began to taunt him. A couple of other boys joined in. The taunting turned physical and he was assaulted. He suffered a cut lip, a deep bruise on his forehead, and a shoe print on his shirt. One of the boys used the N-word and then others did too. When he got home and told his grandmother about what had happened, he found out what the N-word meant. That was the first time he'd ever heard the word—it crashed down on him.

The next day at school his report of what happened was met with skepticism. Despite his injuries and his shirt with the shoe print as evidence, some in the administration didn't believe him. One who did attempted to minimize it, telling Colton he just needed to turn the other cheek. Over the next few years he was confronted with bigotry from time to time, but he always rose above it. He worked hard in school, graduating near the top of his class. Shortly after turning eighteen, Colton ran for mayor of his hometown and won. He served for two years.

When Colton finished his story we compared our calendars, looking for times to meet at the courthouse. Colton said that with school and farm work he has a busy schedule but he would definitely fit in court watching. Even after graduating he imagined he would continue to be a court watcher because it's so important. Colton Morman is a name to remember.

A Parent's Restorative Justice Response

This is a story from a woman who reads the *Justice Diary* blog. She emailed me today, wanting to share a disturbing situation involving her sixteen-year-old son, Sean.

A week ago she read several of her son's texts. He had been in communication with a friend about how to buy a gun, saying that he wanted to arm himself. He was afraid of an older boy who was threatening him. It was apparent from the texts that the friend was familiar with guns—he knew about permit requirements, gun types, and where they could be purchased. But the friend also had some thoughtful advice. He texted that buying a gun was not the answer for Sean and only bad things would come of it.

The woman wrote that after reading the texts she decided to have a difficult conversation. She was reluctant to admit that she'd been reading her son's texts, but she knew it was important that she get to the bottom of things. Fortunately, Sean told her the whole story. He knows a girl who goes to school in the next town and sings in the same choir he sings in. From time to time Sean texts her when he's going to be late for choir practice or unable to attend. The girl passes the information on to the choir director. The girl's boyfriend saw a text from Sean about being late for practice. When he confronted her about it she apparently engaged in some exaggeration about the extent to which Sean has an interest in her. The boyfriend insisted on having Sean's telephone number. She gave it to him. From there matters escalated.

The boyfriend, who has never met Sean, began to bully him with texts about being gay. Sean responded provocatively, and the boyfriend threatened to go to Sean's house and "really hurt him." This lengthy exchange of texts led Sean to begin looking for a gun. He was afraid for himself and his parents. If the boyfriend showed up at the house, he wanted to have a gun for protection.

The woman thought of going to the police but decided against it, concerned with how far the police would take things. She didn't want to get the girl's boyfriend in trouble, but she wanted the bullying to stop. She knew about restorative justice and felt that a response inclusive of everyone involved, parents and children, was the best approach to take. She contacted the girl's and the boyfriend's parents, and they agree that a mediation should take place. A meeting has been scheduled, and the texting has stopped. The woman is hopeful that whatever restorative process is used, it will resolve the situation and also model for everyone a better way to address conflicts in the future.

Unanswered Questions

Once a month I attend a weekend seminar at Macalester College, St. Paul, sponsored by the Minnesota Jung Association. This weekend's presenter taught about the child archetype. For Carl Jung, the Swiss psychiatrist and founder of analytical psychology, archetypes are genetic for the psyche in the same way that instincts are genetic for the body. According to Jung, we are born with certain propensities of the mind. One of these, the child archetype, is a symbol of the developing personality. Our presenter urged us to consider that child images are a way for us to talk about who we are at our core, and that child archetypal images provide the richest way to look at what we are born into.

Earlier this week I met with two fifth grade boys and their mothers at a Des Moines elementary school. The boys are classmates and best friends, and yet are in conflict. Henry has been diagnosed with ADHD. Ben has an anger problem. According to Ben, Henry often makes "silly sounds" that make him really mad. Henry admits this, but silly sounds are what he does. Recently, Henry was making silly sounds; Ben was feeling less than tolerant, so he pulled Henry's chair out from under him. A few days afterward Ben found Henry's math paper stuck under a leg of Henry's chair. Ben pulled it out, tearing it in the process. Henry came along, discovered the torn paper on his desk, and assumed Ben had torn it on purpose. Henry got angry, and a scuffle ensued. After the second incident, the fifth grade teacher asked if I might help the boys have a conversation about the incidents and about their relationship with each other.

When we talked, both boys were able to recall their perceptions and their feelings at the time. In the process, each gained an understanding of where the other was coming from. Both boys accepted responsibility and tearfully apologized. They were then asked if they would like to have a different partner. They declined, saying they wanted to continue to sit next to each other. They were best friends. When asked how they might handle conflict in the future, they agreed that it would be best to approach their teacher and ask for "one of those meetings." They got up from their chairs and shook hands.

A day later I met with two eighth grade girls at a Des Moines middle school. They had been in a fight earlier in the week. Each girl belonged to a group, and the groups had provoked the fight after rumors circulated about what one girl said about the other. They had been friends at one time, but that was "a long time ago, maybe four or five months." Since then they had retreated to the safety of their respective groups, each defined by race.

The three of us were seated around a small table. The girls refused to speak to or even look at each other. The hurt was there, but it couldn't be acknowledged—to do so would be a sign of weakness. We sat with the anger and the awkwardness. An hour into our meeting there was a breakthrough. One girl said she had heard that the other had called her a "ho." The allegation was denied at first, but an acknowledgment followed that maybe it had been said. That led to the turning point. The offended girl said it wasn't so much what she had heard at school, where the term is frequently used. She said it was what the word meant to her. She hung her head and spoke softly, describing how her mother has called her a "ho" for as long as she could remember. She explained that when "ho" is said in her presence she's overcome with shame and rage—she can't help herself. The other girl was humbled and couldn't speak. The anger and bravado had disappeared. There was no real conversation after this, but the pain was felt by everyone. The girls apologized, but there was no inclination to resume a lost friendship or even shake hands.

The years between fifth and eighth grade pass quickly but the world, nevertheless, inflicts its pain. What if these girls had sat across from each other three years earlier? What if the revelation had taken place then? What if the teacher and the mothers had been present? What if the response had been meaningful?

I wonder if the child archetype continues to exert its influence over these girls or if its power has diminished, replaced by the victim archetype. What would that mean for their future?

What Does It Mean to Be Radical?

I realized a few weeks ago that I had frequent flyer miles expiring soon. I hadn't planned a *Justice Diary* trip for March, but New York City was on a short list of possibilities and I was delighted that 20,000 miles would fly me from Minneapolis to LaGuardia and back. It didn't dawn on me until this morning that a four-hour layover in Denver was part of the bargain. That's the price you sometimes pay for a free ticket. And that's why I'm somewhere over eastern Colorado.

There is a freedom in a flight, a freedom from cell phones and traffic and talk radio. And there is a safety too. A safety from the status quo and defensiveness and narrow-mindedness. I say this perhaps because as I look out my cabin window I see no human-made divisions, borders, or barriers. From here the land appears much as it did when first settled, although there are occasional farm buildings, irrigation systems, and ribbons of road redefining it now. But even these suggest a certain vision and risk taking.

There is a safety too in being able to reflect on ideas and concepts. I'm thinking of the word "radical" and how its connotations include "wacky" or "way out" or even "dangerous." I'm thinking of how judges and others have characterized the court watchers at the Polk County Courthouse as "radicals." Among these elected officials and public servants the word is being used along with "intruder," "outsider," and "troublemaker." I can't help but think of how the Pharisees spoke about a certain young Galilean. But if youth is to be feared, those entrenched in the system have little to worry about; the average age of Polk County court watchers is nearly seventy.

What is to be feared of these retirees? Is it their experience and their wisdom? Is it that they have time to think about what they have seen and heard while sitting in the back of our courtrooms? Is it that they have networks within which they might share what they have seen and heard? Is it that they vote?

They Look Like Arnold But Can't Cope

I left the Brooklyn hostel shortly after eight in the morning. Fortunately, I brought an umbrella. I headed south on Bedford then west on Gates. After a few blocks of brownstones with small houses and churches tucked in between, I turned right on Washington and headed north until I found Mike's Coffee Shop. Set back from the intersection and nearly unnoticed, Mike's is a neighborhood institution. Mike himself was at the cash register, where he's been for the past twenty years. Like him, his predecessors served coffee, eggs, and home fries going back to the '50s. I sat at the counter, close enough to the action to discover why it's not just the breakfasts that keep people coming back. Mike inquired of a teenage boy about his mother's health, of an elderly gentleman about his wife, and of a young couple about their newborn. All the while, he was exchanging orders and jokes with his head cook in perfect Brooklyn Spanish.

After a great spinach omelet, I headed west on Dekalb in the direction of the Brooklyn Bridge. Midway I came across Fort Greene Park and what looked like a crime scene. I eventually figured out that something was being filmed. I wandered into the park, where singles and couples were standing frozen, all with black umbrellas. It looked like a remake of *Mary Poppins*. Glad to have a black umbrella too, I coaxed information from a guy with a walkie-talkie—Warner Bros. was filming a pilot for a show called *The Hostages*. He wouldn't give up any more, but I imagined kidnappers would be showing up before long. I wanted to ask if this was true, but he stopped me short to inquire if I was an extra. Admitting I wasn't, he said it was best I walk somewhere else. I exited the park on a side street lined with tents and tractor trailers. Around the middle of the block I stopped to ask directions of a gentleman high up in the cab of one of the trucks. Chris from Queens, a gentle giant of a man, said he was a member of the crew and this is "pilot season," when single episodes are filmed and then marketed in the hope that they will ripen into a series.

Chris then asked what brought me to Brooklyn, surmising, like the guy with the walkie-talkie, that I wasn't a local. This led to a discussion about the courts and then to what he termed the "prison industrial complex." He said he had a problem with child support years ago: He supported his son for the first two years, but the boy's mother moved in with someone else for the next two years. He didn't pay support during that time. The mother took him to court and the judge treated him like a criminal. Fortunately, the mother recognized the boy really needed to be cared for by his father and she dropped the action. Chris has been the sole custodian and supporter for his son for the past ten years.

I asked Chris how things are going with his son now. He said he and his son are fortunate. His son attends a small public high school in Queens—400 students—housed in the same building as LaGuardia College. The teachers and administrators are good, but the key for his son is staying busy in activities outside of school. His son is learning discipline by studying tae kwon do.

We then talked about the larger problems of kids and schools. Chris knows many kids who have dropped out. He said schools have little tolerance for kids who struggle. He added that the kids most likely to drop out or be kicked out of school are the kids who are "low functioning" and on the fringe. He said the way we test kids doesn't identify their unique talents and capabilities. Chris said while there are some specialized schools in Brooklyn and Queens, for the most part there is a one-size-fits-all education system that fails to recognize kids as individuals, resulting in the school-to-prison pipeline. According to Chris, neighborhood kids go into prison and come out men. They come out looking like Arnold Schwarzenegger, but without the skills to cope in today's world. They start using drugs and end up back in prison. Many want to stay there. They have their cell phones and their televisions, and nothing is expected of them. Chris said many of these men feel safer on the inside than on the outside. A guy with a walkie-talkie came up to the truck. Chris had to get back to work.

It Doesn't End

In Brooklyn, New York, five or six blocks north of Lafayette on Bedford, you're in another world. You get a sense that you're approaching it at Willoughby, but once you cross Flushing you're in the heart of it. A block to the west is the Bnos Yisroel School for Girls. A block north is the Yeshiva Mesivta Arugath Habosem. Cross Heyward Street and you find the Beth Jacob School. The neighborhood is home to a large Orthodox Jewish community, most of whom are Hasidic.

Hasidim often keep to themselves. I tried striking up a conversation with several men, young and old, but without success. I wanted to have a conversation with someone about Hasidic justice. The closest I got was a rabbi who seemed intrigued and asked if I was Jewish. I told him I wasn't, but he still took my card.

Failing in my mission, I headed back south. At Classon and Dekalb I found the headquarters for the New York Police Department's 88th Precinct, housed in what had been a neighborhood church. I got the attention of Deputy Inspector Henderson, who gave me the lowdown on the Clinton Hill/Fort Greene section of Brooklyn. He said the 88 is small in comparison with many of Brooklyn's precincts, with fewer than 200 patrol officers. I told him that that was more than half the entire Des Moines Police Department. He said everything is relative and that the NYPD, covering five boroughs, has about 35,000 officers, down from 40,000 a few years ago. He said most precinct calls concern prostitution, drugs, domestics, and petty thefts, adding that crime on the whole is down 75 percent in the last decade. He attributes this to increased community policing and a greater sense of ownership on the part of neighborhood residents. In recent years there's been an influx of people from Manhattan who have taken the chance to purchase old and abandoned buildings and renovate them. He said that that's made all the difference.

After my conversation with Inspector Henderson I headed east on Lafayette.

Eventually I ran into John, a security guard who does apartment maintenance on the side. He was working on one of the neighborhood's many brownstones. I asked him about his experience with the justice system. He said he knows a lot of good cops but also there is a lot of corruption in the system, and once you get into it anything can happen. He spoke about his nephew who went to prison for stealing a car. He did the time, was paroled, violated his parole by using drugs, and went back to prison. One guard didn't like John's nephew so he kept harassing and bullying him. The nephew got fed up and assaulted the guard with a pencil, and is now doing sixty years. John said it's not his nephew he's concerned about, it's the neighborhood teens and young men. There aren't enough jobs, and if they get into any kind of trouble their chances of getting good jobs are slim. His greatest fear is that many of them will go the way of his nephew. It doesn't end, he said.

"Tough on Crime" Should Be for the Bad Guys

There is a little place across from Emmanuel Baptist Church in Brooklyn that has the best black bean burger I've ever had. For ten dollars you get a burger big enough for two with fries to match. I ate my fill, with enough left over for the cat at the hostel. At lunch I visited with Lauren, just arrived from Germany. He's on holiday from his job—doing German–English interpretation at major international conferences. Lauren's English is impeccable. He could easily be from Chicago or St. Louis. We talked about his profession, but what he really wanted to talk about was his dream—becoming a community organizer. Germany has a major problem with refugees and asylum seekers, and he hears horror stories about how they are treated, by the government and by the average citizen. He wants to do something about it, but he doesn't know what. That's why he's in New York. He listens faithfully to *Democracy Now!* and wants to visit their headquarters in Manhattan. He wants to volunteer there and learn how individuals and groups can change systems. He used to think that the only way systems could be changed is from the inside. Recent events around the world have convinced him otherwise. He now believes that systemic change is possible when there is sufficient pressure brought by an educated and organized citizenry. I wished him luck.

On my walk back to the hostel I witnessed an arrest. Three patrol cars with lights flashing had pinned a white car up against the curb. Four male police officers surrounded the vehicle while a supervising officer gave orders. First there was a conversation with the African American driver, and then with a woman in the back seat, also African American. After a couple of minutes the woman was removed, handcuffed, and placed in the back of a patrol car. That car and a second sped off. I approached the supervisor and introduced myself. He was suspicious at first, but it eased his anxiety when I told him I was a retired prosecutor.

His name was Joe. He was fifty-seven, with thirty years on the force and maybe two or three years to retirement. He told me the operator of the white car was a taxi driver who had called the police because the woman had refused to pay her fare. The driver's response was to lock the back doors. That prompted the woman to kick out the rear window. Joe said that taxi drivers getting stiffed is common, as are broken taxi windows. I asked what would happen to the woman. He said she'd be charged with criminal mischief and theft of services. I asked what then? He said most likely nothing. The court system can't handle all of the cases. The judge would probably enter an ACD, an "adjournment of the action without a date ordered, resulting in suspension of the case for six months or so, followed by a dismissal if the woman stays out of trouble. There's no fine, probation, or penalty of any kind. Joe said if a case is dismissed pursuant to an ACD, the effect is that the arrest and the prosecution never happened. I told Joe that where I come from the people who run the system would likely resist the enactment of any legislation similar to New York's ACD statute. He wanted to know why. I said many people think it's necessary to give even minor offenders— juveniles and adults—arrest and court records, and that the labeling of offenders as criminals is important if the goal is being tough on crime. Joe said it's his experience that it's best to save the tough-on-crime stuff for the bad guys.

Knowledge and Responsibility

Some people call it synchronicity—a coincidence of events that seem meaningfully related. I was looking at a subway map, considering a visit to the Brooklyn Art Museum. Just to the south of the large green expanse known as Prospect Park was Flatbush, a neighborhood tucked between Wingate and Prospect Park South. I'd heard of Flatbush and knew it was somewhere in the greater NYC area. I had no idea where, until now. In twenty minutes I was there, up out of the guts of the subway and on the sidewalk. It was past noon, and I debated between the Purple Yam, which featured organic Asian fare, and the Connecticut Muffin, which served soups, sandwiches, pastries, and coffee. I chose the latter, ordering the roasted vegetable soup and a baguette.

As I paid, I asked the cashier if there was a law office nearby. I thought I might visit with a local attorney about justice issues. The young man wasn't aware of one but said I might visit with the council woman whose office is two blocks east on Cortelyou. I asked if she could give me a sense of what goes on in the neighborhood. He said, "For that you have to talk with Raquel. She's right behind you." I turned and saw a petite woman who exuded energy and urgency without speaking a word. I waited my turn while she greeted an incoming customer. I then introduced myself and told her of my interests. She said we had to talk. She had an errand to run and would be back by two. I said I would wait.

Raquel Irizarry is in her early fifties—a late bloomer who didn't finish high school but who is now enrolled in an innovative program at Brooklyn College, where she will earn a four-year degree soon. She said her professors like having her in class. They say she asks good questions and brings experience and a valuable perspective. But that's not what she wanted to talk about. She wanted to tell me what she knows now about injustice, beginning with an incident from a year ago and what has transpired since.

She was at a nearby intersection, standing next to a young Latino man and waiting for the light to change. Just before she entered the crosswalk, a car approached, swerved, and drove up over the curb and onto the sidewalk. Four white police officers jumped out. They ran toward the two of them, encircling the young man and forcing Raquel back so she couldn't see what was going on. She stayed as close as possible, fearing that if she walked away something bad would happen. A few moments later the officers turned away from the young man and returned to their car. As they drove past, one of the officers yelled, "Next time video it." The young man walked toward her, visibly shaken. She asked what happened. He said they wanted to know what he had in his pockets. He told them he had his keys and some money. The officers wanted to know where he had gotten the money. Before he could tell them, one of the officers recognized him and they let him go.

Afterward Raquel walked to the Connecticut Muffin and spoke with friends about what she'd witnessed. She told them she had just seen something very disturbing and thought it was an incident of racial profiling. That evening she told her husband what happened and that it was terribly wrong and shouldn't happen to anyone.

A few weeks later Raquel was at a local restaurant with her husband. They were seated at the window table nearest the street. An African American man with a woman and children as passengers pulled up and legally parked. Before they could get out of the car, two white police officers approached, gestured for the driver to roll down his window, and asked for identification. One officer pulled out a flashlight and began looking in the other windows. Raquel told her husband that something was wrong, that this must be what it was like in Nazi Germany when people were approached, told to show their papers, and asked if they were a Jew.

Raquel started doing research. She discovered that under Mayor Bloomberg police stops increased from 97,000 in 2002 to 724,000 in 2012. She started circulating petitions to educate her neighbors about police profiling and the "Blue Wall" the police hide behind. She reached out to other organizations advocating for justice reform. She made strong connections with a Manhattan organization known as PROP—the Police Reform Organizing Project.

Raquel Irizarry is on a mission. She knows that once you discover the truth you can no longer remain silent. She knows the truth can be a burden but it can't be denied. She knows that communities must organize against police injustice. She's up to the task.

Raquel then told me about her son and the day he was stopped: How he was approached by two men. How he considered pulling a paper punch out of his pocket to protect himself but thought better of it. How they pulled out handguns and pointed them at him. How they then identified themselves as police officers. How they questioned him for no reason. How he got out of what he believed to be a very dangerous situation by telling the officers his father worked for the *New York Times*. How it was only then that they backed off and let him go his way.

Raquel was in tears as she told me her son's story. She said it's a mother's worst nightmare. Last Saturday night in East Flatbush two plainclothes police officers shot sixteen-year-old Kimani Gray. They claimed he had a handgun. He died from seven bullet wounds. He was African American.

A Tale of Two Courthouses

I took the N train to lower Manhattan and Canal Street. I wandered, as visitors do, and found myself adjacent to Thomas Paine Park, named for the patriot. In defense of the American Revolution, Paine wrote: "These are the times that try men's souls. The summer soldier and the sunshine patriot will, in this crisis, shrink from the service of their country; but he that stands it now, deserves the love and thanks of man and woman."

I have to wonder: Who are today's patriots? What crisis calls them to arms, and against whom do they take up arms?

The park sits quietly in the shadow of the New York Supreme Court building, with its Corinthian columns. I ascended the granite steps, entered through massive doors, passed through security, walked down the marble hall, and found myself in the rotunda, encircled by massive columns and crowned by a cupola with elegant windows. I took an elevator to the top floor, intending to work my way down, as I like to do in courthouses. Exiting, I followed the curved hall with windows looking out on the stained glass of the cupola below. Adding yet more elegance, lawyers in tailored suits were meeting with clients in small private conference rooms or with colleagues on benches hugging the wall. All communication was discrete and in a whisper. Privacy is honored here.

I began my search for a courtroom. I peered in five or six, all quiet and inactive with the exception of an occasional attendant. Halfway around I was stopped by a tall, thin gentleman in uniform who offered assistance. I told him I was hoping to sit in on a trial. He said it was unlikely I would find one since it was Friday afternoon. I asked where criminal matters are handled. He said I was in the wrong place, that although many movies and television shows depicting criminal trials are filmed here, the actual criminal courthouse is a block away, "where the crazies are." He said in this courthouse it's about civil matters, about money—real estate, contracts, accidents, divorces. He said if I hurried I could still catch some of the action.

I retraced my steps, exited through the massive doors, and just outside found a well-dressed lawyer-type with briefcase. I asked for directions to the criminal court building. He knew about it but didn't know how to get there. A few feet away was a man sweeping the steps. I asked him the same question. He gave me exact directions. Within minutes I was entering a dark, nondescript building that was more jail than courthouse. Charles Dickens would have fit right in. I again passed through security. There was no privacy here: Handcuffed men and women sat on benches or were led down halls. Lawyers were cajoling. Lawyers were arguing. Faces were etched with pain. Faces were absent of emotion. Absent as well were the rotunda and the impressive cupola. This was a factory. It manufactured justice.

It was easy to find a courtroom doing business. I entered and found a seat near the front. The room was cavernous. The judge sat high up on a bench, the control tower, reading his newspaper in between hearings. On the other side of the barrier from the judge, nearly twenty people were seated around tables, at desks with computers, filing papers, eating, joking, texting—in various states of awareness. Defendants were called up one by one. A bailiff opened the gate, allowing each to approach. A prosecutor stood to the side, reading the charges and stating the State's position. Public defenders took turns at representing their clients. Some were prepared, most not. For the unprepared it was an opportunity to find out what their clients had been arrested for and, in most instances, plead them guilty.

A defendant named Rodriquez had a new charge of public urination and warrants for failing to appear on multiple charges of possessing an open container. He pled guilty to all and was given a $75 fine with an $80 surcharge. Next. Daryl had a new charge of selling heroin. The prosecutor said it was his tenth arrest in a year. She asked for a $25,000 bond. Daryl's lawyer said he's lived in New York all his life, has twin five-year-old sons, and should be released to take care of his family. Bond was set at $12,500. Next. Jerome had a new trespass charge, his fourth in recent months. Five days in jail. Next. Miguel had been charged with assault with injury and damage to property. The prosecutor wanted a $10,000 bond. The defense attorney said that Miguel had been at a restaurant and a female patron didn't like the way he was looking at her. She approached him to take his photo with her cell phone. He struck the phone with his hand and scratched the woman in the process. Miguel's lawyer asked that he be released on his own recognizance. Bond was set at $2,000. Next. Lonte had stolen a coat. He was on probation for another theft charge. Bond was set at $1,000. Next. Jeffrey was drunk in the park. One day in jail with credit for the one day he'd served. Next. And it went on. Twenty some. All Latino or African American. All were charged, defended, found guilty, and processed by public servants, nearly all of them white.

An Island Boy's Story

I met a decent man this morning. I'll call him William.

I was in the lobby of the building where the Brooklyn District Attorney's Office is located. I had a meeting scheduled for 10:00 on the eighteenth floor with the chaplain of the DA's office but found out at the last moment that he'd been called away. I bought a coffee adjacent to security and took a seat on the radiator enclosure that ran the length of the outside wall. Next to me was a handsome man who had a goatee and short dreadlocks pulled back in a ponytail, and was wearing freshly pressed olive khakis. Our eyes met and I stood up, commenting on what a busy place this is. He squared his shoulders and said that his name was William. He was a supervisor with the NYC sanitation department. He said it's busy 24/7. It's overwhelming. There is no way they can keep up. I told him about my experience at the criminal courthouse in Manhattan. He said it's worse in Brooklyn.

Then he started talking about "the kids." He said the kids—twelve, thirteen, and fourteen years old—will kill you without thinking twice about it. He said recently he had seen from a distance two teenage boys rush at an old man and knock him to the ground. He said it didn't appear to be a robbery, just an assault, a vicious one. They struck and kicked the man for a minute or two and then ran to a waiting bus, laughing all the way. He said when these kids get caught judges have no choice but to have them locked up. If they don't, it just gets worse. I asked him what happens when they do get out. He said they are worse and are back in soon enough. He said the sad thing is when a young man rises up out of this, gets a degree, maybe even a master's, and is treated with less respect in the neighborhood than the graduate of Rikers Island. I asked what could be done. He said that he didn't know, that it starts when they are so young.

I told William about being on a subway yesterday and seeing a boy not much older than a year whose mother was in an argument with another woman and had given her son her iPhone so he could play a game. Sitting in his stroller, he was wrecking trains, pushing a button on the screen time after time. He seemed good at what he was doing. William said kids these days are trapped in their devices. They don't know right from wrong, only this from that. He said when they get older they don't know how to make real decisions. They don't even know what the options are. Then he wanted to talk about ethics. He said kids don't seem to have a core from which ethical responses arise. He asked why is it that they fight for the green or the orange of their gangs? Their gangs stand for nothing. Why don't they fight for the red, white, and blue, for the country that has given them so much?

William asked if he could tell me his story. He said he was from the islands. His mother was Hindi, born in India. His father was born in Portugal and raised a Catholic. They met in Guyana. When they married, his mother's family disowned her. William's parents were committed to keeping their small family together. When he was fifteen they moved to Brooklyn and opportunity. William wanted to be a pilot, and as soon as he was of age, he enlisted. Because he was an "alien" his application to flight school was denied. He took another route, serving for twenty-two years and "keeping his country's secrets." He was proud of his service, proud that his superiors had respect for him, proud that he'd become skilled and had done his job well. He said so many kids these days, and adults, are lacking in skills and, therefore, lacking in meaningful pride.

Then William asked if he could tell me the story of his son. He said when his boy was nine or ten he started to become unapproachable and disrespectful. He was having trouble in school. He'd been caught lying. Nothing seemed to get through to him. One evening they had an argument that nearly became physical. William controlled his anger and told his son to go to his room and change his clothes—they were going somewhere. It took nearly an hour, but the boy came out dressed for the weather. They lived in Texas at the time, and it didn't take long for them to drive far enough so that the only light was from the oncoming traffic. William pulled the car onto the shoulder. They had a conversation. William told his son that he was a man now and that two men can't live in the same house. It was time for him to take care of himself. He told the boy to get out and close the door behind him. William returned home alone. When he arrived he told his wife what happened. There were tense moments. Two hours later there was a knock at the door. Nothing was said, but there were hugs. William said that night changed everything. I asked him how his son is doing now. He said his boy enlisted in the navy to serve his country. When he finishes his tour of duty he intends to return to Brooklyn, become a police officer, and serve his country some more.

We Are in a Hell of Our Own Making

Last week I stepped into Emmanuel Baptist Church hoping to speak to the pastor. The woman at the desk said she'd do her best to help. She encouraged me to sit or wander about as I pleased. I chose to wander, discovering that Emmanuel is a Brooklyn institution with a 125-year history. That evening it was alive. Choirs practicing. Classes going on. Conversations in different corners. I wondered, if it's this vibrant on a Wednesday evening, what is it like on a Sunday? A young woman introduced herself and inquired of my interest. When I told her it was restorative justice, she beamed. She said she recently left a position at the Brooklyn District Attorney's Office, where restorative justice is held in high regard. She said I must meet Reverend Tyrone Monro, the associate pastor she'd been hired to replace. She said Reverend Monro has been involved in social justice issues for as long as she could remember. She said he wasn't in at the time, but she promised to connect me.

I met Reverend Monro this afternoon. His business card identified him as the Associate Pastor for Public Witness, but he's much more than that. After a successful business career, he entered the seminary and was ordained in 2001 at the age of fifty-eight. Among many other duties, he's responsible for the HIV/AIDS, Mentoring, Prisoner Re-Entry, and South African Children Ministries, and blood drives. But he's much more than an administrator. Reverend Monro is a man of deep faith, long connected to his church, who responded to a special call at a time when many are nearing retirement. He said he'd read *The New Jim Crow*. He said he's witnessed what Michelle Alexander describes, and it's frightening. He agreed that a social movement is necessary. He said our justice system is embedded deeply in our country, that it's an institution. He paused for a moment and then said, "It's such a monster."

He described how we have always had prisons, dating back to colonial times. But at least then the emphasis was on penance and not punishment. Prisoners oftentimes lived with their families, and there was no intention to completely ostracize offenders from their community. But things have changed radically. It's a business now.

Multi-million dollar, billion dollar industries are dependent for their existence on prisons. He talked about the war on drugs. How it made sense at first, and how we bought into it thinking we would be safer if drugs were eradicated from our streets. But we're not safer. Mass incarceration has resulted in greater disenfranchisement, greater marginalization, greater poverty—particularly for men of color. They get out with little chance of employment. They can't return to their families because they are barred from public housing. The return to prison is inevitable. He said: "At the nexus of poverty and little or no education, there is prison."

Then Reverend Monro talked about kids, the families they are growing up in, the schools they are attending, the pressures from our consumer culture. He told me a story about a minister friend of his from the West Coast. His friend was at a family gathering and came to the realization that he was the only adult male who had not been incarcerated: his father had been in prison, all of his uncles had been, all of his cousins. Even though he was a minister, he suddenly felt the great weight of being a role model, not only for those in his congregation but for those in his extended family. Reverend Monro said he felt the same pressure. More than anything the young, and the not so young, need mentors, positive role models to emulate. We talked about a model program in Boston for ex-offenders. Harvard studied it. While many things are needed for those re-entering society after imprisonment, the most critical determinant of success is the existence of a successful mentor relationship.

Reverend Monro is a man of faith. By nature he is an optimist. He believes people can change. He believes our country can change, that sooner or later we will wake up to the fact that being tough on crime is not working. But Reverend Monro is also a realist. He said when it comes to how we are addressing poverty, education, and crime in our country, "we are in a hell of our own making."

Nearly seventy, Reverend Monro will soon retire from his present position. I asked about his plans. He said he's not sure but he is sure he will be doing justice work of some kind.

Stop and Frisk

Testimony started Monday at the federal courthouse in lower Manhattan in the *Floyd* case brought by four New Yorkers who claim that stop-and-frisks conducted by New York City police officers are unconstitutional and racially biased. Plaintiffs say the NYPD has a pattern and practice of disobeying constitutional limits by engaging in suspicionless stops and arresting people, mainly blacks and Latinos, without probable cause. They also claim that some police supervisors have set quotas on the number of stops. According to the *New York Daily News*, Darius Charney, a lawyer for the Center for Constitutional Rights, alleged in his opening statement that "the NYPD is laying 'siege to black and Latino neighborhoods'" and that "'thousands if not millions of New Yorkers have been subjected to a 'frightening and degrading experience.'" The *Floyd* case is national news. Police and community organizing groups around the country are taking notice and awaiting the outcome. Those who favor the stop-and-frisk approach say the NYPD targets crime and not members of minority groups. They cite favorable statistics documenting the dramatic reduction in crime in New York City since Michael Bloomberg became mayor in 2002.

I decided to observe the trial firsthand. This morning I arrived early and waited in a long line. Only after going through security did I find I was in the wrong courthouse. I was told to go next door to the federal courthouse. A shorter line, security, and, again, the wrong courthouse. I was in a federal courthouse, but the *Floyd* trial was being held at a second federal courthouse down the street. I was told by a security officer that if the courtroom filled up before I arrived, I could return and watch the trial on a monitor set up in the overflow courtroom on the fifth floor. I walked the block to the second courthouse, went through security, found the *Floyd* courtroom, and was told it was full. On the way to the overflow courtroom I struck up a conversation with attorney Peter Gleason, who had also been turned away. Gleason said he represented Adrian Schoolcraft, an NYPD police officer who blew the whistle on arrest quotas leading to police abuses. I had read in yesterday's paper that lawyers for the *Floyd* plaintiffs expected to introduce as evidence audiotapes Schoolcraft secretly recorded that documented numerous instances of police misconduct within the NYPD's 81st Precinct. Schoolcraft released the tapes to the *Village Voice* in 2010 and has since filed a separate lawsuit against the NYPD claiming retaliation and seeking $50 million in damages. He claims his six-day involuntary hospitalization in Jamaica Hospital Center's psychiatric ward was ordered to discredit his allegations.

Gleason was attending the *Floyd* trial in anticipation of his client's future trial. We passed through security and found our way to the overflow courtroom, the first to arrive. The monitor hadn't been turned on, so we had time to talk. Gleason told me he had been a cop with the NYPD in the '80s, during the time when the Lower East Side was at its worst. He said prostitution and drug dealing were rampant. Buildings had been vacated and were crumbling: "It looked like a war zone." He said something had to be done, but the response went too far. Blacks and Latinos were routinely stopped for no reason, harassed, and thrown up against a wall, and worse. He said that for the most part, the beat cops didn't want to do it. It was directed from the top down. I asked why others didn't come forward as his client had. He said most cops are afraid and he understands that. His own client has been suspended for three years without pay and fears for his life. The others can't afford to lose their jobs. They have families and bills to pay. There is no other work they can get with the salary and benefits given to a New York City cop.

At that point a bailiff arrived and turned on the monitor. A black police officer was testifying. He was telling how kids, twelve and thirteen years old, were stopped and handcuffed for no reason. He testified that on several occasions he was called to a scene by a supervisor and told to write a summons for an offense that hadn't occurred. He said he complained many times, he'd gone to internal affairs, but nothing ever happened. Seated next to me was a young woman, a filmmaker. She was taking notes feverishly.

"I Hate Injustice"

In midair over Ohio and I can't shake New York City. It's a rush. It's a drug. It grabs you like no other place I know. Maybe one of the great cities of China or Japan or India are like it. I don't know. But those cities are also part of the fabric of Manhattan and Brooklyn and Queens. America as melting pot describes the City up to a point. But it's not homogenous. The dress and food and languages of other lands, the faces, remain distinct. The rudeness and indifference some speak of is overstated. When it does present itself, it has its own charm. Delivered with a Brooklyn accent, it has a familiarity. Sitcoms and television dramas prepare you for it. Perhaps the beauty of being a visitor is you don't know where you shouldn't go. I'm not a fool, and I understand the world is different at night, when the protection of people and daylight are diminished. And some neighborhoods I passed on the train to Flushing or Flatbush are probably best not explored after dark. A cop in Harlem spoke with pride about how safe his neighborhood is these days, but he also said there are some Brooklyn neighborhoods he couldn't say the same for.

New York City is far more than its theaters, restaurants, and museums. The trains and buses get you to the starting point and your feet get you into it. I was a foreigner there, but not treated as one. People will talk with you. There is not a shyness. They readily share their stories. And on the subway they don't care who is present.

I stood next to two school girls yesterday on the eastbound R train. They spoke of love with the wisdom of grandmothers. They talked about how there can be no love without respect, no matter what the boys say. They agreed that respect means you think about what you say before you say it. They talked about their futures and what they wanted in a man.

There are some other conversations I hope to write about, after I get home and have a chance to review my notes. I need to talk about the young community organizer who teaches faith groups to use social media and whose mother, a minister, learned about community organizing the old-fashioned way—from Saul Alinsky—years ago. I need to write about a much older man who still fights for police reform even after retiring as the head of a statewide corrections association. I need to talk about the Brooklyn minister who treats gang members like his own kids and who runs a gun buy-back program out of church basements while serving as the chaplain for a district attorney's office.

But for now, some images from the past ten days: The Martin Buber quote on the wall of the Jewish Museum on the Upper East Side: "I cannot accept the laws and statutes blindly, but I must ask myself again and again—is this particular law addressed to me and rightly so." The film *The Gatekeeper* that tells the story of Shin Bet from the perspective of six former heads of Israel's secretive internal security service and their reflections on the mistreatment of Palestinians. The Gordon Parks black-and-white photography exhibit in the basement of the Studio Museum in Harlem that documents the poverty and squalor of tenement life in 1967. The elderly Jewish woman who spoke of the death of her husband and the discovery of love late in life. The reminder during the Sunday jazz Mass at the Church of the Ascension of the weekly gay fellowship meeting on Wednesday. The garment salesman from Bombay who held back tears as he spoke of family difficulties he could not attend to. The poetry jam at the Brooklyn Academy of Music where talented artists of the word—black, white, and Latino—spoke with eloquence and fire about violence, oppression, death, respect, and hope. The beautiful black child sleeping in the arms of her sleeping father on the E train. The *Gravity and Grace* exhibit at the Brooklyn Museum of Art—a display of the genius of El Anatsui and the skill of thirty young Nigerian men working in his shops transforming aluminum bottle caps into incredible wall-sized tapestries of color and delight. The plaque with the quote from the Lithuanian-born artist Ben Shahn: "I hate injustice. I guess that's about the only thing I really do hate. I've hated injustice ever since I read a story in school, and I hope I go on hating it all my life."

Restorative Justice with FaceTime

Over the past year and a half I've been helping members of First Parish Church in Portland, Maine, start a community-based restorative justice center. On three occasions I've made the trip to train them on the principles of restorative justice and the basic techniques of facilitating victim–offender dialogues and mediating conflicts between school kids. In addition to the onsite trainings, we've used FaceTime, allowing me to work with the church's restorative justice team remotely. iPads are wonderful tools. They've made it possible to sit at home and mentor new mediators fifteen hundred miles away. By placing an iPad strategically, I can observe a facilitator and two people role-playing kids having a conversation in the aftermath of a fight or a bullying incident or damage done to a relationship by an inappropriate Facebook posting. The experience is an intimate one. With the iPad in the middle of a table, two or three feet from each of the participants, I'm able to be right there—listening, stopping the action to slow things down a bit, gently coaching them to really hear what's been said.

The leaders of First Parish's restorative justice initiative are now training a new group of church members. The people in this group want to become involved in working with kids in trouble and in conflict, helping them to problem solve and to learn new ways to respond when they are frustrated or angry.

This evening I met with the group via FaceTime. A dozen people were seated in the first row of the church's sanctuary. I was plopped on top of the ebony piano. Faithful to the restorative justice way of doing things, it wasn't a lecture but a conversation with examples and storytelling and the sharing of opinions and insights. After a brief history of the growth of restorative justice dating back to the '70s, we considered what restorative justice has the potential to offer that our present retributive response to criminal wrongdoing does not. Through role-play they put themselves in the positions of victims and offenders.

The volunteers at First Parish Church in Portland are not naive. They don't believe in being soft on crime. They also don't believe that being tough on crime is the answer. It makes sense to them that holding offenders accountable, rather than punishing them, has the greatest chance of success, whether the offenders are juveniles or adults. They want to be part of the growing effort in which ordinary citizens are demanding to play a part in helping to make things right.

We Don't Want a System That Just Fills Prisons

Twenty people gathered this evening at the home of former Iowa lieutenant governor Joy Corning. It was the study group's final discussion of Michelle Alexander's *The New Jim Crow: Mass Incarceration in the Age of Colorblindness*. The class was facilitated by Cameron Barr, associate pastor at Plymouth Church, who is passionate about justice. Cameron knows about injustice, having ministered to death row inmates while a seminarian at Vanderbilt. He preaches about justice whenever he's given the opportunity.

This past November Cameron spoke eloquently about restorative justice. His sermon created quite a stir, particularly among several judges at Plymouth who took issue with Cameron's statement that AMOS intended to recruit court watchers to sit in the Polk County Courthouse, taking note and publicizing the insensitive actions of indiscriminate prosecutors and judges who are too punitive. Cameron's sermon was printed and circulated among judges outside the Plymouth community, even getting into the hands of the chief district court judge, who expressed his own displeasure. Perhaps he was angered by Cameron's insistence that "We don't want a system that just fills prisons. We want to tend to broken relationships."

Two Sundays ago Cameron again preached about justice, referencing Alexander's book and her argument that our society openly discriminates against people labeled as criminals in the same way that we once openly discriminated against people of color. In one succinct and powerful paragraph, Cameron got to the heart of our collective culpability:

Jail or prison is hardly the end of a criminal's punishment. Once released they cannot find jobs or housing.
They typically cannot vote or serve on juries. They are
ineligible for many forms of government assistance.
And they are saddled with debt for days spent in jail,
for court costs and fines, and for a multitude of other
unexpected fees and penalties. Most debilitating is the
stigma that a former prisoner carries. As a society we
fear people who are called criminals. We won't trust
them. This is not a problem just for the people who
work in the system every day—judges, prosecutors,
police officers, defense attorneys. This is a system that
we have built together, election by election and vote
by vote. We bear a collective guilt for a system biased
against the poor. We bear a collective responsibility to
discern together what justice ought to look like.

It is this "hell of our own making," as a Brooklyn minister
recently put it to me, that Cameron's study group has been wrestling
with. The challenge for this final class was to answer the question,
What can any individual or group do to push back, to make a difference? It was agreed that there are no easy answers, that there is no
single solution. Even at the local level there must be a multifaceted
approach: Court watching must continue. More people should be
trained. Accurate statistics must be gathered and disseminated. The
public needs to become better educated. Public forums need to be
held. Elected officials need to be asked the tough questions about
their policies and practices. The media needs to be called upon to do
its job. And, above all else, kids need to be helped early. The school-
to-prison pipeline must be disassembled. The community must be
enlisted to help teachers and administrators work with kids in conflict to make conversation and dialogue the norm.

As this evening's discussion drew to a close, plans were being
made for the next steps toward a goal of placing trained volunteer
mediators in every school in the city. Everyone agreed that this is a
doable goal, a goal that, if realized, can make a very big difference.

Go Out to the Outskirts

Pope Francis celebrated Holy Thursday Mass at St. Peter's yesterday. His homily was an admonition to those who remain on the sidelines while others suffer. Though gentle in its delivery, the homily was a call to action:

> We need to "go out," then, in order to experience our own anointing, its power and its redemptive efficacy: to the "outskirts" where there is suffering, bloodshed, blindness that longs for sight, and prisoners in thrall to many evil masters. It is not in soul-searching or constant introspection that we encounter the Lord: self-help courses can be useful in life, but to live by going from one course to another, from one method to another, leads us to minimize the power of grace, that comes alive and flourishes to the extent that we, in faith, go out and give ourselves and the Gospel to others, giving what little ointment we have to those who have nothing, nothing at all.

* * *

I had a conversation earlier this week with an astrologist who said we are in a time of change unlike any witnessed in this country since the '60s. The corruption and inertia within many of our institutions is causing them to weaken to the point of crumbling, and the astrological sign for justice has a strong presence on the astral charts right now. For those who would be change makers there is and will be for the next few years a strong wind at their backs.

Last Saturday there was a follow-up training for volunteers from the community who want to be school mediators. Many of the trainees are retired, but there is an energy and an urgency when they speak of their desire to get into schools and help kids resolve conflicts and mend broken relationships.

* * *

This morning a woman who works with a church-based restorative justice program called to tell me of her recent experience observing juvenile court in her city's courthouse. She spoke of how shocked she was to see that the justice system is just a machine, even when it comes to kids. She's not sure what she'll do next, but she's going to do something because "you can't be complacent once you know."

* * *

These are interesting times. As Pope Francis told the world yesterday: "We need to 'go out' . . . to the 'outskirts' where there is suffering, bloodshed, blindness that longs for sight, and prisoners in thrall to many evil masters."

Should School Misconduct Be Treated as Delinquency?

The full house at the Drake Law School Legal Clinic this evening listened to a panel discussion on school discipline. Brent Pattison, director of the clinic's Children's Rights Center, stated at the outset that the challenge for panel members was to address the question, When should student misconduct be treated as delinquency? Pattison commented that, in the interest of school safety, there is a growing risk that schools will outsource and rely too much on juvenile court.

Panelist Marilyn Lantz, the chief juvenile court officer, spoke first, saying that we need to think back to the 1990s. In response to heightened fear of gang activity, mostly on the East Coast, many states became reactive and moved to a much more formal juvenile justice system. This was accompanied by the enactment of get-tough laws, more kids being moved to adult court, previously confidential juvenile records being made public, and schools adopting zero-tolerance policies. Lantz said many states have revisited the enactment of get-tough laws and policies, but Iowa hasn't. She said research in the area of juvenile delinquency has increasingly forced those who supervise juveniles to move away from the trail-'em-nail-'em-jail-'em approach to one focusing on a change process in the after-math of delinquent incidents.

Kathy Nesteby, with the Iowa Division of Criminal and Juvenile Justice Planning, projected a chart showing Des Moines school district removals of students from their classrooms by race, ethnicity, and gender. The statistics show the number of minority students removed was nearly 67 percent. The primary reasons for removals, adding up to nearly 60 percent, were disruptive behavior, absenteeism, and fighting. Nesteby said research shows the one-size-fits-all approach to school discipline is just not working, and zero-tolerance policies in schools need to be dumped.

Connie Cook, a retired associate superintendent and high school principal, was brief in her remarks. She said that kids have to get through school; that the kids who drop out are destined for problems, if not with the courts then certainly with trying to make a living. She said that schools need to put as many steps as possible in place to keep kids out of the formal justice system and that we must address the school discipline problem lovingly.

Randall Wilson, legal director of the Iowa ACLU, was the most blunt. He acknowledges being a "system critic" and sees a racial justice issue, not only when looking at school removals but when

The one-size-fits-all approach to school discipline is just not working, and zero-tolerance policies in schools need to be dumped.

looking at the rate of arrests of minorities in relation to whites and the rates of convictions. It's a pattern repeated all the way through the system. Wilson said the real problem comes with the exercise of discretion. When it comes to minorities, they always lose. Instead, Wilson said we need to take advantage of our discretion and look at the school-to-prison pipeline as a challenge, not an accusation.

What Justice Demands

Michael Byars was an eighteen-year-old high school senior when he was sentenced to prison for the offense of lascivious acts with a child. That was in 2008. He had been accused of having a short, consensual relationship with a freshman who was thirteen years old at the time. The girl became pregnant and gave birth to a boy. Michael spent less than a year in prison, but he was placed on parole for life. He was also placed on the Iowa sex offense registry. Michael, now twenty-three, wants to help raise his son, but being on the sex offense registry has made that virtually impossible. With guts, determination, and the ability to persuade, he has helped fashion legislation that should ultimately allow him to get off the registry and on with his life.

State Senate File 385 has passed the Senate and the House public safety committee. All that's left is approval on the House floor. If it passes, a judge will decide whether or not Michael should be discharged from the registry. Michael would first have to complete sex offender treatment and be rated as at low-risk to reoffend. But the legislation is the key. With full approval by both the House and the Senate, it's likely Governor Branstad will sign the bill. Things are looking up for Michael. For the first time in years people are on his side.

But others are out to get him. Last Friday someone put a call in to the Scott County Sheriff's Office (Michael lives in Davenport) and alleged that he had "failed to register as a sex offender" under Iowa Code Section 692A.104. That someone claimed that on March 7, Michael registered his "relevant information" with the Scott County Sheriff's Office but did not include his employment as a lobbyist or his email address. Apparently, employment and email are considered "relevant information" required by the keepers of the registry. Michael was arrested for an aggravated misdemeanor, punishable by a maximum of two years in prison, and taken to the Scott County Jail. Michael's parents posted bond to secure his release.

Also, someone, probably the same someone who called the sheriff, put a call in to the corporate offices of Michael's employer. On

Saturday Michael was fired. The papers Michael was given at court this morning don't identify who the caller is. There is no hint as to what their motivation might be. All that's known is that Detective Peter Bawden signed his name to an affidavit in the presence of a notary stating: "The following facts known by me or told to me by other reliable persons form the basis for my belief that the Defendant committed these crimes."

The system is a machine. Machines don't call people to get their side of a story. Machines don't give people the opportunity to turn themselves in or, better yet, give them a court date at which they can voluntarily appear. Machines, operated by individuals lacking either discretion or compassion, have people arrested, jailed, required to post a bond, with the sorting out of things to happen at a later date.

A young reporter with the *Des Moines Register* is out to determine the truth of things, out to determine who the someone is. Let's hope he does. Justice demands it.

The Poorest of the Poor

Busy day today. The highlight was the hour I spent this evening on FaceTime with my daughter Sarah, who is volunteering in Guatemala. Sarah starts medical school in August, having taken the year off to recharge after a grueling four years of pre-med work. Of my five kids, she is the one I never expected to be a backpacker. But she certainly is one. Sarah spent the fall and early winter traveling in Thailand, Vietnam, Cambodia, and India. Now she's tutoring kids in Guatemala City through an organization called Safe Passage that helps families whose sole source of income is derived from what they can scavenge from the mile-long municipal dump.

I visited Safe Passage a couple of years ago—it's an amazing effort. There is now a school adjacent to the dump, and also a workshop and a store where visitors purchase craft items and jewelry made from what's been salvaged from the garbage heap. It's amazing how resourceful those who have almost nothing can be.

Sarah works with eighth graders in the morning and second graders in the afternoon. She says no matter what the age, the kids are a delight. Her only concern for herself is that she will get lice. It's inevitable.

Sarah had planned to volunteer for only four weeks and then travel throughout Central America until the end of July. But she's rethinking her plans. The kids are feeding her soul, and she knows she's better off for it.

The Buddha's Truths

I had coffee this afternoon with a Drake student at Mars Cafe. She's trying to decide what to do with her life between graduation and applying to law school. I first met the young woman in an honors' class where I was training students to become court watchers. I asked her today: Why law school? Why be a lawyer? She said she first thought about it in high school, but the court watch experience has reinforced her belief that she can help people by having a law degree. I asked what kind of law. She said she wants to be a public defender because everyone charged with a crime is presumed innocent and deserves to be represented.

On my walk home from Mars Cafe I listened to a Jack Kornfield lecture on the Four Noble Truths. Kornfield is one of the best at translating the Buddha's teachings into a language accessible to the Western mind. The Four Noble Truths speak to the suffering of the world. I'm not very disciplined, so my mind wandered. I reflected on a question that has long challenged me: If suffering is universal and inescapable, then why are some people sensitive to the pain and suffering of others and some not? I've thought that our own pain should lead us naturally to a sense of justice. Empathy—the ability to understand and share the feelings of others—should cause us to want others to be treated with fairness and compassion, just as we would want for ourselves. But human history suggests otherwise, so it's not surprising that the words of the Buddha, Jesus, and the other great teachers so often fall on deaf ears.

I thought back to last fall, when I taught a course on justice at First Unitarian Church. I expected a dozen people at the first class. Forty-five showed up. We gathered in a circle, spending two hours sharing memories of our first awareness that there is this thing called justice. For a few, an awareness of justice came from parents who taught them in the context of a particular faith tradition. But for most, an event—at school, in their neighborhood, at home, on the job—had made them sensitive to injustice because of the pain it caused them. And then I thought about a conversation I had this morning with a good friend who shared a story I hadn't heard her tell before. She grew up in a close community, attending Catholic church and Catholic school. Her parents were well respected and of adequate means. But one day her family "became poor," and life changed. It happened at the end of her junior year in high school. Tuition at the school was free, so when her father went to enroll her for her senior year he didn't expect a problem. But he was told he was too late to register his daughter and she would have to go elsewhere. She said it was on that day she learned that money and status means everything. Those who have it are treated differently than those who don't.

People medicate themselves with alcohol, drugs,

gambling, and pornography.

People also medicate themselves with power.

My friend could have become bitter, but she didn't. She has a sensitivity for others that is palpable.

So why do many who experience similar injustices respond otherwise? Why do some embrace the poor and others reject them? Why do some seek to repair while others seek to punish?

Finally, my mind wandered back to this afternoon, before my coffee with the Drake student, when a court watcher told me about a recent experience with a juvenile court officer. Following a judge's sentencing of a young boy to a correctional facility and the family tears that followed, the officer said it should have happened a long time ago and the boy deserved to be punished. There are some good juvenile court officers, just as there are some good prosecutors and judges. But there are just as many with cold hearts and quick pens. It's easy to know what justice is and how it should be administered when you are in power. You have to wonder what happened to those prosecutors and judges who are so certain in their judgments. We know from the Buddha that they've suffered. Do they hide behind the law for self-protection?

People medicate themselves with alcohol, drugs, gambling, and pornography. People also medicate themselves with power.

Kundalini and Delinquent Kids

I'm in St. Paul for the monthly weekend seminar of the Minnesota Jung Association. The assigned reading was from *The Psychology of Kundalini Yoga*, a collection of notes from a series of lectures given by Carl Jung in 1932. Although the connection between Western depth psychology and an ancient Eastern practice was intriguing, it didn't take long for the Hindu concepts and Sanskrit terms in the book to wear on me. So my arrival at Macalester College was accompanied by some trepidation. My anxiety dissipated, however, when we were introduced to Dr. Charles Zeltzer, a Jungian analyst from Los Angeles, who immediately delighted us with childhood tales about being raised by a Catholic mother and a Russian Jewish father. Following the stories, we learned soon enough that in Kundalini yoga the body consists of a series of chakras linked by channels. Chakras are not thought of as physiological reality in the Western sense; rather, they represent a subtle or mystical body. Jung wrote about Kundalini to provide a modern psychological interpretation of the chakras.

There are seven chakras, depicted as rising vertically from the groin area. They can be seen as a spiritual ladder, with spiritual consciousness ascending from lower to higher. The first chakra, the lowest, is the condition of everyday life. The true Self is asleep, and we are entangled in the roots of our existence in this world. According to Zeltzer, when we are in the first chakra we are in the "mother," so to speak—psychologically we are children, and our needs revolve around comfort and protection.

But a dramatic change comes with the movement from the first chakra to the second, which occurs during the teenage years. This is where it gets interesting for those concerned with delinquent youth. Moving from the first to the second chakra involves the release of significant energy. The myth within which the typical teenager lives, whether a boy or a girl, is one of risk, adventure, and taking chances in life. What we see as aberrant behavior is actually symptomatic of spiritual growth. Zeltzer said: "You look at adolescents and wonder: What are they doing? They treat their parents like crap. Adolescence is a violent event that both parent and child must go through. It goes much better if the parent doesn't take it personally."

The argument can also be made that it would go much better if society and, specifically, the justice system, didn't take it so personally either. In earlier cultures, teenagers were inducted into adulthood through an initiation process. Rites of passage were essential to the continuity of the group. Indigenous communities recognized that the teenage years are a great awakening and that the symptoms of this time must be met with a sacred attitude. According to Zeltzer, we must meet these symptoms with love and not disdain, as challenging as that might be. Just as we must now consider the latest findings by neuroscientists concerning the development of the adolescent brain and its limitations, we should also consider the adolescent psyche before we pass judgment on kids who disturb us with their incorrigible and disruptive behavior.

Justice the Mozart Way

There is nothing quite like a fine symphony orchestra performing classical music in a medieval church to remind you of the stark contrast between the sublime and the profane. St. Michaelis, in Lüneborg, Germany, was built by Benedictines in the fourteenth century. This evening it was home to the Prague Symphony Orchestra. Pieces by Mozart captivated locals, students, and visitors in a building designed to elevate the soul of peasants and nobles alike. For two hours I was transported to a time when the sacred held sway over the secular, and belief in the possibility of perfection was manifest in the arts and architecture.

But near the end of the evening I was overcome with sadness, thinking about the tragedy of American culture where the only possibility of a town on the order of Lüneburg would be in the corner of an Anaheim amusement park. I remembered a philosophy course at

Pity the prosecutors, public defenders, and judges who toil behind the counters and at the grills, preparing and selling a justice that poisons both those who serve it and those who ingest it.

Saint Louis University and a lecture on the four classic virtues: temperance, prudence, courage, and justice. I wondered whether any of these are valued by our consumer culture, which has taken over the world. Of the four, justice seems to be the most diminished.

A friend emailed today a list of quotes on justice. One by William Penn hit home: "Justice has only one scale and weight—for rich and poor, great and small."

Can we say that about the American justice system? Does Penn's definition bear a resemblance to how we do justice? Would Plato, Aristotle, or any of the great theologians give credence to what we call "justice" in our courthouses and in our communities? Shouldn't we just drop the pretense and label what we have "the American punishment system"?

Whether it be the Polk County Courthouse or a courthouse in Brooklyn, Chicago, or Santa Fe, what any curious visitor would find is a justice system reflective of our culture, a system that dispenses justice to those of color, the poor, and the disenfranchised the way the fast food industry peddles its burgers, fries, and shakes. Pity the prosecutors, public defenders, and judges who toil behind the counters and at the grills, preparing and selling a justice that poisons both those who serve it and those who ingest it. We are all dying a slow death because of our punishment system gone awry.

Mass incarceration resulting from draconian policies and punishments gets the most attention in the press these days. But just beginning to creep into the back pages are stories of the mounting cost of punishment to low-level offenders and taxpayers alike.

Imagine for a moment what justice would look like in the hands of those with imagination, or the truly creative, like Mozart, Bach, or Beethoven.

A Party Not to Be Missed

While I was visiting my daughter Mary in Germany, she asked if we could go to Majorca for a long weekend. She said most of her friends at the university had gone at least once and it's the number one destination for Germans wanting to get away. I said sure, having no idea where Majorca is on the globe. I found out soon enough. It's a Mediterranean island belonging to Spain. Palma is the capitol.

Yesterday we got up at sunrise and walked the mile to the Lüneburg train station, arriving an hour later at the Lübeck airport. We took the three-hour flight to Palma, sharing the jaunt with a groom and his stag buddies, a bachelorette group, and two or three knitting clubs.

We landed at Palma's state-of-the-art airport and took a bus to our hotel on the most efficient system I've ever seen. At the stop, a screen displays each approaching bus, the number, and the minutes to arrival. When you pay the fare, you receive a computer-generated receipt with the location, date, time of departure—to the second— and the final destination. Once on board, you track your progress on a digital monitor displaying each upcoming stop. The bus purrs along, propelled by an electric motor probably manufactured by Mercedes Benz. I imagine the Des Moines metro transit has a similar system on the drawing board.

Last night we ate at a wonderful place near the waterfront. I think the waiter had a crush on Mary. We had excellent service. I ordered the corn pancake veggie burger and a local beer. As we finished, the proprietor, a stout man with a Dutch accent, showed up. Christian Van Maanen left Amsterdam twenty-five years ago, spent a decade exploring the Canary Islands and then landed in Palma, where he's entertained locals and tourists ever since. He's a congenial guy, probably because he likes where he lives and what he does. He asked what I did. When I said I'd once been a prosecutor, he launched into a tirade. Five minutes into it he excused himself and returned shortly with newspapers from the last three days. He read the headlines of each edition. Three stories, three tales of corruption. He turned the pages. More stories, more corruption. He said no one trusts the government. The bad are thrown out and replaced with worse. The son-in-law of the king was just exposed for diverting millions of euros from a charity to a Swiss bank account.

I asked about the justice system. Corrupt too, judges and lawyers alike, Christian said. I asked about the police, assuming more of the same. But Christian's answer surprised me. For the most part, people trust the police. It's an honorable profession. There are three levels. The national guard goes after the big-time criminals. The state police handle customs matters, border patrol, and the areas outside the municipalities with a no-nonsense approach. And the local police are efficient and responsive, and they take into account that they're members of the community. It's been Christian's experience that the police do their best to keep order in a nonpunitive manner.

It was nearly ten and the place was starting to fill up. Christian asked if we were going to be around on the 30th. It's the Queen of the Netherlands' birthday and the day she passes the crown to her son. He said it's a once-in-a-lifetime day and he's throwing a party not to be missed.

When Mercy Is Equal to Justice

I spent most of Sunday in Hamburg, returning from Majorca about noon. Hamburg is Germany's second largest city and has little charm compared to nearby Lüneburg.

I was told to skip the city center and head to the harbor. A walk along the water led me to a green-domed building resembling the

Pantheon. I expected an exhibition space inside. Instead I found a circular staircase descending forty feet. At the bottom was the entrance to a 425-meter tunnel under the Elbe. My quarter-mile walk ended with a companion staircase. On the surface, vendors served coffee and ice cream to sunbathers and strollers.

I found myself observing a conversation between a woman in her sixties and a younger man, about forty. Standing nearby was a man about the same age as the woman. I understood none of the German, but it was evident that this was a mother with her son. She spoke softly, covering his massive hands with her left hand and stroking his deformed face with her right. He was barely articulate, drooling as he spoke. She understood every word and calmed him with her voice and touch. I wondered how it is that six million Jews were murdered by men who were once little boys. I looked at the man who bore a strong resemblance to the boy. He paced in a small circle, disinterested and impatient.

Perhaps the problem of violence is less one of nations and more one of gender. I imagined Justice, blindfolded, with scales in hand. I wondered what our justice system will look like when female lawyers and judges outnumber their male counterparts. Women already outnumber men in American law schools. It's only a matter of time when the profession is in the hands of women. What will our justice look like then? Perhaps then mercy will bear a weight equal to that of justice.

The mother stood up with her son. She continued to hold his hand, leading him to the staircase. They walked slowly, stopping every few steps so she could put him at ease and draw his attention to something of interest. The boy's father hurried ahead, alone.

Prisons Are Profitable

A friend recently emailed a link to a short video titled "Wealth Inequality in America." It's based on the findings of a Harvard business economist. The statistics are startling: 1 percent of Americans have 40 percent of the nation's wealth, whereas the bottom 80 percent of the population has only 7 percent of the wealth.

This got me thinking about the prison industrial complex and the contributions private prison companies make to the U.S. inmate population. The giant of the industry is Corrections Corporation of America. CCA manages more than sixty facilities that, combined, have a capacity of 90,000 beds. It's a multi-billion-dollar company with 2012 fourth quarter profits of nearly 10 percent. Easy to see that the more people go to prison, the more money goes into the pockets of CCA shareholders. Mass incarceration is good for a lot of people.

Damon Hininger, president and CEO of CCA, made $3,688,705 in 2012 in total compensation. Quite a contrast to what the citizens of Iowa pay Director of Corrections John Baldwin. He received a salary of $151,252 in 2012. You have to wonder where the incentive lies. Hininger is paid to be creative, to make money for CCA. He's rewarded handsomely; in 2012 he also received a bonus twice his annual salary. Apparently, increasing the number of people incarcerated in prisons managed by CCA increases the bonus given to Hininger and the trading value of a share of CCA stock.

What about Baldwin? What are his incentives? Is he paid to be creative? Is he paid enough? Iowa football coach Kirk Ferentz was salaried at $3.7 million in 2012, twenty-five times Baldwin's salary. Ferentz is paid to produce winning football teams, a questionable value in the bigger scheme of things. The Hawkeyes finished the 2012 season 4–8. Iowa's prison population is 8,249, spread across nine facilities having a capacity of 7,209 beds. As the director of the DOC Baldwin is charged with the task of successfully reintegrating offenders into the community and protecting the DOC staff, victims, and the public from victimization. Perhaps Ferentz and Baldwin should swap salaries. Surely what taxpayers hired Baldwin to do is more important for the public good than what they hired Ferentz to do. If Baldwin were paid more, he'd have an incentive to really get creative at figuring out how to successfully integrate offenders back into the community. Perhaps the DOC wouldn't have a 50 percent failure rate experienced now, like the Hawkeyes.

A final note. If you go to CCA's website, CCA.com, you find that its vision is "To be the best full-service adult corrections system."

A look at their numbers shows that CCA is much closer to its stated purpose than either the Hawkeyes or the Iowa DOC.

Re-Visioning Justice

Howard Zehr, often considered the grandfather of restorative justice, emailed the other day. He has to give a talk outlining his vision of what restorative justice will look like in ten years, a vision of what's doable. He wanted to know what I thought.

James Hillman, a psychoanalyst and the founder of archetypal psychology, wrote a book titled *Re-Visioning Psychology*. Hillman says that it's not easy to re-vision something that's become systemized or strongly believed in as empirically verified; that when you attempt this you are challenging very deep ideas. I imagine the same would be said if we attempted a re-visioning of justice. A consideration of justice in this country must include the justice system. Many would assert that our justice system has been empirically verified and that there is no other way to do business. But what if we tried?

Molly Rowan Leach, a peace activist and restorative justice expert, wrote a piece for the *Huffington Post*, "American Justice—For Profit Prisons or Truth?" Leach writes about how backward and corrupt our criminal justice system has become and how restorative justice not only "opens the door to the humanity of wrong-doing," but also saves money. She concludes that a "death knell is sounding in the United States—it is that of the paradigm that punishment works and that of the complacency that we all have been mostly unknowing and complicit in to support an industry motivated by something other than what it proclaims itself to be."

Let's assume we are witnessing the death of our system of justice, even though it's fighting violently to stay alive. What could replace it? Is restorative justice up to the task? Does restorative justice offer a vision comprehensive enough to withstand the onslaught of criticism from those who benefit from the current system? Does restorative justice have the capacity to anticipate the myriad details that must be taken into account in order to construct an alternative system better than the status quo?

Perhaps Howard is right to consider only what is possible in ten years.

A friend once sent me the keynote address from a restorative justice conference held in Ontario, Canada. The keynote speaker predicted we would have a restorative justice system in a hundred years. Twenty years have passed since then, so we have about eighty years left on that speaker's timeline. But how do we get there? What will happen between now and then? What could we have in 2093?

When I replied to Howard I told him that we need a justice system that shifts the focus—the time, effort, and expense—from minor transgressions to serious offenses such as abuse and violence.

Does restorative justice offer a vision comprehensive enough to withstand the onslaught of criticism from those who benefit from the current system?

I said where we will be in ten years depends on how much worse things get between now and then. Will there be a sense of urgency that can't be ignored? There isn't one yet. The most serious cases continue to grab the headlines. There is little interest in questioning how business is done every day in thousands of courthouses around the country. I told Howard it seems that with dwindling resources there must be prioritizing, with the major emphasis on those offenses that really cause harm. An argument can be made that the adult criminal justice system should be run like the best juvenile justice systems. We'd have a system in which the majority of police referrals result in a diversion from the formal system. Emphasis would be placed on the determination of what really needs to be in court and what doesn't. The concept of "punishment" would be replaced with one of "accountability." Without that paradigm shift, business will continue as usual.

Racial Profiling Project Initiated in Des Moines

The ACLU reported today that a black person in Iowa is more than eight times as likely to be arrested for marijuana possession as a white person, even though whites and blacks use marijuana at about the same rate. In Polk County, blacks are five times as likely as whites to be arrested for marijuana possession. The ACLU report comes on the heels of a study released a week ago by the Iowa Division of Criminal and Juvenile Justice Planning (CJJP), which cited a 767 percent increase in the number of African American youth detained in Polk County for simple misdemeanors from 2010 to 2012. The CJJP report also revealed that the number of delinquency petitions filed against African American juveniles by the Polk County Attorney's Office increased 182 percent. These reports paint a picture that can't be ignored. None of this is new for the people who are directly affected by the justice system. For others, particularly white middle-class people, the statistics are a revelation. What can be done? Media exposure is a start. Better education of law enforcement is too. But what about the prosecutors and judges who make the filing and sentencing decisions? Should racial bias education be required of them? Can we wait for the legislature to address the issue?

A few years ago a group of Yale Law School students addressed the problem of racial profiling in New Haven, Connecticut, by initiating a project to document racial bias practices by local law enforcement. Their approach was a simple one: interview the victims and tell their stories. The project was a success, resulting in a Department of Justice investigation and sweeping reforms. A similar project is being initiated in Des Moines. A Mid-Iowa Organizing Strategy (AMOS) is partnering with the ACLU of Iowa and the Des Moines Chapter of the NAACP to develop and implement a comprehensive response to racial profiling practices in the Des Moines area. Like the Yale model, interviewing victims of racial bias will be at the core of the project. It's hoped the project will be up and running soon, supported by local churches and Drake University law student interns.

In *The New Jim Crow* Michelle Alexander calls for a new social movement led by a new generation of activists. And Valarie Kaur, a Yale Law School graduate and the founding director of Groundswell, says that social change must be a product of "storytelling plus advocacy." I'm eager to witness the telling of stories by our black and brown brothers and sisters in Des Moines and the advocacy that will follow.

Road Trip West

I've made it to McIver State Park south of Portland, Oregon. My tent is up, nestled between two giant redwoods with canopies so thick the rain fly isn't necessary. I'm always amazed at how far you can drive with coffee and munchies. Regular West Coast road trips should be mandatory. After a day, limits give way and the expansiveness begins to creep in.

I'm here to attend the Northwest Justice Forum in Oregon City. Restorative justice in the schools is the hot topic. I'm particularly interested in Howard Zehr's keynote, which will outline his vision for restorative justice.

* * *

At ten this morning I descended from the Blue Mountains of eastern Oregon and began the drive west along the Columbia River. As I was driving, a friend called wanting to know if I'd seen the piece in the morning's *Des Moines Register* written by County Attorney John Sarcone. I hadn't, so he read it to me. Sarcone's letter was in response to one written by two local ministers and published in the *Register* a week ago. It was clear Sarcone thought he had been wronged. While not directly addressing the concerns of the ministers, he wrote that there is a lot of lying going on and that a recent report by the Iowa Criminal and Juvenile Justice Planning Agency addressing disproportionate minority contact in Polk County was suspect. The letter cast blame without accepting responsibility. After a brief conversation, I told my friend I had to go.

My thoughts turned to a biography of American psychoanalyst James Hillman. The author traces the history of psychoanalysis, stopping at points along the way when new ideas began to eclipse old ones. He describes the defensiveness on the part of the old guard, manifesting itself in anger and recrimination. I thought of those in the criminal justice business who have built their careers on the bedrock of "law and order" and being "tough on crime." They assert that these are the only legitimate responses to criminal wrongdoing, despite a growing body of research showing that this approach has failed. Is Sarcone a member of the old guard, which has yet to come to grips with the changing times? Does he have a death grip on the retributive approach to justice even though it is questioned by growing numbers inside and outside the system, even conservatives who are waking up to the waste of money and human potential the traditional system fosters?

In the 1960s adherents to the law-and-order approach clashed with people who were demanding rights and freedom. Trust in traditional American institutions was at an all-time low. Aging leaders fought to hold back the tide, but to no avail. Many say our present decade is the closest we've come to the pivotal days of fifty years ago.

A wave of pity for Sarcone and those of his mind-set and generation washed over me.

A Vision for Restorative Justice

The Northwest Justice Forum was great, including Howard Zehr's keynote.

I first heard of Howard in 1991. I read *Changing Lenses* and, inspired, I purchased twenty-five copies for our neighborhood mediators. Now there is a new generation learning about Howard, his work, and his ideas, which planted the seeds for a new paradigm of justice that continues to move forward.

Young lawyers attended the forum—prosecutors and defense attorneys—along with mediators, juvenile and adult correction officers, administrators, teachers, and community organizers. They are witnesses to the ineffectiveness of our present justice system. Some have been harmed by it. Others work in it and know there must be a better way. They attended the Forum to find out what that might be. The Forum posed the question "What is a realistic vision of restorative justice for the next decade and beyond, and how do we get there?" Howard articulated his own vision, drawing on his wisdom and experience as well as the ideas and efforts of other pioneers. He said of himself that he is a synthesizer, which is true. But he has also been an innovator and a catalyst. Time will tell if the new generation will be up to the task of carrying his vision forward—through education, implementation, and risk taking. The presentations and the private conversations have given me encouragement.

Back home things are heating up. The question of what justice should look like in Polk County, particularly for our youth, is being asked by many.

Given that the United States has the highest incarceration rate in the world, two questions must be considered: How can our communities engage in a dialogue with justice system professionals to look at what works and what doesn't work? and Whose role is it to commence this dialogue and sustain it? Growing awareness of disproportionate minority contact in Polk County has raised questions about the approach of the Polk County attorney when it comes to juvenile justice. Editorials by County Attorney John Sarcone and Sheriff Bill McCarthy attempt to shift the attention and blame away from the justice system and toward AMOS. Sarcone and McCarthy are elected officials and public servants. They have a duty to invite AMOS representatives and other concerned citizens to the table rather than continuing to suggest that the community doesn't have a right to question how justice system professionals go about their business. The questions remain: How can the community be engaged in a dialogue with the justice system, and who should sustain that conversation?

No direct conversation has taken place yet, but people are beginning to clarify their positions. It's to be expected that there would be tension, even anger, when positions are challenged. Ruling orders are by nature self-protective. Reform is rarely initiated from within. Stability takes precedent over creativity. Those who have built their careers on a foundation of law and order value safety over the more ambiguous and less easily defined work of justice.

The *Des Moines Register* should be lauded for its even-handed approach in allowing community representatives and justice system officials to articulate their respective views. Statement, response, and counter-response are the first steps toward conversation. Perhaps it's time for the *Register* to take a role in moving the process forward by sponsoring a series of community forums so citizens can be educated on critical justice issues. How else will the electorate become educated so when the time comes to vote they can make informed decisions?

Lawyers As Healers, Not Hired Guns

My son, Phil, graduated from the University of Iowa College of Law in May and will soon take the bar exam. He was a far better law student than I was, and, I suspect, he will be a better lawyer than me. When, at the age of ten, he told me he was going to be a lawyer, I had feelings of foreboding. They remained as his commitment grew. I feared that the law school experience would dramatically change him and that his innate sense of justice would be eclipsed by the law's tendency to favor winners over losers. I'm relieved and proud to say that three years of law school have not damaged Phil and that he's chosen to pursue a career of public service rather than a six-figure salary and a steep climb up the partnership ladder. This morning I reflected on the elemental ideas of the spirit of the law and the letter of the law. I grabbed hold of a thread of time and followed it back to my early years as a father, listening to my son announce his future. I wondered why I had feared for my son's future because he aspired to do what I was doing.

Warren Burger, a former chief justice of the U.S. Supreme Court, observed in 1984 that: "The entire legal profession—lawyers, judges, law teachers—has become so mesmerized with the stimulation of the courtroom contest that we tend to forget that we ought to be healers—healers of conflicts. Should lawyers not be healers? Healers, not warriors? Healers, not procurers? Healers, not hired guns?"

Justice Berger's questions, like Phil's announcement, have haunted me. Restorative justice has helped to answer the questions. But the answers give rise to more questions: How can a lawyer make a living, represent a client zealously, abide by ethical rules and professional norms, and yet be a healer rather than a hired gun in the adversarial culture that dominates our existing American justice system?

Abraham Lincoln had a vision that our country could be free of slavery. He had the courage to fight a war in order to realize that vision. Few, however, think of the Lincoln who made a living as a lawyer long before becoming president, the lawyer who advocated for peacemaking first and litigation only as a last resort. In notes

"As a peacemaker the lawyer has a superior

opportunity of being a good man.

There will still be business enough."

—Abraham Lincoln

prepared for a lecture and preserved in his *Collected Works*, Lincoln called upon the lawyers of his day to: "Discourage litigation. Persuade your neighbors to compromise whenever you can. Point out to them how the nominal winner is often a real loser—in fees, expenses, and waste of time. As a peacemaker the lawyer has a superior opportunity of being a good man. There will still be business enough."

Many lawyers today fail to heed Lincoln's admonition and find themselves faced with a crisis of meaning, distrusted by the public, stressed by overwork, and questioning the value of their contribution to society.

Addressing the spiritual crisis afflicting American lawyers, Joseph Allegretti paints a portrait of the sad state of the legal profession in *The Lawyer's Calling*:

Lawyers are almost four times more likely than other
people to be depressed. . . . Forty-four percent of lawyers
report not having enough time for their families; fifty-
four percent report not having enough time for themselves. . . . In 1990 only one-third of lawyers report that
they are 'very satisfied' with their work. . . . In 1986,
seventeen percent of Americans believed lawyers were
less honest than others. By 1993 the figure had risen to
thirty-one percent. In 1986, eighteen percent of people
thought that there were too many lawyers; in 1993 the
figure had soared to seventy-three percent.

In *Transforming Practices* Steven Keeva addressed the same spiritual crisis. He argues that many lawyers undergo a disintegration as
human beings, a process that begins in law school. He characterizes
this process as a "map without a meaning" that is followed by the
"law firm map," which compels the lawyer to win at any cost.

In *Lawyers as Peacemakers*, attorney J. Kim Wright concurs that
the problem begins with our law schools, where young minds are
exposed to the adversarial paradigm in overt and subtle ways. Wright
speaks from experience: "The competition started when we applied
and vied for a seat in the class, continued with the fight for grades
and rank, and extended into law practice. We are trained in the skills
of litigation . . . we watch our backs, we hide the ball . . . the view is
of a world where individuals protect their rights, territory, property,
and selves from other individuals." For Wright, this paradigm results
in a separation of a lawyer's needs from his or her values, and places
needs and values at odds with each other.

Attorney John Allen, writing in the *Michigan Bar Journal*, stated
that many in the legal profession argue that a lawyer's ethics require
that every cause be pursued with zeal, bound only by the outer
requirements of law. He quotes a colleague who observed that "too
many lawyers hide behind the ethical duty of zealous advocacy to
justify all manner of outrageous misconduct."

Most who go to law school enter with noble intentions. The traditional American legal education, however, with its embrace of the

adversarial system, makes it difficult for the pure of heart to remain that way. Well before graduation, dreams of serving the poor and disenfranchised give way to a desire for the comfortable life. In the past, once the new lawyer entered the mainstream of legal practice, it was unlikely that a win-at-all-cost career could be avoided. That may not be such a sure thing as the present century moves forward. There are signs that a healing model of law practice is gaining momentum. Law students, law professors, judges, and practicing lawyers are taking a second look at what they want for themselves and for the legal system they work within. The desire for personal satisfaction and meaningful work may be on the ascent at the same time that an emerging generation of educated Americans is placing lifestyle ahead of status and big bank accounts. A second trend, already witnessed in the health care field, is patients/consumers insisting on being more involved in their care. If legal clients begin to demand results that are less divisive and more satisfying, then a paradigm shift could occur.

It's difficult to predict what effect the Great Recession and "jobless recovery" will have on the legal profession. Will the shrinking economy result in lawyers remaining entrenched in the business-as-usual mentality, or will it empower clients to demand satisfactory outcomes without the time and expense of litigation and roll-the-dice trials? Will law schools embrace the healing model and reform their curriculums? Will judges take a leadership role and insist that mediation become the norm for cases lingering on their overcrowded court dockets? Will attorneys hang up "healing lawyer" shingles rather than give in to the lure of security and financial reward?

Only time will tell if what is now an experiment by the innovative and courageous will become the new reality. I am hopeful that my son and his classmates will become practitioners of a new reality.

Report from Managua

I'm in Managua, the capital of Nicaragua, which is the second most impoverished country in the Western Hemisphere. I was last here in December of 1978, less than a year after the murder of Pedro

Chamorro, the liberal editor of *La Prensa*, and less than a year before the Sandinista forces descended on Managua, bringing an end to the Somoza regime. The thirty-fourth anniversary of that event was yesterday. For years Chamorro used his pen to denounce the brutality of Somoza and his military. He was jailed and tortured many times, but he was never silenced until a Somoza bullet ended his life.

I'm not in Managua to celebrate the Sandinista victory of 1979. I knew nothing of the people's struggle when I arrived as a gringo backpacker, amazed to find sandbag barricades and government tanks in the streets. I'm here because of another brutality, one inflicted six weeks ago on my daughter Sarah.

Sarah is an intrepid traveler and a savvy one. She's seen and experienced much, having backpacked through Thailand, Vietnam, Cambodia, India, Guatemala, and Honduras. She is always prepared—traveling with others, booking ahead, carefully choosing her transportation. But nothing in her experience prepared her for what happened at 1:00 in the morning at the end of a long dirt road through the jungle, twelve miles from the resort town of San Juan del Sur.

In her room at Camping Matilda's, Sarah and her traveling companion were awakened to violence at their locked door. It was their second night at Matilda's, a remote hostel known for its hospitality, charm, and access to Playa Majagual, one of Nicaragua's finest beaches. Sarah and her friend had little time to respond and no time to prepare. The force inflicted on the door by the attackers was sufficient to break both the heavy chain attached to the inside of the door and the lock used to secure it. What happened in the minutes that followed is a woman's worst nightmare, and her father's. What happened was the unimaginable. Only now can I begin to grasp it, having stepped across that threshold and stood next to the bed Sarah was awakened from. I can imagine but I can't describe it. I can't write about it. I can only say that Sarah and her friend feared for and fought for their lives at the hands of five men—five men armed with guns and crude machetes. When it was over, and their hands and feet bound with plastic restraints, the men left.

A short time later there was a gunshot. Sarah and her friend assumed the two British girls who were also staying at Camping Matilda's had been found. Sarah feared she was next. There was a long silence and then the start of a car and the sound of tires on gravel. Sarah waited. She doesn't recall for how long. Time for her on that night was not time as we know it.

Finally the owners arrived, Antonio and Matilda. Shaken but unharmed, they have their own stories of terror. I have always been proud of Sarah, but never more proud than when Matilda told me that Sarah's first response was to hug her and assure her that everything would be alright.

I came to Nicaragua to make sure that my daughter and what happened to her would not be forgotten. I've met with U.S. embassy staff. They've provided wonderful support. I've met with the chief of police, who is overseeing the investigation. He assured me that this is the case of his career. His oldest daughter was raped and murdered when he was a captain. I've met with the chief prosecutor, who assured me that her best trial attorney will prevail in court. Hostel owners Antonio and Matilda have assured me that they will testify and see this to the end. I've been encouraged by what I've found here, by the professionalism and by the compassion.

Sarah can't sleep alone or go out alone at night. She starts medical school in two weeks, but her life has been changed forever, as have the lives of those who love her. But Sarah is taking care of herself. Therapy, yoga, meditation, a healthy diet, sleep when she can find it, and close contact with family and friends provide needed support for body and soul. And Sarah is not afraid to tell her story so that it's outside of her and not the source of her fears and nightmares.

Two men are being held in the Rivas jail. Three are at large. Arrest warrants have been issued. The trial starts on August 5 for the two in custody. We pray that justice prevails, but justice is just the beginning. Sarah says she wishes she had never come here, but I've learned from my experience with restorative justice that crime creates relationships. Sarah will always be connected to this country of incredible contrasts.

Restorative justice is about harm and the repair of harm. Every crime is different, every case is different. Restorative justice provides a vision but, in Sarah's case, not the specifics. Only time will tell. I'm certain that I will return to Nicaragua. There is a story here without a conclusion. Perhaps there is a source of healing here as well.

* * *

Sarah's journey since Nicaragua has been a painful one. It has also been one of determination and courage. At Sarah's request, I've made no mention of her ordeal throughout the rest of this book, except on a few occasions and with her permission. Sarah will tell her own story someday, when it is right for her. For now it is enough to say that Sarah is in the second semester of her second year of medical school and she is frequently called upon to speak publicly about sexual violence and the marginalization of women.

Black in America

A week ago I was in Managua. Nicaraguans were celebrating the fall of the Somoza regime and the government was giving away free alcohol. I spent most of the day in the lobby watching dignitaries come and go and keeping an eye on the festivities from a safe distance—in front of the hotel televisions. In the afternoon I received a news alert from NPR about a just-concluded talk by President Obama at the White House. He had appeared unannounced, hoping to help white Americans comprehend black Americans' reaction to the acquittal of George Zimmerman. The NPR story was brief, so I went to the official White House website for the complete speech.

The president focused on why many African Americans reacted the way they did from the time of the shooting of Trayvon Martin until the verdict. He didn't attempt to explain whites to blacks. Citing his own experience, he said: "There are very few African American men in this country who haven't had the experience of being followed when they were shopping in a department store. That includes me."

This week I had coffee with a young African American man. His father is a physician and his mother a lawyer. He graduated from a prestigious East Coast university with a degree in economics. He is a lawyer for the State of Iowa. We talked about Trayvon Martin, President Obama, racial profiling, and what it's like to be black in America. He told me if there are any black men in this country who haven't been the victims of racial profiling, then they've been living on another planet.

Also this week I spoke at an undoing racism conference in Des Moines. As I approached the room where I was to give a talk called "The New Jim Crow—And a Restorative Justice Response" I ran into a longtime Iowa civil rights leader. He had heard about the AMOS racial profiling project and wanted to know more about it. He told me that as a young man he twice had a gun held to his head by police officers.

Near the end of my presentation a black man raised his hand. He works with at-risk kids for the Des Moines Public Schools. He said wherever he goes he has to be "on top of his game." A middle-aged black woman then rose. She talked about her young-adult son who was recently sentenced to twenty-five years in prison for a robbery involving less than two hundred dollars. He'll spend seventeen years in prison before he's eligible for parole. She said there was no restorative justice in her son's case; he wanted to apologize but wasn't allowed to. She ended by saying that there needs to be a revolution in this country.

I had coffee with the woman two days later. She looked me in the eye and told me that no matter what I read or how many people I talk to I will never know what it's like to wake up in the morning and go out into the world with black skin.

On my flight back from Managua I sat next to an older black couple. The husband had been a police officer with the Lexington, Kentucky, police department for thirty years. The wife worked on a Toyota assembly line. Our conversation eventually turned to racial profiling. The man acknowledged that it's a problem. The woman told me that earlier this month she was driving in a white neighborhood of Lexington. A white police officer driving in the opposite direction noticed her. He went by, made a U-turn, and began following her. After three blocks she pulled over. He stopped and approached her car. She asked what she had done wrong. He said she had a tail light out.

President Obama's remarks focused on African American boys and how they are "painted with a broad brush." He would have done well to have talked about African American men and women as well.

There's No Going Back

I knew it would happen, and yet it still sickens me. The Polk County Board of Supervisors approved the request of the County Attorney to fund two new juvenile prosecutor positions this morning. The vote was unanimous. It's craziness. The research shows the deeper you put a kid into the system, the deeper he or she will stay. And yet the system continues to build capacity.

Because of the tremendous increase in court filings, the judiciary has created a sixth juvenile judge position. This comes at a cost of at least $200,000 a year, what with salary and benefits for both a judge and a court attendant, plus the increased use of a court reporter. The Polk County Attorney followed suit, saying he needed two new lawyers because of the new judge—another $200,000 a year. No one has said "Let's slow this train down and look at what's going on here." We study the migratory habits of monarch butterflies flying from Mexico to Iowa, but we don't study the question of why there is an increase in the number of juveniles in court when there is no related increase in juvenile crime and juvenile arrests.

There are presently five juvenile judges. Each sees 20 percent of the problem. With a sixth judge, each will see 17 percent. There will be even less of a sense of urgency to do something about the problem than there is now. With one-sixth of the pie, a judge will be less inclined to consider the impact of each individual decision. There will be no decrease in court filings, but there will be an increase in detention holds.

There is no collective wisdom when it comes to these matters. Consider what happens when we build a new jail or prison. As the saying goes, "If you build it, you will fill it." I talked recently with an architect about the notion of capacity and control. He said there is a recognized precept in neighborhood and town planning that you control capacity in order to control for a desired outcome. You don't widen streets unless you're prepared for increased traffic, and you don't increase the capacity of utilities unless you are planning for an increase in the density of construction. By adding a judge and two juvenile prosecutors, the system has just widened the transportation

The research shows the deeper you put a kid into the system, the deeper he or she will stay. And yet the system continues to build capacity.

corridor. There is no going back. It will be interesting to look at the statistics in five years. The past two years have been bad enough when it comes to the number of youth in detention and those pushed through the formal juvenile justice system. Five years from now we will be wishing for the good old days of 2013.

What If Law Schools Taught Justice?

I was thinking about racial profiling last night. The campfire at Ohiopyle State Park, Pennsylvania, was just right—warm enough to take the chill off and menacing enough to keep the bugs away. The day before, I'd met with law professor and racial profiling expert David Harris at a café near his office at the University of Pittsburgh. This evening I was still in the mood to delve into the national discourse on the death of Trayvon Martin and the acquittal of George Zimmerman. I'm partway through Harris' book *Profiles in Injustice: Why Racial Profiling Cannot Work*, and I'm intrigued by his assertion—and the documentation he has to back it up—that racial profiling has failed as an effective tool for crime prevention in the United States. I set up shop on my small camp table only to find that my iPad was dead. The muses fled just as quickly as they'd arrived. There was nothing to do but brush my teeth and turn in for the night, hoping the ideas and the mood would be present in the morning. But morning came and racial profiling seemed too complicated to tackle on an empty stomach. As often happens, sunrise brought with it its own agenda and subject of inquiry.

In addition to the Harris book, I'm reading one by psychologist James Hollis titled *Hauntings: Dispelling the Ghosts Who Run Our Lives*. Hollis writes about those memories, events, ancestors, and traumas that inhabit our unconscious, every bit as real as the family, friends, colleagues, and acquaintances of our daily lives. This morning my barely awakened consciousness nudged me with more foundational questions. Questions that precede and should inform our conversations about racial profiling. Questions that frequently haunt me: What is justice? What is its source? What does it look like in our day-to-day treatment of others? How should it be taught? What is its relation to the law? Where should it fit into the law school curriculum? Should it be the framework around which all law school courses are organized? What does it mean that prosecutors are "to do justice"? What is the role of the community in defining justice? Are justice system professionals informed by basic notions of justice? Are there standards that should guide the administration of justice and, when in conflict with rules and statutes, should supersede them? What do we mean by "the spirit of the law"?

* * *

This past fall I was asked to give a talk on restorative justice to students at Campbell Law School in Raleigh, North Carolina. They were mostly third-year students enrolled in the school's legal clinic who were trained to go into the public schools and serve as mediators for kids in conflict. They were also trained to facilitate victim–offender dialogues in cases referred by the juvenile justice system. After I spoke about my own experience, we launched into a wide-ranging discussion about what the system would look like if it were guided by restorative justice principles. We talked about the relationship between law and justice and about how they might, as lawyers, engage in the practice of law as healers. I asked the group of about thirty if, in other law school classes, anyone had ever had a discussion about justice. Not a single hand went up. Several said they'd been motivated to attend law school by basic notions of justice and they had dreams of becoming "justice crusaders." But they acknowledged that precedent and procedure, winning and losing, soon became the focus of their law school education. They said it was only in their legal clinic work that they got a glimpse of what justice might look like in a human context.

What if the first two days of my law school experience had been an exposure to poverty, the inequities of our legal system, and the possibilities of equal access to justice for everyone?

* * *

I spoke last night with my daughter Sarah. It was her first day as a student at the University of Minnesota Medical School. Formal classes start next week. This week the students are attending a conference focusing on poverty, the inequities of the health care system in the United States, and access to affordable and quality medical care for everyone. I was impressed. And I was jealous. I wondered, What if the first two days of my law school experience had been an exposure to poverty, the inequities of our legal system, and the possibilities of equal access to justice for everyone? What if that exposure provided the framework around which all subsequent classes had been organized? What if law schools graduated lawyers who were not only technically skilled but also sensitive to issues of justice and injustice? What if understanding and healing were the focus of the law, not winning and retribution?

Poverty, Drug Abuse, and Crime

As you enter Uniontown, Pennsylvania, from the south, Highway 40 takes a sweeping turn to the west and you are immediately struck by the clock tower at the top of the Fayette County Courthouse. With its high arched entrance, the courthouse, the oldest in Pennsylvania, is an impressive stone structure reminiscent of one you might find in old London. But the clock tower holds a dark history. It wasn't until I met Judge Wagner's court attendant that I learned of that history.

As I walked the nearly vacant halls of the courthouse late on a Friday afternoon, Mike greeted me. A graduate of the University of West Virginia, Mike had been an undertaker for a while but had to quit his job and go to work for the county to get health care benefits. He has been Judge Wagner's bailiff for nearly five years and has seen a lot. He could easily be the courthouse tour guide with his knowledge of the building and the people who have walked its halls. I told Mike I thought there was an eeriness about the clock tower. He wasn't surprised. He said the ghost of an innocent man haunts the tower. The man was wrongly charged with and convicted of murder in 1795. His sentence was death by hanging. The execution, a public event, was carried out in the tower. A noose was placed around the man's neck, and he was dropped four stories through the center of the courthouse. It was the first of many hangings, which continued until 1914. According to Mike, the clock tower is still the home of the hangman's hook, and of the innocent man.

Mike knows more than just history. He has a present-day knowledge of Uniontown and its decline as a prosperous center of commerce; the coming of Kmart, Walmart, Target, and the strip malls that have led to minimum-wage jobs; the boarding of downtown storefronts; and the ensuing poverty. He talked about the kids who can't afford college and can't get decent work. He talked about the malaise that has set in and the prescription drugs and heroin that offer short-term relief but long-term problems. He pointed out the window behind Judge Wagner's bench toward the Fayette County Prison, just a few feet away. The prison has a capacity of two hundred, but going into the weekend it houses more than four hundred, with many people sleeping on the floor. The Department of Justice has threatened a lawsuit to force the county to address the deplorable conditions. Mike says there are no easy answers because the poor economy leads to underemployment and unemployment, which lead to self-medication, which leads to crime. Mike says the shrinking tax base means there are few dollars for effective drug treatment. He said in Pennsylvania an inmate can be sentenced to up to two years in a county jail and in Fayette County in-jail treatment can't exceed ten days.

I asked Mike what the future holds for him, his wife, and his children. He said he hopes somehow his two daughters will be able to go to college and make lives for themselves elsewhere. He and his wife have to stay where they are. There are no better prospects. Mike said he makes only $9.50 an hour, but at least when he hits the five-year mark he will get a 3 percent raise.

A Canadian Perspective

Psychologist James Hollis tells the story of his preparation for a trip. Thinking ahead to a long layover he would have at a connecting airport, he decided it was time to reread the *Meditations* of Marcus Aurelius. Hollis writes that he read *Meditations* as a young man but had no idea why it had just come back to mind. While looking for his worn copy, he received an email from a friend he'd not heard from in decades. His friend thanked Hollis for introducing him to *Meditations* many years before, which he had forgotten until just recently. Most of us have had similar experiences. Depth psychologists call it "synchronicity," a manifestation of energies moving through the invisible world and entering the visible world as seeming coincidence.

Yesterday afternoon, while walking the beach near Braddock Cove in South Carolina, two streams of thought entered my mind. One concerned my hope to finish David Harris' book about racial profiling while on vacation. The second was a reminder that later in the evening CNN would be airing a documentary called *Weed*, in which Sanjay Gupta would explain why he had reversed his position on marijuana. Just as I was about to head back, a young couple caught my eye, a black couple. They were seated under two shade umbrellas, each with a book in hand. I approached and introduced myself as a retired attorney researching the experiences people have with the criminal justice system. The man, I guessed in his early thirties, said he had a lot to say about that. He was tall, fit, good looking. I expected him to tell me about his encounters with law enforcement. He said he was a prosecuting attorney from Toronto and that for most of his career he has prosecuted drug dealers and traffickers. He asked why I was interested in the justice system as a research topic. I told him I'd once been a prosecutor and that I'd been challenged by James Baldwin's admonition to find out how justice is administered by listening to the unprotected. He told me Baldwin is his favorite author. From there we had an easy conversation.

We talked about marijuana, racial profiling, poverty, families, schools, and the pipeline to prison. He told me that while the use of marijuana for medicinal purposes has long been legal in Toronto, the possession of marijuana is not. He said, however, that the recreational use of marijuana is tolerated, and law enforcement efforts are directed at the big players, not casuals users. He said, unlike in the United States, racial profiling is not a significant problem. One reason is that blacks have greater representation within law enforcement, the legal community, and the judiciary. A second reason is that the greater the number of blacks and other minorities in the general population, as in Toronto, the less likely racial profiling will be used as a law enforcement tactic. We talked about the recent ACLU study documenting disproportionality when it comes to blacks arrested for marijuana possession. He said the problem with the justice system in the United States is money, that justice is big business at so many levels.

This young man is extremely well-read, from Emerson to Maslow to the ills of American justice—the privatization of prisons, the flow of federal money to local law enforcement, the fact that so many justice system leaders are elected officials rather than civil servants. He said until the profit motive is taken out of the administration of justice, our problems will continue. Beyond that, the problem resides within each one of us. As a nation we've not moved beyond slavery and racism, no matter how much we insist we have; many Americans, including those in the business of administering justice, believe their decisions are not racially motivated. He said that the problem is our unconscious racism and that until it is brought forth from the depths and scrutinized in the light of day, the past will continue to be the present.

Recipients of Privileges We Did Not Earn

I am so heartened by the decision handed down on Monday by Judge Shira Scheindlin in the civil rights case of *Floyd v. the City of New York*. The trial blew the cover on the stop-and-frisk practices of the NYPD. Testimony exposed several troubling realities, including the fact that for every one hundred individuals stopped and frisked in New York City, only six were arrested, often for minor offenses; and the fact that the success rate for finding a gun borders on nonexistent: one in every one thousand stops. The trial exposed the fact that for many officers of the NYPD, male + black = reasonable suspicion.

In March I observed a morning of the *Floyd* trial at the federal courthouse in lower Manhattan. A Latino police officer testified that, more than once, he'd been called by a supervising officer to a location where a black or brown youth had been stopped, frisked, and handcuffed. The supervisor would tell him there was no legitimate reason for the stop and that he was to make up something and put it in his report.

The day before, I visited with Bob Gangi, director of the Police Reform Organizing Project (PROP) in Manhattan. We talked about the work of PROP and other NYC organizations to push back against the stop-and-frisk approach. He said that since 2004 police have stopped more than four million people, almost 85 percent of whom have been black or Latino. In a recent year, stops of whites amounted to 2.6 percent of the white population while stops of blacks amounted to nearly 22 percent of the black population. Gangi pulled open the upper left-hand drawer of his desk, removed a sheet of paper, and read a statement made by a high-ranking official with the NYPD after being asked why police aggressively pursue stop-and-frisk: "We do this because we want every black and brown boy in this city to think twice before they leave their homes."

* * *

Mark Stringer, pastor of the First Unitarian Church in Des Moines, emailed today to let me know about his last sermon, written following a month of reflection on the George Zimmerman acquittal. Mark wrote eloquently about his responsibility "to resist the systems that unjustly keep those unearned privileges in place and to do what I can, as a person with more influence than I sometimes understand or accept, to try to see the world through the eyes of the oppressed, to stand up not only for their right to name reality as they see it, but to stand with them and work for the just society for which we should all be yearning."

Never Again

I'm at O'Hare. My flight to Beijing has been delayed. A two-hour delay on a Des Moines–to–Chicago flight is a pain, but on a fourteen-hour flight it's just a little extra time to settle in. I have biographies of Confucius and Genghis Khan, Alan Watts' *Tao: The Watercourse Way*, and Stephen Mitchell's translation of the *Tao Te Ching*. I've read Lao-Tzu's 2,500-year-old classic on the art of living at least a dozen times, and it never grows old. A wonderful combination of humor, lucidity, and deep wisdom, Lao-Tzu's slim volume should be required reading for any young person contemplating a life course, every leader or future leader, and every retiree or near-retiree who again is contemplating a life course. For the next two weeks I'll be in and around Qufu, the birthplace of Confucius. Mary, my youngest, will be studying kung fu at the Qufu Shaolin Kung Fu School, and I've been given the enviable task of delivering her safely to the school. I imagine that after two months in a boot camp–like environment run by monks she'll be well equipped to find her way back home.

Even with China less than a day away it's difficult to disconnect from the last couple of weeks. I've spent a fair amount of time on the AMOS/NAACP/ACLU racial profiling project. The draft questionnaire has passed through many hands. It's incredible to witness the passion those committed to racial justice bring to the task of fine-tuning a data collection tool designed to document the encounters people of color, and others, have with law enforcement and other government entities. I've heard many stories over the years—"anecdotes," as some say dismissively. But in the last several months the number of firsthand accounts from victims of discriminatory profiling has increased.

This past winter I taught a justice class at Bethel African Methodist Episcopal Church on the east side of Des Moines. Listening to the stories, it's hard to imagine that there are any African Americans who've escaped the sting of racial profiling.

A couple of weeks ago I met at the Drake University Law School with about a dozen young lawyers and law students eager to help with the profiling project. Six or seven were African American, and each of them acknowledged that they've been targeted by law enforcement because of race. The mood in the room was somber as we discussed how prevalent profiling is. At the end of the meeting I encouraged everyone present to read, if they hadn't already, Michelle Alexander's *The New Jim Crow: Mass Incarceration in the Age of Colorblindness*.

A few days ago one of the lawyers emailed to let me know he'd finished the book. Alexander's impact on this young man was considerable:

> *The New Jim Crow* is the most profound and insightful piece of contemporary literature I have read in my entire life. I will never again be able to take seriously anybody discussing equal justice policy who has not read it and dealt with its implications. It speaks directly to me in a way that I wish everybody has the ability to experience. It activates my intellect, charges my passion, and sharpens my understanding of race in America. I have long

decried the war on drugs and its implications. Undeniably this book sets forth concepts that I have long known, observed, and experienced intimately. But they were conceived piecemeal and often viewed in artificial isolation. I have never seen them articulated with such coherence, historical reflection, and vision. I will forever be a better human rights advocate as a result.

And it's not just the young who have been influenced by Alexander. Drake University Law School Professor Russ Lovell read *The New Jim Crow* while on a recent trip. He returned determined to revamp his civil rights class and has made Alexander required reading for this semester's class. I met with Lovell's class this past Tuesday. Of the twelve students in attendance, eight signed up to be trained as interviewers for racial profiling clinics that will be held at the law school legal clinic this fall.

Racial Profiling Does Not Make Us Safer

I was at a meeting the other day at Bethel African Methodist Episcopal Church. The single-story wood building, painted barn red, looks as though the next summer storm could blow it onto the nearby East High football field. But it has stood the test of time, and other tests as well. Declining attendance threatened its existence. But then Brigitte Black arrived. Pastor Black is a dynamo. Movies are made about her kind.

I love going to meetings at Bethel. If you're lucky you'll get a piece of Pastor Black's sweet potato pie or some other incredible dessert, perhaps served at a funeral lunch the day before. But more than the sweets, I love going to Bethel because of its vibrancy. Its people are real, and they have suffered. I taught a series of classes at Bethel this past fall. I learned more about discrimination, racial profiling, and about how a system can grind a people down from the people there than from anything I've ever read.

At this recent Bethel meeting a court watcher spoke passionately about the needs of our youth and how the justice system often fails them. Another spoke about how prosecutors attempt to dissuade court watchers from sitting in on juvenile hearings, suggesting that there are better things they could do with their time and perhaps they should look into mentoring. There was talk about the school mediation program, the volunteers who have been trained to facilitate conversations with kids in conflict, and efforts by the Polk County Attorney to prevent the program from getting off the ground. Testimony was given by the mother of a young man, a victim of racial profiling. An honor roll student and a football player at one of Iowa's best private colleges, the young man has no criminal record and has never been arrested—only stopped, questioned, and searched. A second mother spoke of her son, who had recently been sent to prison—another wasted life. A pastor from a suburban Methodist church encouraged those in attendance to remain committed to repairing our unjust justice system.

As we were leaving, I was stopped by a man and woman in their early forties. The woman asked if I would listen to her partner's story. Soft-spoken and slightly built, he told me of a recent encounter with the police. It was late evening and he had just left his workplace. As usual, he was riding his bicycle the six blocks from work to his apartment. When he was halfway home, riding on the sidewalk, a patrol car pulled up and two officers got out. They approached and ordered him off his bike. When he asked why, one said, "Don't you know it's illegal to ride a bicycle in the dark without a headlight?" They handcuffed and searched him. At the same time, a white youth rode by on a bicycle without a headlight. Nothing was said or done. After telling his story, this gentle man hung his head and asked what can be done. I gave him my card and encouraged him to come to the upcoming racial profiling clinic, where he could tell his story again, perhaps leading to a change for the better.

* * *

Appearing before the United States Senate Judiciary Committee last year, racial profiling expert Dr. David Harris testified that: "The evidence is clear: using these types of profiling does not make us safer; it makes us *less safe*. It takes law enforcement's eyes off of behavior, upon which our agents need to have a laser-like focus. It wastes our resources. . . . The costs of using profiling in the currency of safety and security are overwhelming. It is high time that these practices end."

It will be interesting to see how justice system professionals in Des Moines, predominately white, accept the stories of racial profiling victims, the overwhelming majority of whom are innocent of any crime when stopped and questioned, oftentimes searched and handcuffed without cause. Beyond acceptance, will these stories bring about a change not only in attitudes but in policies and practices that are not only immoral but waste resources and fail to secure public safety?

How Do I Know What Justice Is?

It's been six months since Sarah called from Nicaragua. She's nearly finished with her first semester of medical school. I'm amazed by her capacity for recovery and her creativity in dealing with the symptoms of post-traumatic stress disorder. She is a hero for me. I can also see, after six months, the effects of the assault on my own psyche. As a typical American father, if there is such a thing, I raised my children to go out into the world—to make their way. In the process, my role as father was slowly redefined from storybook reader, fort builder, and chauffeur to mentor and advisor. It seems to me that this is the natural order of things. But when there is a rift in the natural order and an adult child, like Sarah, has the needs of a child again, the archetypal energies of early fatherhood return in full force. Energies I had recently devoted to retirement were redirected to a more ancient and primal response. But Sarah is doing better now, much better than was hoped or expected. And despite everything, Sarah knows that she will be a better doctor than she would have been, and a better human being too.

Sarah's courage has prompted me to return to the reflection and writing that I was engaged in on a regular basis before the attack. This time around, however, my interest is less about the present and the failures of our local justice systems, and more about where we've come from. When I was a prosecutor I'd often witness a colleague pronounce judgment on an offender. I'd ask myself, What in his life experience gives him the wisdom to know what is best for another? In other words, how does he know what justice is and how it should be defined and applied in a given case? Lawyers are not taught about justice in law school. They don't learn about justice at lawyer conferences. They are not mentored in the ways of justice by their supervisors. They don't talk about justice among themselves. I ask myself, How do I know what justice is? Can I presume to know from my own life experiences? The justice lens through which I look at the world may be just as blurred as that of a lawyer I have misgivings about. If there is to be a reimagination of justice in America, and perhaps a redefinition, then we must look further back than Ronald Reagan and the war on drugs. Although law schools don't teach justice, countless books have been written about it. An Amazon.com search for "justice" yields 259,903 results. Which of these might provide the necessary insight? Perhaps the answers aren't to be found in them at all. Maybe the prophets are the better teachers, the Chinese scholars, the Zen masters. What might great literature teach us, and poetry, not to mention myths, legends, and fairy tales?

I don't know the answers to any of these questions, but I'm intrigued by the notion of applying Suzuki's "beginner's mind" to my own inquiry. In *The New Jerusalem*, G. K. Chesterton once said that a modern person is like a traveler who has forgotten the name of his destination and has to go back from where he came to find out where he is going. Perhaps in attempting to define justice for myself I need to do the same thing. What is justice? I don't know, but I am interested in knowing.

"Throw Away Morality and Justice . . ."

The American mythologist Joseph Campbell believed that one of the best things that ever happened to him was falling short of getting his PhD. There are differing accounts as to why—the Great Depression hit and he couldn't afford the tuition, or he didn't want to write a doctoral thesis. Whatever the reason, the result was that he moved to the countryside and spent five years reading. He'd go from one book to another, each suggesting what the next should be. He didn't have a reading list or someone telling him what to read. His guides were his intuition and his intellect. Campbell said that had he gone on to study for a doctorate, his education would have been defined by others and narrowed in the process. Instead, his approach was one of turning over one rock after another and finding delight in each new discovery.

I've long admired Campbell for his approach. A person pursuing an inquiry into justice would do well to follow Campbell's approach. I have neither the discipline nor the stamina to read eight to ten hours a day as Campbell did. I can, however, wake up every morning and consider what the previous day's reading and my own intuition suggest for a place to start.

This morning I woke to thoughts of Lao-Tzu. An older contemporary of Confucius, Lao-Tzu wasn't a prolific writer. The story is told that he would never have written but for a chance encounter with a minor official at a remote outpost. He'd retired as a royal archivist and was leaving the country in search of a solitary life. The official asked if he would write a manual on the art of living. The *Tao Te Ching* was the result. I dip into it regularly, but this morning I couldn't recall to what extent he wrote on justice. It turns out he wrote very little, at least explicitly. He did intimate, however, that if people would throw away morality and justice, they would do the right thing. Lao-Tzu believed people are inherently good and do not require laws to know how to conduct themselves. He also had a bias against labeling and its tendency to marginalize. To characterize some people as holy or wise is to label others as unholy or ignorant. To define what is moral or just results in a limiting categorization of others and their conduct.

Most moderns would say that without laws there would be chaos and anarchy. But there is a wisdom in Lao-Tzu's admonitions. They cause us to pause and consider: How far do we go? When does further law making and labeling create more harm than good? These are not just questions to be asked in an undergraduate philosophy class. They are increasingly relevant in our age of overcriminalization.

Judge Neil Gorsuch of the Tenth Circuit Court of Appeals delivered a lecture this past month at the Federalist Society's National Lawyers Convention in Washington, DC. He didn't reference Lao-Tzu, but he easily could have. Judge Gorsuch called into question legislation that gives an inordinate amount of power to prosecutors:

> Whether because of public choice problems or otherwise there appears to be a ratchet, relentlessly clicking away, always in the direction of more, never fewer, federal criminal laws. Some reply that the growing number of federal crimes isn't out of proportion to our population and its growth. Others suggest that the proliferation of federal criminal laws can be mitigated by allowing the mistake of law defense to be more widely asserted.
>
> But isn't there a troubled irony lurking here in any event? Without written laws, we lack fair notice of the rules we as citizens have to obey. But with too many written laws, don't we invite a new kind of fair notice problem? And what happens to individual freedom and equality when the criminal law comes to cover so many facets of daily life that prosecutors can almost choose their targets with impunity?

I am reminded of a question attributed to one of the early Roman poets: Who watches the watchmen?

Rehabilitation in Warehouses

The New Melleray Abbey is a Trappist monastery founded in 1849 on a thousand acres of rolling prairie and woodland southwest of Dubuque. It's a refuge. The monks trace their lineage to the sixth century and the *Rule of St. Benedict*. I've stopped here a few times over the years, sometimes for an hour or two, sometimes a day or two. This is my first week-long stay.

My first exposure to the monastic life was in the fall after college graduation. I'd been hitchhiking since May and had made it

from St. Louis to the West Coast and back. I took a job in Illinois
long enough to watch the World Series. The A's played the Dodgers.
(Not a real World Series—the Yankees weren't playing.) Restless, I
hitchhiked to the southern tip of Illinois and then east on two-lane
country roads through Kentucky. A farmer picked me up somewhere
halfway across. We rode in silence. A sign for a monastery caught
my eye. A couple of miles afterward, I asked to be let out. I walked
the two miles back. As I approached the main building, I met an old
monk picking apples off the ground. He pointed to a bucket suggesting I do the same. An hour passed with several buckets filled. The
old man said it was time to eat and that Brother Jerome would show
me my room. I left a month later, having gained some understanding
of solitude.

The silence here at New Melleray, inside and out, becomes a
companion. Without meetings to drive to or errands to run, time
takes on a different meaning. You can see it in the older monks. They
are like ancient trees. The rhythm of their lives is rooted in nature. I
wonder how much they think about it—their lives without change.
Of course that's not entirely true. They have their aches and pains
and their illnesses. They have the graying of hair, the loss of hair,
the loss of fellow monks, the arrival of young men and old wanting
a different kind of life. Perhaps they get letters from the outside.
From time to time they are given new tasks. The guest master here,
Brother Paul, assumed his present duties in January after several
years in the garden and around the farm. Raised a Methodist, he left
his office job at the age of forty-four and never returned. He says his
fifteen years as a monk are all he knows.

I wonder where justice is to be found here? Where are the transgressions and how are they remedied? Surely there are slights that
fester, resulting in distance and alienation. Brother Paul says that
occasionally an outsider with a history of neglect and turmoil will
arrive. Such a life can upset the delicate balance. The monks do their
best to accommodate the visitor, but those who have been damaged
too much are asked to leave. They must find their lives elsewhere.

I've been thinking of Benjamin Franklin and the Philadelphia
Society for Alleviating the Miseries of Public Prisons. Franklin and

others proposed a radical idea: to build a true *penitentiary*, a prison designed to create genuine regret and penitence in the offender's heart. It took thirty years to convince the Pennsylvania Commonwealth to build Eastern State Penitentiary. Opened in 1829, it broke with the prisons of the day. Its goal was not to punish but to move the offender toward spiritual reflection and change. The method was a Quaker-inspired system emphasizing solitude and labor. Proponents of the system believed that offenders, exposed in silence to thoughts of their behavior, would become genuinely penitent. There are elements of the Trappist life in the Quaker model. Reading, reflection, prayer, work, and meals constitute the daily schedule of the monk. Silence is the norm. Quite a contrast from the conditions we often hear about in our modern prisons.

Alexis de Tocqueville visited Eastern State Penitentiary in 1831 and wrote in his report to the French government:

> Thrown into solitude . . . [the prisoner] reflects. Placed alone, in view of his crime, he learns to hate it; and if his soul be not yet surfeited with crime, and thus have lost all taste for any thing better, it is in solitude, where remorse will come to assail him. . . . Can there be a combination more powerful for reformation than that of a prison which hands over the prisoner to all the trials of solitude, leads him through reflection to remorse, through religion to hope . . . [?]

There are certainly deficiencies in the Quaker model. Humans are social animals. They have a need for contact with others. Even in their silence, Trappists come together seven times a day in prayer. They acknowledge each other and raise their voices in common. There must be a balance between solitude and society, labor and leisure. Our prisons can do much better. Any reform, however, must start with fewer inmates and shorter sentences. Rehabilitation cannot take place in warehouses.

Nelson Mandela Did Not Simply Visit This World

I had intended to write this morning on racial disparity and death row inmates, but Nelson Mandela died. I've long had an image of Mandela as ageless, like rocks are. I marveled at his stamina and grace during his years of imprisonment. I have imagined Mandela, carrying his grief as a nobleman, living out his life in a cell, as much for others as for himself. How many of his fellow South Africans thought, "If Nelson can carry his burden as he does, surely I can do as much?" How many others in prison cells around the world have thought the same?

I grew up knowing of Nelson Mandela, but no more than I knew about Abraham Lincoln or John F. Kennedy or Dr. Martin Luther King Jr. I carry images of each, before crowds and in solitude. And I have bits and pieces of their souls, tucked away and rising like white doves in times of my own solitude—the Gettysburg Address, the speech at the Berlin Wall, the speech on the steps of the Lincoln Memorial fifty years ago this past August.

On the fiftieth anniversary of JFK's death, my daughter Juliann said that her generation gives little thought to President Kennedy or his life; that what is important are the issues of today. Juliann was not alive during the Kennedy presidency. But I have to think that his admonition that Americans ask what they can do for their country lives within her as a silent reminder that we each have an obligation to act beyond our own self-interest.

Sometime after his release from prison in 1990 Mandela reflected on his years of imprisonment and on continuing to work toward peace:

> It was during those long and lonely years that my hunger for the freedom of my own people became a hunger for the freedom of all people, white and black. I knew as well as I knew anything that the oppressor must be liberated just as surely as the oppressed. A man who takes away another man's freedom is a prisoner of hatred,

he is locked behind the bars of prejudice and narrow-mindedness. I am not truly free if I am taking away someone else's freedom, just as surely as I am not free when my freedom is taken from me. The oppressed and the oppressor alike are robbed of their humanity.

Generations from now, what child or young adult or restless mid-lifer will read of Mandela, of his life and his words, and be moved to action within the context of their own times?

Justice in Mississippi

When my daughter Mary returned from China she asked if she could go with me "on one of those *Justice Diary* trips." I said sure, but told her that she had to pick the destination. We left Des Moines early yesterday and arrived at our B&B near Hernando, Mississippi, well after sunset. It was night, jet black, when we crossed the border south of Memphis into Mississippi. There was a subtle eeriness as we drove on narrow blacktop roads, the moon illuminating fields tucked between pockets of woodland, fields that had once been worked by slaves. This was a different country. My imagination, informed by a rudimentary history of the Old South, brought forth slave quarters dwarfed by antebellum mansions. Recently, a viewing of *12 Years a Slave* sickened me with its graphic portrayal of horrid conditions and bare-back whippings.

We woke to a different world this morning. Sunshine on iced branches brought a civility to the shadow land of the night before. After a breakfast of baked oatmeal and black coffee we drove into Holly Springs, Mary's choice for a few days with dad. Holly Springs is its own oddity, ghostlike at first glance. But like a hundred out-of-the-way towns, it has a charm that belies its weariness. We decided to spend the morning in the Marshall County Courthouse, where we walked in on a battle over an old dirt road, claimed to be public by the plaintiff and private by the defendant. Two witnesses in their eighties, one a former state legislator and sheriff, and the other a once-wealthy businessman, testified from teenage memories about the use of the road in the early 1940s. The judge, who knew everyone on a first name basis, was seated high up on the bench, which was draped on one side by the Stars and Stripes and on the other by the flag of the Confederacy. It was a civil trial in the best sense of the word—the opposing lawyers probably roommates at Ole Miss. With the noon recess, everyone paraded out of the courtroom and headed to JB's on the Square. Mary and I ate fried green tomatoes and listened to an elderly farm widow and her daughter talk about the "cloud on the title" and the injustice of it all. The young man who bought the adjacent farm and who padlocked the gate nearly six years ago ate lunch two tables down. The lawyers for both sides ate lunch together.

Later at the courthouse I had the good fortune to meet some Holly Springs residents: the deputy sheriff who had wanted to be in law enforcement since he was a little boy when his father introduced him to Buford Pusser, the sheriff of *Walking Tall* fame; another deputy who works exclusively with juveniles and who said his biggest challenge is marijuana use by local youth; the mother of a young marijuana user who said that, for the most part, the people who run the system try hard to keep kids in school and keep the stupid things kids do from ruining their lives; the frightened sixteen-year-old boy waiting his turn to see the judge because he had violated his probation.

In mid-afternoon Mary and I drove the back roads of rural Marshall County and witnessed firsthand the poverty behind the statistics that place Mississippi, with a 9 percent unemployment rate and 24 percent of its population below the poverty line, dead last among the poorest states in the country.

My Conversation with Al

I had an interesting conversation with a friend Friday evening. I see Al once a year, at one of the obligatory Christmas parties. Some people mellow with age. Al has always been mellow. He is the only person I know who can sleep anywhere better than I can. In his early seventies and recently retired from the government, Al is a proud conservative. While not a card-carrying Libertarian, he nevertheless considers himself one. He is also a staunch Catholic, raising four children Catholic and putting them through Catholic schools. Al has values. He believes in hard work, honesty, responsibility, and accountability.

Friday evening Al wanted to talk about kids—kids who make mistakes. He told me that since we last talked he had read quite a bit in the newspaper about what's going on with kids in our juvenile justice system. He had read about the big increase in juvenile court filings and the addition of a sixth juvenile judge and two more juvenile prosecutors. Al said that it looks like people who run the system prosecute and punish these kids just because they can. That they do it to justify their existence and to keep their jobs. He said it doesn't make sense to him that we criminalize behavior that wasn't criminal when he was a kid. Al told me he made mistakes when he was a teenager but that the government didn't need to be involved. It was enough that his father and his teachers cared. Al said he wonders what is going to happen to these kids when they are adults, having been labeled by the schools and courts as delinquents. He said he has heard from his own children about difficulties some of their friends have had because of mistakes they made when they were in high school. Al said he is no longer confident in the political process. He doesn't care for any political party. He said that politicians are like prosecutors—they just want to keep their jobs.

Al told me he is interested in what AMOS is doing. He has heard of retired people being trained as court watchers and school mediators, and that makes sense to him. He likes the idea of average people actually being able to do something about justice, particularly about juvenile justice. We then got to talking about social movements. I asked Al if he had heard of Michelle Alexander's book *The New Jim Crow* and her conclusion that a social movement is needed in this country to bring about significant changes in our justice systems. Al said he hadn't heard of the book and that he has always been skeptical of social movements. He also said, however, that his ideas on this have changed lately—that people just can't sit on the couch anymore and expect things to get better. Al said we get what we deserve and if people don't actually get involved and demand change, then we have only ourselves to blame.

I thought all weekend about my conversation with Al. As often happens, I picked up a book that spoke to the conversation. It was a book of essays by Vaclav Havel, the Czech playwright and poet and, later, the first president of the Czech Republic. Havel, in writing about the power of the powerless, posed these questions: "Who are these so-called dissidents? Where does their point of view come from? What importance does it have? What is the significance of the dissidents' initiatives? What real chances do such initiatives have? Is it appropriate to refer to dissidents as an opposition? What is this opposition within the framework of the system? What does it do? What role does it play in society? What are its hopes and on what are they based? Can they actually change anything?"

Havel's questions were answered, and the Czech Republic was the result. I wonder what Michelle Alexander would say about Havel's questions. Are they relevant to her imperative? I wonder what Al would say about Havel's questions. Are they relevant to the rest of his life, and the lives of his children and grandchildren?

Ubuntu

I had breakfast this morning with an attorney who told me she is struggling with her chosen profession. She said she is more and more convinced that if the profession is to survive, then the adversarial posturing must give way to compassion and collaboration. She spoke of her recent experiences at the courthouse and asked why it is that prosecutors are so often mean-spirited. She wondered what role power plays in the harshness of the prosecutorial attitude.

A law professor told me recently that a friend of his, a businessman who is African American, had just moved back to his home state and bought a house in a predominately white suburb. On three occasions in less than a month the man was stopped by police and questioned about what he was doing there.

At about the same time, I had a conversation with a young man who was admitted to the practice of law in Iowa in September. He told me that a few months earlier, while driving to meet a friend, he was stopped by police. An officer approached his vehicle, and the first question the officer asked was "Do you have drugs in your car?" The young man, an African American, was told to get out of his car so it could be searched. Nothing was found.

Following a recent church service, I was approached by an African American woman. I learned that she is an opera singer, has been nominated for a Tony Award, and has performed around the world. She told me that in recent years she has been harassed for no reason by police in several U.S. cities. A graduate of Juilliard, she said that she no longer considers this to be her country and that she must find another to call her home.

Desmond Tutu has written that in his culture the highest praise that anyone can give to an individual is to say that he or she possesses the quality of ubuntu. Ubuntu has to do with how individuals regard others and how they see themselves within their intimate relationships, their familial relationships, and within the broader community. In reflecting on the end of apartheid, he knew that ubuntu would be put to the test, but he believed in its power of reconciliation. Tutu tells the story of a man by the name of Malusi Mpumlwana who, even while being tortured by security police, looked at his torturers and realized that these were human beings too and that they needed him to help them recover the humanity they were losing.

Why Restorative Justice Works

I've been thinking lately about why our present way of doing justice—retributive justice—doesn't work and why restorative justice does; why it is that punishment doesn't get the necessary results and why the restorative justice approach, which requires an offender to be accountable, does. When we punish people by incarcerating them, we really don't expect anything of them. We sequester them from society, locking them out of sight, and requiring them to eat, sleep, and exercise at specific times. But there is no requirement that they do anything, at least nothing directly related to the offense they committed. Punishment is passive. And because it is passive there is no sense of accomplishment. There is no growth.

In a restorative justice system, on the other hand, when we say that an offender must be accountable for the conduct that caused harm to another, we are saying that the offender must be active, that he or she must do something. It is in the doing that there is efficacy.

> *When we punish people by incarcerating them,*
>
> *we really don't expect anything of them. . . .*
>
> *Offenders must be held accountable*
>
> *for the harm their criminal acts cause others.*
>
> *If we allow them to be accountable,*
>
> *they will heal in the process.*

I had a conversation today with a psychologist friend. Our conversation centered on agency, the ability of humans to affect the world that surrounds them. As we talked it became clear that to have agency is to know meaning. When a potter is at her wheel she experiences agency, and the creative process engenders meaning. The act has much more meaning than the adulation that might come from those who praise her for her work. The basketball player, in a zone, knows agency. My guess is that Michael Jordan would trade all of his records for the opportunity to know that agency again. My grandson, heading toward the terrible twos, knows agency on a daily basis. He experiences the ability to make things happen. He is filled with joy when he does and frustrated when he is unable to.

As we continued our talk I had an aha moment. The accountability that restorative justice requires of offenders is directly related to agency. When offenders engage in an act of accountability, they experience agency. They are doing something, and they are doing it because they agreed to do it. Whether the doing arose out of a victim–offender conference or a Circle process, what is important is that offenders at some point make a commitment and follow through with it. For offenders, much of the healing of the soul that is needed occurs during the actual doing of the things they have committed to doing to make reparations. It is no wonder that there is a growing body of research documenting the fact that offenders who participate in restorative justice processes reoffend at a lower rate than those who do not.

Offenders must be held accountable for the harm their criminal acts cause others. If we allow them to be accountable, they will heal in the process.

To Be as Good as Good Old Mr. Scrooge

I finally found it—up on the top shelf, a little dusty, but the same book I'd read to my own children many times and, sadly, many years before that. It is ageless though. *A Christmas Carol* is new for each succeeding generation. It's time for me to open it up for my grandson, just in time for his second Christmas. I'm sure we won't get through it all this year; many of the words are beyond him, but the pictures tell so much and it's not too early to learn of Tiny Tim. As I paged through the book I was reminded of how quotable Charles Dickens is: "Christmas is a poor excuse every 25th of December to pick a man's pockets." "It is always the person not in the predicament who knows what ought to have been done." "He told me, coming home, that he hoped the people saw him in the church, because he was a cripple, and it might be pleasant to them to remember upon Christmas Day, who made lame beggars walk and blind men see." "Charity begins at home, and justice begins next door." "For it is good to be children sometimes, and never better than at Christmas." "For not an orphan in the wide world can be so deserted as the child who is an outcast from a living parent's love."

This last quote has me reflecting on the dark side of Christmas—the reality that for many children Christmas is not the best time to be a child. Right now more than two million children have parents behind bars in this country. The number of children with parents in prison increased 80 percent between 1991 and 2007. One in eight children has experienced parental incarceration at some point in their lives. Half of all juveniles in custody have a father, mother, or other close relative who has been in jail or prison. Black children are 7.5 times more likely and Latino children are 2.6 times more likely than white children to have a parent in prison. Nearly half of all parents in state prisons lived with their children before being sent to prison. Sixty percent of parents in state prisons and 45 percent in federal prisons have not had any personal visits with their children while in prison.

Tiny Tim, at that famous Christmas meal, prayed simply: "God bless us every one!" My prayer, while not so simple, is that every prosecutor think twice before recommending to the court that the parent of a child be sent to prison, and that every judge think twice before handing down a sentence that would do the same. And for those of us who get discouraged at times by how justice is often administered in this country, we can all find hope in the change of heart of good old Mr. Scrooge. For as Charles Dickens tells us: "Scrooge was better than his word. He did it all, and infinitely more; and to Tiny Tim, who did not die, he was a second father. He became as good a friend, as good a master, and as good a man as the good old city knew, or any other good old city, town, or borough in the good old world."

Where Would Jesus Stand?

On Christmas Eve I went to Mass. A young woman sitting in front of me was wearing a "WWJD" bracelet. I've never worn one, but I'm told the bracelets have informed the personal actions of many. Millions have been sold. I wonder if "WWJS" bracelets would be just as popular? What if millions asked themselves daily: "Where would Jesus stand? On what issues would he stand? Who would he stand with?" I've also wondered, What if Jesus had lived a long life, like the Buddha? What if he had been born into our time? What if he had been born in Delhi, Cape Town, Harlem, or inner-city Detroit? Who would have attended his birth?

There is a beautiful book titled *Works of Mercy*. It's a collection of wood engravings by Fritz Eichenberg, who had a forty-year association with Dorothy Day and the Catholic Worker movement. At first glance Eichenberg's *Christmas 1954* depicts the typical manger scene. But soon you see that there are no wise men, no gifts, no shepherds. There are three homeless men, and in the background are a half dozen or so tenement buildings. A stray dog is at Mary's feet as she holds her newborn.

If Jesus had been born in the last hundred years, would he have been an activist or would he have sat at home? Would he have been a pacifist or would he have sat at home? With whom would Jesus have stood? Would he have been with Gandhi on the Salt March or with Dr. King on the March on Washington? Would he have stood with the students at Kent State and Tiananmen Square? Would he walk hand in hand with those marching for food freedom and against Monsanto? If Jesus had gone to law school, would he stand with the government as a prosecutor or with the accused as a public defender? If he had studied business, would he be a hedge fund manager or a micro-lender? If he were a teacher, would he teach MBA students or kindergarteners? If he coached, would he coach the Yankees or Little Leaguers? Would Jesus have been born white, or is it more likely he would have been born black or brown or yellow or red? Would Jesus be a Christian? A Catholic? Would he be a priest? Would he advocate for women to be priests, to be bishops, to be the pope? Who would Jesus have come for—the CEOs, the senators, the Silicon Valley millionaires, or would he have come for the poor, the undocumented, the imprisoned?

A Vanished World

Yesterday a friend loaned me a prized possession. It was *A Vanished World*, a book of black-and-white photographs taken by Roman Vishniac in the decade before World War II. Vishniac's photos evoke compassion and sorrow for the Jewish world in Germany and eastern Europe shortly before it was engulfed by fire and darkness. My friend is a student of Jewish history and the Holocaust. Raised on a small farm in northern Iowa, he knows bigotry. He is a gay man. He grew up at a time when to come out would have meant social suicide.

Many still live in that time. So my friend shared his book with me so I might see the faces of those who lived in a world that did not love them. I spent time this afternoon looking at those faces, imagining their lives, their loves, their families, their dreams and aspirations—knowing that death had already marked them for its own. I couldn't help but make the connection between their lives and the lives of Native Americans before the genocide, or between the lives of African Americans before the war on drugs and mass incarceration. I understand that the parallels are not perfect, but the wiping out of any people, either by murder or by marginalization—on reservations, in prisons, or in ghettos—deserves our sustained attention.

This past August, Attorney General Eric Holder ordered a fundamentally new approach in the federal prosecution of many lower-level drug offenders. Holder said that it's past time to take concrete steps to end the nation's four-decade incarceration binge. In Holder's words,

> Today, a vicious cycle of poverty, criminality, and incarceration traps too many Americans and weakens too many communities. And many aspects of our criminal justice system may actually exacerbate these problems, rather than alleviate them.
>
> It's clear . . . that too many Americans go to too many prisons for far too long, and for no truly good law enforcement reason. It's clear, at a basic level, that 20th-century criminal justice solutions are not adequate to overcome our 21st-century challenges. And it is well past time to implement common sense changes that will foster safer communities from coast to coast.

The harsher-is-better mind-set is giving way to a recognition that widespread incarceration is both ineffective and unsustainable.

One need only go to the website of Right on Crime (righton crime.com) to find that conservatives are taking up the cause of reform. According to Newt Gingrich: "There is an urgent need to address the astronomical growth in the prison population, with its huge costs in dollars and lost human potential. . . . The criminal justice system is broken, and conservatives must lead the way in fixing it." Grover Norquist agrees: "Today's criminal justice system is big government on steroids, and the responsibility for taming its excesses falls to those committed to smaller government: conservatives. We fight against big government, excess spending, unaccountability, and bureaucracy in nearly every other segment of spending." As does William Bennett: "Conservatives are known for being tough on crime, but we must also be tough on criminal justice spending. That means demanding more cost-effective approaches that enhance public safety."

Restorative justice holds out the only true promise for a just justice system in our country.

I have believed for more than two decades that restorative justice holds out the only true promise for a *just* justice system in our country. I still believe that, but those of us who are true believers must embrace others who have similar goals and are approaching those goals from a different direction. When I look at my home state and my home community I witness very little, if anything, being done by liberals and Democrats. Iowa continues to be a leader in the arrest and prosecution of African Americans for drug offenses even though the use of drugs by African Americans and whites is nearly the same. There is no real debate here about the legalization of marijuana or doing away with harsh sentences and mandatory minimums. It is an embarrassment. But beyond embarrassment, it is a tragedy. As Holder said, "too many Americans go to too many prisons for far too long, and for no truly good law enforcement reason." And in the process we marginalize more and more people. Years from now, in the not too distant future, if we do not fix what is so terribly broken, we will look back on another people and their vanished world.

Nobody Can Make It Out of Here Alone

Columnist Ellen Goodman once said, when giving a Harvard commencement address, I think, that her favorite people are those over forty who haven't decided what they want to do with their lives. I think my favorite people are those over sixty who have decided that they are called to be radical.

When I was in my thirties I got to know Phil Riley. Phil had been the city attorney for Des Moines but was retired when I first met him. I was representing homeless and nearly homeless people as a Legal Aid lawyer, and Phil was passionate in his belief that we could do much better when providing for the least fortunate. Phil was also an outspoken opponent of the nuclear arms race and was deeply involved in the Plowshares movement, advocating that military weapons be converted to peaceful civilian applications. I would sit with Phil on his front porch and listen to him articulate a vision for a peaceful world. I imagined being like Phil Riley when I grew up.

I had the pleasure this morning to sit in a Circle with about fifteen others at an inner-city church. A few I have known for decades, dating back to when I first met Phil. I know them because of their commitment to nonviolent protest against war and oppression of all kinds. Some of them have served jail time for their beliefs. This morning the conversation was wide-ranging, from the need for mediators in schools, to the failure of our local justice system, to racial bias and mass incarceration, to the marginalization of the poor and the privatization of prisons. Nearly everyone spoke, and nearly everyone agreed that profit making is behind all of it.

On Christmas Day, a friend, a wonderful man born in Iran who has experienced more injustice than anyone I know, sent me an email. It was a simple one, prefaced by "You will find this of interest." In the body was a simple statement of fact: "The combined net worth of 48.8 million low-income households matches the worth of just six billionaire members of the Walton family." You have to think that the one-tenth of the One Percent who own and control most of our country must find it very amusing that the rest of us, in our failure to work together, do such a poor job of managing our communities and providing the most basic of human needs—decent housing, decent education, decent employment opportunities, and decent justice. They, in their palatial homes and on their monstrous yachts, must think they are immune from the impending collapse of our institutions and systems. But the prophets and poets among us know better.

Out with the Old

I know I'm not alone in believing that our justice system is broken. William Pizzi says it in *Trials Without Truth*. Dick Snyder says it in *The Protestant Ethic and the Spirit of Punishment*, as do Angela Davis in *Arbitrary Justice: The Power of the American Prosecutor*, Michelle Alexander in *The New Jim Crow*, William Stuntz in *The Collapse of American Criminal Justice*, Glenn Greenwald in *With Liberty and Justice for Some*, and Stephanos Bibas in *The Machinery of Criminal Justice*. Critics will say that these are just academics or that they are lawyers with an ax to grind or a book to sell. The critics generally have their own agenda, and that agenda is to maintain the status quo. To do that, it's critical that they dismiss the outsider, no matter how cogent the argument or compelling the facts. This is to be expected. But the truth is that the broken system will not embark on a course of self-correction until those who make the pivotal decisions within the system begin to question their own values and the foundation upon which they are constructed. Unlike the critics, however, it is highly unlikely that judges or prosecutors will read Pizzi or Snyder or Davis or Alexander or any of the rest. If they know these books exist, most are frightened of them or dismissive of them because they don't support the worldview that makes their lives comfortable.

I know a college professor who reads everything in his field, not for the purpose of building a case or supporting a position, but because he wants to have the broadest understanding possible. Lawyers aren't like this, at least those lawyers who make their livings as courtroom warriors. If they read anything at all about the other side, it is to better defeat it. They don't read to discover the truth, they read to win. It's ironic that our adversarial system is touted as the best system humanity has created to discover the truth of a matter in contention, and yet the litigator seeks to build an argument that is unassailable. What litigator of any competence argues the merits of the other's case while at the same time arguing her own? This may be the best system possible when it comes to determining the guilt or innocence of an accused person. But what happens when a community or a society begins to question the way justice is administered, since those who defend that system are litigators and prosecutors?

A second irony in all of this is that prosecutors are public servants. Prosecutors serve at the will of the people. They are custodians of justice and have a duty to not only participate in the fair administration of justice but to diligently strive to correct any flaws that system might have. Where is the prosecutor who is doing that? Last week the editorial board of the *New York Times* lauded President Obama for commuting the "outrageously long drug sentences" of eight men and women. The *Times* said that this showed a "measure of compassion and common sense" but that it also served to highlight the injustice being done to thousands of other prisoners whose sentences have not been commuted. The *Times* reported that when Obama issued the commutations, he blamed the "unfair system" that is keeping thousands behind bars. The *Times* didn't stop there. It said that federal drug laws are "far too harsh and inflexible" and that "their burden falls most heavily upon the poor and racial minorities." The *Times* concluded by recognizing that Obama "did not create the broken criminal justice system, but he can do much more to lessen its impact on those who have been most unfairly punished by it."

I doubt that many prosecutors are familiar with the books listed above, let alone have read any of them. But prosecutors certainly do know of the *New York Times*. Perhaps somewhere along the way a prosecutor will send out an email with a link to the *Times*' opinion piece about President Obama's commutation of "outrageously long drug sentences." And maybe the email will go viral among prosecutors. And, if we are fortunate, some eyes will be opened and some values will begin to be questioned. It is New Year's Eve. For as long as I can remember, Americans on this day have joined together and said, "Out with the old and in with the new." We can only hope.

Midwives to a Healing Process

I had a conversation today with an analyst I know—a Jungian, a doctor of the soul. She does not consider those who come to her to have a disease or an illness. Neither does she label. She practices in the spirit of Carl Jung, the founder of analytical psychology. She's learned everything she can about the human psyche; and then forgets it when she enters into a relationship with a client. She practices what Jung famously preached: "It is what you are that heals, not what you know." For her, analysis is a process of discovery. The analyst doesn't administer or sedate or surgically remove. It might be said the analyst merely holds the light while the client examines himself. This self-examination in the presence of a compassionate, nonjudgmental analyst is the prescription for healing.

This afternoon we talked about the alchemical process as a metaphor for individuation, the process by which an individual becomes psychologically whole. According to my analyst friend, it was the task of the alchemist to transform base matter—iron, lead, salt, sulphur, vinegar, blood, poison, and a host of other materials and substances—into something of great value: the philosopher's stone, a symbol of perfection. For the alchemist, even the most vile substance or material was a necessary element in the transformation process. Likewise, for the Jungian, a client's most disturbing symptoms as well as her deepest fears, regrets, and shames—conscious and unconscious—are the stuff from which one becomes one's own self.

Earlier today I had coffee with a local minister. It was our first meeting. She recently completed an intensive mediation training and is interested in opportunities to develop her new skills. She's known of restorative justice for a long time, having worked in prison ministry and with re-entry programs. We talked about victim–offender dialogue and the use of restorative practices in schools. She said the need for restorative practices is endless—in prisons, schools, the workplace, neighborhoods, and even within church congregations. She added that she has had opportunities over the years to be present, in a nonjudgmental way, to people in spiritual and psychological pain and that she knows of the healing nature of such a presence.

Late this afternoon, while walking along the river, a connection was made, the kind that happens at times as geese pass overhead. I recognized a similarity between the role of the "doctor of the soul" and the role of the "keeper of a process," whether it is a victim–offender dialogue or conference or a Circle meeting. I understand the roles are not the same. The keeper or facilitator does not and should not engage in therapy. But both the analyst and the facilitator bring to their respective practices compassion and attention. Both sit with pain, anger, and hurt—and ugliness at times—without judgment. Neither offers a prescription, but both, if all of the elements are present, serve as midwives to a healing process.

Infusing Kids with Hope

I was at a meeting this morning at Trinity United Methodist Church. It is a jewel on the near north side of Des Moines, in the heart of the River Bend neighborhood. Trinity quietly proclaims that it is a place of "radical hospitality and holy chaos." The hospitality offered is "not only to those who are like us but to those who may be quite different from us." Hundreds of people pass through Trinity's doors daily. Some show up for a loaf of bread, a bag of vegetables, or some rice and beans. Others arrive to learn English or take a citizenship class. Trinity has re-entry teams to assist people coming out of prison, an ongoing relationship with a village in El Salvador, and it supports a legal service project for immigrants. Far too many show up at Trinity because life has become so overwhelming there is nowhere else to turn. Pastor Barb Dinnen says, "As we see the many needs on a day-to-day basis, we cannot help but work to alleviate suffering by addressing and advocating for the elimination of systemic causes of poverty and injustice."

As I was leaving the church I picked up a copy of Trinity's weekly newsletter. The cover story was about Father Greg Boyle, the Jesuit priest who has worked with Los Angeles gangs for nearly three decades. Father Boyle founded Homeboy Industries, the largest gang intervention program in the nation, operating seven social enterprises: a bakery, a café, a farmer's market, a diner, a grocery store, a catering operation, and a merchandising operation. The newsletter contained an excerpt of an interview that NPR host Krista Tippett did with Father Boyle in which he tells the story of a gang member's experience of Christmas. The gang member had been abused and abandoned by his parents, and now worked on Homeboy's graffiti crew.

> "What'd you do for Christmas?" "Oh, just right here." I said, "Alone?" And he said, "No, I invited six other guys from the graffiti crew who didn't had no place to go," he said, "and they were all . . ." He named them and they were enemies with each other. I said, "What'd you do?" He goes, "You're not gonna believe it. I cooked a turkey." I said, "Well, how'd you prepare the turkey?" He says, "Well, you know, ghetto style." I said, "No, I don't think I'm familiar with that recipe." He said, "Well, you rub it with a gang of butter and you squeeze two limones on it and you put salt and pepper, put it in the oven. Tasted proper," he said. I said, "Wow. What else did you have besides turkey?" "Well, that's it, just turkey. Yeah, the seven of us, we just sat in the kitchen staring at the oven waiting for the turkey to be done. Did I mention it tasted proper?" I said, "Yeah, you did."

I couldn't help but think of the prosecutor's office I used to work in and the disdain for "gang bangers" held by many in the office. I hurried home to try to find Tippett's interview, which I did in the archives of her On Being website.

To listen to Father Boyle is to listen to a man who truly lives the gospel message. Near the end of the interview, done in front of a live audience, he was asked by a member of the audience about his interaction with the justice system. The question was preceded by the statement that "so many in the area where I come from, the way you deal with gangs is you incarcerate them." Father Boyle responded that he has testified in about fifty death penalty sentencing cases around the country involving gang members, and he has never encountered a gang member who, as a defendant in one of those cases, was not a deeply disturbed, mentally ill person:

> No one wants you to say that. The prosecution refuses you to say anything. Even the defense says don't say anything like that. Why? Because then you're forced to in the face of somebody who's mentally ill, you can only have one response and that's compassion. And this freaks us out because, oh, what happens to responsibility, and he knew what he was doing. Prosecutors always say to me, well, he could choose.
>
> I go, gosh, you know, not all choices are created equal and a person's ability to choose is not created equal. I don't know. If we were more sensible, you know, at an early age, we'd be somehow infusing kids with hope when they can't imagine their future and they're planning their funerals, or we'd heal kids who are so damaged that they can't see their way clear to transform their pain, so they continue to transmit it, or to deliver mental health services in a timely, effective, appropriate way. If as a society we did those things . . . we wouldn't be at the place we're at.

And if we did that, maybe we would see that every young person is worth saving, that no child should be thrown away, and no child should ever be labeled a "gang banger."

Reverence for Life

There was a time when I thought anything was possible. I was twenty-four, driving an ambulance, and working in the emergency room of a small hospital. I don't recall if I had a dream or not but I got it in my head that I should work with Mother Teresa. With that in mind I quit my job, hoping to get to Calcutta. (I never made it.) I rode a freight train to Colorado and then headed south for Panama. It was in September and the hitchhiking was good for a while. However, the farther south I went, the fewer the rides. The buses weren't much better. Fortunately, I wasn't in a hurry. I arrived in Panama City in early January. Along the way, I stopped in Cuernavaca, Mexico. For about a hundred dollars I got a bed for a month, three meals a day, and four weeks of Spanish instruction. The owner of the little school had a friend in a local prison serving a one-year sentence for selling marijuana. He asked me if I wanted to go with him to visit his friend. I ended up going seven or eight times.

At first I was appalled. The inmates lived in small huts surrounding a large area I would call a courtyard. It was hard-packed dirt, except when it rained. The huts had floors of the same material, which stayed dry most of the time. The inmates, all men, had to cook for themselves and rely on family and friends to bring them food. No visitors, no food. I thought this was the height of cruelty. But after a couple of visits I began to see the humanity in it. None of the men were starving; in fact none of them looked like they ever missed a meal. They had visitors every day, and if one of them didn't, the others shared. Families stayed connected. Friends brought games and laughter and sometimes music.

I had forgotten about these visits to a Mexican prison until just the other day. I was thinking about Albert Schweitzer, who, as a young doctor, established a hospital in the middle of an African jungle. Schweitzer had been a theologian, composer, and a world-class organ builder, but he gave it all up to attend medical school so he could care for Africans in need. The story is told that shortly after Schweitzer arrived in Gabon he embarked on a journey by boat to care for a dying woman. On the evening of the third day, at sunset, he had a revelation that all ethics, all life-affirming principles, could be boiled down to a single phrase: "Reverence for Life." This revelation deeply influenced Schweitzer and the way he would establish his hospital. Instead of building a modern one, by European standards, he duplicated a traditional African village and attached a clinic for dispensing medical services. Schweitzer realized that he had to meet Africans on their own terms—he had to have reverence for them—knowing they had a strong sense of family and would not be inclined to go to a hospital in which sick family members were separated from relatives and friends.

Hospitals and prisons both isolate. Our American models do little to encourage connection with family and continuity with community. Fortunately, hospital stays are often short. The same can't be said for prison sentences. Once an inmate is released from a state or federal facility, a great deal has been lost. Families move on as best they can when a loved one is incarcerated. Inmates remain stuck, with little to show for having done their time.

Justice for Fort Lee and for Bridget Anne Kelly

Bridget Anne Kelly. A household name because she apparently initiated, as political retribution, the closing of entrance ramps to the George Washington Bridge, which connects New York City and Fort Lee, New Jersey. She has already become an icon for the deceitful and the despicable. The feeding frenzy has begun. The media hounds are in attack mode. The politicians are piling on. A federal investigation is underway. No doubt multiple indictments will be returned and the federal guidelines will require a prison sentence. And to what end? Given the facts as they have been reported, Kelly's actions can't be excused. She was wrong, probably criminally wrong, if politics motivated the part she played in the closing of two lanes of traffic on the George Washington Bridge this past September. But where do we go from here?

In the last couple of days I've talked to a half dozen people about Kelly. To a person, they want to see her punished. She should do jail time. In addition, there should be a lifetime ban on Kelly ever holding a position of trust.

I will never forget the first time I heard Robert Yazzie, the former chief justice of the Navajo Nation, speak about his people's response to the most serious of crimes. Yazzie said that before the white man came, the Navajo practiced restorative justice. He said that when there was a murder within the tribal community, the offender was given the choice to remain in the community, providing support to surviving family members, or to leave the community, never to return. No one died as the result of Kelly's apparently politically motivated stupidity. As far as I know, there were no injuries either. Nevertheless, Kelly should be held accountable for the harm done to the people of Fort Lee, New Jersey. Her accountability should be direct and in person. Assuming that Kelly will be prosecuted and found guilty, or pleads guilty, what if she were ordered to serve a probationary term and, as a condition of her probation, must reside in Fort Lee?

What if a peacemaking Circle were held, maybe several? What if community members participated and the anger could be transformed into healing? What if over the two or three years Kelly lived in Fort Lee, she visited personally with people residing there who had been affected by her actions? What if, over time, she participated in the community life of Fort Lee? What might life look like for Kelly in a few years if she were sentenced to Fort Lee rather than to a federal penitentiary? It's not hard to see that a life might be salvaged rather than destroyed.

There are those of us in the justice field who believe that a justice of accountability, compassion, and restoration is the justice we are called to practice. Isn't the case of Bridget Anne Kelly a call for restorative justice leaders and others to stand up and call for a healing response to the harm she caused the people of Fort Lee?

The Apparatus

Two Court Watch trainings were held this weekend. Twenty-five people attended, adding to the nearly one hundred court watchers trained in the last twelve months. Almost everyone expressed concern for the local juvenile justice system. They believe something is wrong but don't know what to do. Most have had contact with the system. They are retired teachers or social workers, even retired lawyers, or they have had a child or a grandchild go through the system. They feel a general uneasiness about the way power is wielded by those who run the system, but they don't feel competent to speak out. They do, however, want to learn and observe how the system works. They believe that's the first step. They want to see what justice looks like firsthand and to gain an understanding of the intricacies of the justice machinery so they might influence decision makers.

At a meeting this morning a woman spoke about her adult daughter, who is now doing fine, but who suffered greatly as a teenager at the hands of juvenile justice professionals who said they knew what they were doing. She struggled to find a word to describe the system as she had experienced it. A woman sitting across from her, a woman with years of experience advocating for social justice, interrupted her friend and said the most accurate description of our system is that "it is broken." We then talked about how the system appears to be mindless—that there are powerful people throughout the system, but no one is in control. It is like a runaway locomotive without an engineer.

Simone Weil, the French philosopher and mystic, witnessed firsthand the suffering endured by average people as the result of society's machinery. As a young teacher she became involved in local political activity, supporting unemployed and striking workers. While initially attracted to the Communist Party, she never joined it, and in her twenties she became increasingly critical of Marxism. Weil was one of the first to identify a new form of oppression not anticipated by Marx, one in which bureaucrats could make life just as miserable for ordinary people as did the most exploitative capitalists. A friend told me that 70 percent of those surveyed in a recent poll said their number one fear is big government. Weil would have understood. She wrote:

> Whether the mask is labeled Fascism, Democracy, or Dictatorship of the Proletariat, our great adversary remains the Apparatus—the bureaucracy, the police, the military. Not the one facing us across the frontier or the battle lines, . . . but the one that calls itself our protector and makes us its slaves. No matter what the circumstances, the worst betrayal will always be to subordinate ourselves to this Apparatus, and to trample

underfoot, in its service, all human values in ourselves and in others.

I admire those who have taken the time to be trained as court watchers. They are taking a first step in their refusal to be subordinated to the Apparatus.

Responding to the Real Needs of Victims

I ran into an acquaintance yesterday while on a late-night walk. We exchanged updates on our children and, in the process, he told me that his son-in-law is now an assistant U.S. attorney prosecuting white-collar crimes. I told him that in the mid-1980s I had been a white-collar crime prosecutor and was fascinated by the holes people dug for themselves. Almost without fail, white-collar offenders started small and were convinced that sooner or later they would pay back what they had taken. Another trait of these offenders was that early on the amounts were small, and rarely was there a clear pattern in their activity. But once they got a head of steam, the amounts grew significantly and a clear pattern of deception would emerge. I later came to understand that the more blatant the behavior, the more likely it was that the offender was crying out to be caught.

As I continued on my walk, I recalled the anger of the victims of these crimes. Vengeance was more important than getting their money back. They wanted the thieves to rot in prison. If the amounts taken were large enough, they got their wish. Oftentimes, however, an interesting thing would happen. Victims would call after an offender had been sent to the penitentiary and would express dissatisfaction with the outcome. It wasn't that they were unhappy with the prison sentence, it was that they felt something was missing. They couldn't articulate what it was, and I couldn't either. It wasn't until I discovered restorative justice and sat in on victim–offender mediations that I began to develop an understanding of the underlying reason for victim discontent.

The victim—a CEO or business owner—would attend a mediation with bank records, logs, internal memos, and ledgers in hand and demand that every penny be accounted for and be repaid. The process was a tedious one, often taking two or three hours. But almost always something would be said and the course of the meeting would be altered. Frequently the offender would accept full responsibility, agree to whatever amount was asked for, and begin to apologize profusely, sometimes tearfully. This was the threshold moment. Without knowing it, this is what both victim and offender had been waiting for. Ledger books would be closed. Stacks of records would be pushed aside. The victim would slowly state the one thing that had remained unsaid: "You betrayed me." At this moment the government's role became inconsequential to the needs of the real parties to the crime. The real loss became the subject of the conversation. Money, like the State, became secondary to the broken trust.

As an observer of human nature, these encounters were invaluable. Over time, my sense of justice was redefined. I began to see that the rightful role of the State is to make available healing processes that are urgently needed by victims and offenders. Restorative justice advocates and practitioners assert that the rightful response to criminal wrongdoing is accountability, not punishment. Accountability begins when victims and offenders come together in safe and private spaces and have conversations about the harm that has been caused and how that harm might be repaired.

Where Are They to Learn Peace?

Thomas Merton took a walk on a sunny January afternoon forty-five years ago. It was near St. Bernard's pond on the grounds of Gethsemani Abbey, where he had lived the past twenty-seven years. He wrote in his journal that day that he had intended to read from Martin Buber's *Ten Rungs*, but instead could only look at the sun, the dead grass, the green soft ice, the blue sky. And then his solitude was disturbed. He wrote: "Will there never be any peace on earth in our lifetime? Will they never do anything but kill, and then kill some more? Apparently they are caught in that impasse: the system is completely violent and involved in violence, and there is no way out but violence, and that leads only to more violence. Really—what is ahead but the apocalypse?"

Isn't that the question? Isn't that the specter that haunts our children as they consider their future and try to sleep at night? Where is the system that teaches peace, not violence? Where are the leaders who model peace for us and for our children and grandchildren? Nelson Mandela is dead, and who remembers Gandhi, and what leader quotes from the Sermon on the Mount? Those who we pay to deliver us justice, where in their words and in their actions do we find compassion? Are we beyond the tipping point?

Our school children are our future leaders, our future soldiers, our future Peace Corps volunteers. Where are they to learn peace but in our schools?

I have a vision, naive I know, that in a generation every school in this country will have become a restorative justice school. Every conflict, involving every child at every age, would be brought to the table, or into a Circle. No transgression would be too small or too large to be inappropriate for a peacemaking process. The modeling we would like to see from our leaders would, instead, be provided by volunteer mediators and facilitators from our communities. There would be an army of them, mostly retired people, because they would have the time, and they would know that nothing is more important. Our school children are our future leaders, our future soldiers, our future Peace Corps volunteers. Where are they to learn peace but in our schools? If they do not feel it in their hearts and know it in their bones before they become adults, when will they?

To Be an Icarus

It was dark when I left our cabana in Puerto Morelos, Mexico. But daylight comes early to the Yucatan peninsula. As I walked the beach toward the first pier, an orange line appeared on the horizon, immediately followed by the glowing orb. Sunrise is a silent shattering, as was the Resurrection. At just that moment a pelican, resting on a sea pier, took off from its solitary perch and flew straight up. The underside of its body and wings appeared to catch on fire and the bird was lost in the rising sun. It soon reached its apogee and just as quickly plunged to the sea—a powerful image of Icarus and the myth that some say is to remind us of the folly of the flight of the ego. But the truth of a myth is in the mind of the beholder. Some say the story of Icarus is one of failure. I say it is one of celebration and heroism. Those who take flight from the pedestrian life reflect back for the rest of us the light of the sun, even if death is the result. Witness Jesus of Nazareth, Simone Weil, Dietrich Bonhoeffer, and Martin Luther King Jr. Martyrdom is not necessarily a prerequisite to salvation, but waking up is.

Dr. King reminded us that: "One of the great liabilities of history is that all too many people fail to remain awake through great periods of social change. Every society has its protectors of status quo and its fraternities of the indifferent who are notorious for sleeping through revolutions. Today our very survival depends on our ability to stay awake, to adjust to new ideas, to remain vigilant and to face the challenge of change."

A friend sent me a link yesterday to a video clip. Al Levie, a high school social studies teacher from Racine, Wisconsin, was one of three recipients of a Dr. King humanitarian award during a celebration at which Representative Paul Ryan was on hand to present congressional recognitions. After speaking, Ryan stepped behind the podium to hand Levie his award. Levie backed away and turned toward the audience, refusing to accept the award. He said later that, as a humanitarian: "I would not accept the award from Paul Ryan because Paul Ryan is a lackey for the 1 percent. Paul Ryan had no business at a Martin Luther King event, it's totally hypocritical. On the one hand he votes to slash health care, while on the other hand, King dedicated his life and he died for it, for people to have adequate health care, to have adequate jobs. King made it very clear that he was on the side of working people. Ryan on the other hand, he has absolutely no affinity for the working class and for him to come to an event where somebody of King's stature was honored is wrong."

Paul Levie has chosen to stay awake, to face the challenge of change. He may not be a Dr. King, but he has chosen not to sleep-walk, not to value survival and comfort over the imperatives of our times.

I told Sandy, a friend of mine, about the pelican I saw this morning. She said he was probably just looking for fish. I would like to think that something else moved inside of him, at least for a moment, to seek something greater.

All the Fishermen That Are Needed

In Puerto Morelos, Mexico, there are the beachcombers, in search of seashells or sea glass or lost coins. I admire their single-mindedness, their focus. There are also the beach walkers. Whether their gait is brisk or leisurely, the solitary ones, they have a goal. There are the pairs—some are friends, some are lovers, some are in love, some carry the heavy years of their union. There are the old ones, strolling gently through their final days, each step an affirmation, an anticipation. There are the sun bathers, some with clothing and some without.

And then there are the fishermen. They stand apart, waist-deep in the surf, in touch with their inner selves and the unseen hook and leader at the end of the line. Tony is one of them. He has stood in the same spot, with the same distant gaze, the last three mornings. This morning we talked. He told me about the one that got away. He hooked it yesterday—a shiny, purple three-footer. He'd never seen anything like it. There was a struggle, just as there always is between a competent angler and his competent prey. Yesterday, the native won out. This was of no concern for Tony. He was back this morning—prepared, watchful, hopeful.

Tony and all good fishermen are great teachers. First and foremost they teach us patience. They teach us that there will always be another day until the last day. They teach us that it's not in the winning or losing. They are like baseball players in this way. It's in the game. There is something Eastern in this as well. The cyclical nature of life—the rise and fall, the ebb and flow, the give and take. Perhaps I should think of justice in this way—two steps forward, one step back. The rise and fall of systems. The birth and death of philosophies. The birth and death of those stuck in the past, clinging to old ideas, old values, old prejudices. There is a peace that comes from knowing we are small, that our actions, while meaningful perhaps, are limited and soon forgotten. Tony, as skilled and prepared as he is on any given morning, does not fret over his inability to land the big one, let alone the countless others that are out there.

I think of the wise man I read about twenty-some years ago who said we would have a restorative justice system in one hundred years. I think of all the fishermen needed to make that come to pass. I think of a poem written thirty-some years ago by Bishop Ken Untener:

> We cannot do everything, and there is a sense of
>   liberation in realizing that.
> This enables us to do something, and to do it very well.
> It may be incomplete, but it is a beginning, a step
>   along the way, an opportunity for the Lord's
>   grace to enter and do the rest.
> We may never see the end results, but that is the
>   difference between the master builder and the
>   worker.
> We are workers, not master builders; ministers,
>   not messiahs.
> We are prophets of a future not our own.

Drive Around for a Year and Listen

She said I could call her Mari or Mary. Her friends and coworkers affectionately call her Godzilla. She is Mayan, maybe five feet tall, and she has fingers of steel. There are many things I can imagine that might be similar to the experience—professional wrestling, professional football, getting thrown around by a gorilla. And she does it all with a smile. Mari has been giving massages at the Ixchel Jungle Spa in Puerto Morelos for about seven years. But she didn't learn her art there. She grew up with it. It is the medicine of her people. In Mari's community, twenty miles into the jungle, Mayan massage is used to treat a host of maladies including indigestion, bowel obstructions, infertility, and impotence. A Mayan massage isn't just about fingers and hands. Mari uses her forearms and elbows and even her feet. My tour group was told that a Mayan massage is where heaven meets hell. It's that and more. Throughout the hour and a half, moans and groans are interspersed with laughter and muffled screams. It's been twenty-four hours and I still don't know what happened to my body.

When it was decided we would visit the Jungle Spa I wasn't concerned about the massage. I was concerned that this would be another tourist rip-off—both for tourists and those employed at the spa. It wasn't. Sandra, an expat from Texas who was beyond normal retirement age, settled in Puerto Morelos in the early '90s in the hope of establishing a small jungle tour business. She did, and she discovered Mari's people. She was immediately taken by their natural beauty and their friendliness. She was also disturbed by their poverty. Sandra developed relationships with many in the community and offered to help them develop a market for their crafts.

As time went on Sandra and her husband purchased a single hectare in the jungle and built a home there. About twelve years ago, with the help of friends, a nonprofit was created to allow for the creation of the Jungle Spa, which is much more than a spa. There is a community center where workshops and classes are held to teach craft making and English. During the winter months there is a Sunday market. Local women sell homemade crafts and regional food.

Jungle tours are offered, as are jungle camps for families. The actual spa offers facials, masks, pedicures, manicures, braids, energy treatments, sweat lodge, natural remedies—and massages. And Mari, along with her Mayan coworkers, receives 75 percent of every massage and treatment provided, plus tips. This money goes back into their community and allows families to educate their children in a way never before possible. All of this comes under what Sandra calls "community tourism," a broad term for tourism that helps local residents—often rural, poor, and economically marginalized—earn income as entrepreneurs, service and produce providers, and employees, with most of the earned income going into the pockets of the locals.

About five years ago I volunteered for two weeks with a small nonprofit serving remote villages in the mountains of northern Guatemala. While there, I met a young professor who teaches nonprofit organization to local students. The professor told me that there are approximately 3,000 nonprofits doing work in Guatemala and that much of the work is inefficient and redundant. He said the American way of helping a developing country is to send in a research team for ten days to study a problem. After that the team returns to the States and writes a report. He said the best thing any American, or any other would-be do-gooder, can do is travel to Guatemala, buy an old car, drive around the country for a year, and listen. At the end of the year the do-gooder might have an inkling as to what help is needed and how the locals can bring that about. I don't know if Sandra ever received similar advice before leaving Texas for Mexico, but she certainly got it right.

A Restorative Justice Ethic

I woke this morning at about three, having just left a dream. Sitting up, leaning back against the wall, I had a vision—a daydream in the dark—of children fleeing something. They were flowing down long hills and running across a field, away from parents and the adults of the world. The children were fleeing our culture of consumption and craziness. They gathered in the woods around an open shelter they had built. A young girl, wise for her age, was speaking. The other children, seated around her, knew that they had been neglected by "the older ones" and knew that adults wouldn't save them—that they must save themselves. The image is reminiscent of *Lord of the Flies*, but not the same. There is a feminine wisdom missing from William Golding's novel. The children in my vision realize they must stick together. To survive they must cooperate and care for one another. If they don't they will die.

What are the children fleeing from? Did they know that Little League and soccer, quizzes and Game Boys are not enough? Did they yearn for a structure that they can push back against—even if it be community, church, or country? Did they yearn for a solid place to stand before being launched into the larger world of complexity and paradox? Children are hardwired to rebel. They need something substantial to rebel against. As the poet Rainer Maria Rilke said, "When we are only victorious over small things, it leaves us feeling small." Did the children yearn for parents who care enough to provide structure beyond entertainment? Parents who are larger than them, who put down the television remote and game controller and engage in the battles that really count—against pollution, discrimination, and poverty, and for better education, better health care, better justice? It's difficult for a child to find a model worth emulating if that model isn't the parent. And what if that parent is stuck in adolescence?

I've been thinking about the role of restorative justice in all of this—its emphasis on accountability and restoration through responsibility. Is restorative justice large enough? There are those writing now about restorative justice beyond the legal system—restorative justice in schools, the workplace, in the community, in churches, within families. To be this large, restorative justice must be more than programs and even more than a philosophy. It seems to me that it must be an ethic, one akin to Albert Schweitzer's "Reverence for Life." If to restore means a return to reverence—for the earth, for others, for self—then restorative justice might serve as an ethic large enough to embrace believer and nonbeliever, those who have and those who don't.

If our children could see and experience a world of reverence around them, perhaps they would have nothing from which to flee.

An Allegory

On a plane leaving paradise there was a man, a very large man, who appeared different from the rest of the passengers. His hair was long and gray. It was unwashed and uncombed. Perhaps he had not bathed for a while. And he wore clothing from another time. This man moved slowly because of his weight. The seating of passengers behind him was delayed. He had difficulty fitting into his seat because of his size. But his wife didn't mind. She was much smaller and she loved him. Despite the slowness of the man, the plane from paradise was on time as it pulled back from the terminal and approached the runway. But something happened. The man rose quickly from his seat and ran as well as he could toward the front of the cabin. His goal: the toilet. He initially was denied entrance. The toilet was for business-class passengers only. The man pleaded, and again he was denied. The captain was informed, the plane was stopped, and the man was finally allowed in.

A few minutes passed, the door opened, and the man slowly returned to his seat. He was followed by a flight attendant, a very efficient woman who informed the man's wife that she would have to clean up her husband's mess. The wife refused. An argument followed. The wife said it was not her job. The flight attendant said it was not hers. The flight attendant threatened that the plane would have to turn back. The wife did not budge. The flight attendant did not budge. The plane turned back. The flight was delayed. Forty-five minutes passed before the door was opened; an hour and forty-five minutes before the flight resumed.

In the meantime, members of the ground crew entered the plane. The man and his wife were asked to leave. They refused. Another argument. The wife said her husband has an illness—he is on multiple medications and it was an accident—he couldn't help it. The flight attendant returned. She took control. She was angry. She demanded they leave. The wife pleaded. The flight attendant prevailed.

The passengers sat silent.

The man and his wife were last seen entering an airport bus, the man in a wheelchair. The flight from paradise eventually landed in a very cold land, two hours later than advertised. Several passengers missed connecting flights. Vouchers were issued for hotels and meals. The flight attendant went on her way.

I suppose our story is, technically, not an allegory. The characters are real and the events happened—earlier today. But it is an allegory in the sense that it can offer a truth for what justice often looks like when an individual comes up against a system; when there is an imbalance in power; when those in control act without compassion; when there is an us-versus-them attitude that informs the decision makers.

And, of course, the question must be asked: What if there had been a restorative justice response? What if the passengers—the community—had become involved? What if they had advocated for the man and his wife? What if they had tried to facilitate a conversation between the couple and the flight attendant? What if the passengers had taken it upon themselves to clean up the mess? What would have been the risks if such actions had been attempted? What would have been the rewards? Perhaps the man and his wife would not have been ostracized. Perhaps they would not have been left in Mexico to fend for themselves. Perhaps they would have made it home tonight. And the passengers. It's likely that there would have been no missed connections and they would all have made it home tonight too. And what about the system? What might the airline have gained? Certainly it would have saved money, and perhaps it would have saved face. And what did it lose?

Bridging the Paradigm Divide

Psychologists tell us that people can only stretch themselves just a bit when attempting to comprehend others beyond themselves. Some researchers say that a person can't stretch more than one step beyond his or her own consciousness. This is a problem when those who advocate for a paradigm shift attempt to have a conversation with those who resist or are opposed to the shift. The result is those at higher levels of consciousness often appear wrong, heretical, or even dangerous. This is a big problem for advocates of restorative justice who embrace a paradigm of accountability, reparation, and healing and seek to dialogue with those who embrace the traditional justice paradigm of retribution and punishment. This is not a mere problem of language, of reaching an agreement on common terms. Nor is it likely a matter of intelligence or education. Those who are charged with the responsibility of administering justice in our communities are generally bright people, often with advanced degrees and years of experience. And it's not likely a matter of religion. At least in the United States, there are representatives of the major faith traditions on either side of the paradigm divide. What is it then? What gives rise to or brings about a higher level of justice consciousness if it is not education, intelligence, or experience?

It may be that it's necessary to drill deeper, to inquire further into the particular education, intelligence, and experience that can open the door to the heart of restorative justice, to an understanding and acceptance of a justice response that values equally, whenever possible, the victim, the offender, and the community in the justice equation. I've talked with several people who have said they didn't "get it" until they read Howard Zehr's *Changing Lenses*, or Rupert Ross' *Returning to the Teachings*, or Desmond Tutu's *No Future Without Forgiveness*. Or they didn't get it until they heard a compelling sermon or lecture or took a restorative justice class. Others have said that their emotional intelligence is such that when they were first introduced to restorative justice it immediately resonated with them. Or that a past harm or trauma had sensitized them to the emotional needs of victims, which are rarely met when a case is handled in the traditional manner prescribed by the retributive system. For many, it takes participating in a restorative justice process to really understand the healing nature of the approach.

I have sat in on many victim–offender meetings in which defense attorneys skeptical or suspicious of the process had an aha moment, much like their clients after hearing victims describe the extent to which their lives had been significantly altered after having been victimized. The challenge, then, is to bridge the divide, to narrow the gap between those who maintain the status quo within the system and those on the outside, and to advocate for a re-visioning of justice.

Restorative justice is process driven. The bridging of the gap must be process driven. Within each community there must be found individuals with the requisite competence, stature, and clout to convene and facilitate the dialogues that must take place between system representatives and those within the community who seek justice reform. Study groups and committees are not enough. Sustained and committed conversations that are open to the public, though, would be a beginning.

A Crime Peace Plan

I've had a license to practice law for over thirty years. There have been enough high points to satisfy me, to convince me that selling my bicycle shop and going to law school at the age of twenty-eight was the right decision. But today may have been my proudest moment—sitting in a third-floor courtroom of the Johnson County Courthouse, a few feet away from eight empaneled jurors, and not saying a word. I was second chair for my son, Phil, licensed since September but every bit a seasoned lawyer. When he was ten I predicted he would be a better lawyer than me. I was right. He is what every client deserves—bright, articulate, prepared, a good listener, tough when necessary, not afraid to represent the underdog. And he has a heart. Today he represented a man who has waited nearly five years to tell his story. Phil gave him that opportunity. It was a good day for the man and it was a good day for the system. Today I was proud to be a lawyer and even prouder to be the father of one.

During a break, however, I was brought back to earth a little. While the jurors mingled outside and the lead attorneys spoke with the judge, I opened a letter from a friend. Sister Jeanie, now in her late seventies, has been a nun for more than half a century. Her sister Elaine is a year older and has been a nun for just as long. They live in Des Moines and together are the most passionate advocates for social justice I know. If they were a generation or two younger they might be priests, or they might be public defenders—lawyers for the poor and the powerless. No matter their age, they have given to the world far more than they've taken.

Sister Jeanie's letter was a Christmas one, printed with alternating paragraphs of red and green. At the bottom was a short note acknowledging that "Elaine never gets Christmas letters out on time." Tucked inside the letter was a copy of an article from the *National Catholic Reporter*. It was about a man by the name of David Link—a trained lawyer, a former federal prosecutor, the dean of the Notre Dame Law School for twenty-four years, and then dean and president at three other universities. In 2003 his wife died. David Link the lawyer went back to school and became Father David Link, a priest. Father Link's primary ministry now is within the Indiana prison system. He has seen a lot, working in a maximum security facility for about 2,400 men, 70 percent of whom are convicted murderers. As a result of his experiences Father Link is proposing a "Crime Peace Plan" for healing the criminal justice system. What Father Link is proposing is nothing short of revolutionary, and it is in the spirit of a plan proposed more than two thousand years ago. These are the plan's objectives:

1. Change the mission of the system from punishment to healing
2. Change the system from adversarial to collaborative
3. Appoint rather than elect prosecutors
4. Oblige all lawyers to engage in or to support criminal defense as a condition of practice
5. Establish a special code of ethics for prosecution and criminal defense
6. Establish an accurate and uniform definition of crime
7. Establish indeterminant and consistent standards of sentencing
8. Convert jails and prisons to places that are concerned with the diagnosis of and treatment for the

social illnesses that have brought each person to
incarceration

9. Have sentence modification determinations made by
people who know the present status of the incarcerated
and the readiness of the receiving community

10. Provide tax incentives to employers who hire
recovering ex-prisoners

Every point in Father Link's plan deserves reflection and writing
about. And I hope to. But not tonight. Phil needs help with his closing argument. He has a client who is deserving of his best.

When Prosecutors Become Criminals

Last week the Seventh Circuit Court of Appeals ruled that a prosecutor is not protected by immunity when allegedly coercing false
testimony. Two prosecutors, Lawrence Wharrie and David Kelley,
were accused of egregious misconduct in a case that resulted in the
conviction in 1986 of Nathson Fields for two murders. Fields was
sentenced to death, but in 1996 was granted a new trial based on
the discovery that the trial judge had accepted a $10,000 bribe from
Fields' codefendant, Earl Hawkins, for his own acquittal. Judge
Thomas Maloney later returned the money after Hawkins' conviction and the disclosure of a federal investigation. The second trial
resulted in the acquittal of Fields after various witnesses recanted
their testimony. That trial revealed misconduct and coercion by the
prosecution to secure false testimony. Fields sued both prosecutors,
who argued that they had immunity. The trial court initially agreed
but later stripped Wharrie of qualified immunity for his role in the
investigation. The matter went to a Seventh Circuit panel where
Judge Richard Posner held that it would be absurd to allow prosecutors to claim immunity in such cases.

The conduct by Wharrie, while hopefully an exception to otherwise honest behavior by most prosecutors, is not surprising given
how and why certain lawyers become prosecutors. These days, most

new prosecutors are recent law school graduates. They have had little, if any, legal experience except law school itself. They have not represented a client and they grew up in a win-lose culture. They look at life and the law through a good-vs-evil lens. Most learned about the law through the mock trial experience, beginning as early as sixth grade. If they are good at it—good at being adversarial—they continue with it, all the way through undergraduate studies and law school. By the time they have their law degree and are licensed, they cannot distinguish themselves from their role. It's sad to say, but these are the young lawyers who aspire for the life of the prosecutor, and who are sought after by elected prosecutors who believe that re-election is dependent on their tough-on-crime record. For most prosecutors, young and not so young, the background, education, and culture that molded them is manifested in a particular attitude—aloofness and superiority, and a penchant for punishment.

And then there are those, like Wharrie, who cross the line and become criminals, oftentimes worse than the ones they have taken an oath to prosecute.

If I Could Run a School

I spent the night in Newburgh, about an hour and a half north of New York City and just west of the Hudson River. I look forward to crossing the great river with the sun still to the east. Yesterday, at about this time, I left South Bend. The 700-mile drive was uneventful—just enough simple beauty to offset the desecration. These long road trips are the best. Like a long bike ride, you get into a groove. I alternated the Crosby, Stills, and Nash channel on Pandora with Jack Kornfield's talks on Buddhism for beginners. Kornfield is such a gentle man, with generations of Buddhist monks and Zen masters coursing through his veins. I have heard that some schools now are teaching mindfulness to grade schoolers. Moving forward, it may be that mindfulness and restorative justice become essential components of the curriculum. Of course that will require a different attitude from school board members and school administrators.

Last July, on my drive back from the Northwest Justice Summit in Oregon, I stopped for gas in Cozad, Nebraska, population about 4,000. It turns out that the painter Robert Henri lived there as a boy. He was Robert Cozad then, but after his father shot a man, the family thought it best to relocate and have a change of name. The town is proud of him now, and nearly a hundred years after his death it boasts the Robert Henri Museum. Located in a little house off Main Street where he lived for a few years, the museum offers a second reason for driving across Nebraska. I knew only that Henri had existed before stopping in Cozad. Now I know that he was a great artist and a great educator.

After spending the afternoon with Henri's paintings, I stopped in the small gift shop and bought a copy of *The Art Spirit*. It's one of those books you wish someone had given you when you were young. It's as much about life as it is about art. Compiled by one of Henri's students, it's an anthology of thoughts, reflections, anecdotes, articles, and lecture notes spanning the last couple decades of the artist's life. It's one of the books I pick up regularly to read just a page or two.

I was thinking about Henri yesterday and his fondness for Walt Whitman. Henri thought Whitman was an example of what the real art student should be. He saw Whitman's work as an autobiography—not of successes and failures, accomplishments and mishaps—but of his deepest thought. Henri recognized that even in death, Whitman lived on in his work and, like Shakespeare's, the body of his work would expand and become greater the more it became known. Henri wrote that Whitman thought of *Leaves of Grass* as an outcropping of his own emotional and personal nature, as an attempt to put a human being truly on record.

Thomas Merton is another of those I try to read from regularly. Were he still alive, yesterday would have been his ninety-ninth birthday. In reflecting on his life, Merton wrote: "If I don't make it to sixty-five, it matters less. I can relax. But life is a gift I am glad of, and I do not curse the day when I was born. On the contrary, if I had never been born I would never have had friends to love and be loved by, never have made mistakes to learn from, never have seen new

countries and, as for what I may have suffered, it is inconsequential
and indeed part of the great good that life has been and will, I hope,
continue to be."

So many of our children these days do not see their lives as gifts
and do not have a vision of a good life before them. That is our fault.
If I could run a school, be in charge of the curriculum, I would make
sure the students practiced mindfulness and restorative justice, and
that they knew there had been lives like Robert Henri's, Walt Whitman's, and Thomas Merton's.

An Educational Model Worth Studying

I arrived in Maine on Saturday. Sunday morning I attended a
memorial service for Pete Seeger at the First Parish Church in Portland and sang "If I Had a Hammer" and "Turn, Turn, Turn" with
twenty or so other retired hippies. Sunday afternoon I moved into
my room here at the Wayfinder School at Opportunity Farm. The
school serves at-risk youth from all over Maine who would have little
chance of graduating were it not for Wayfinder.

Monday was my first day on the job with the Restorative Justice
Institute of Maine, the beginning of a half-time commitment with
the Institute through November. The day started with a meeting
at the Topsham police station and a conversation about community
boards and keeping young people out of the formal justice system.
Tuesday morning I met with a school administrator in Biddeford.
We talked about keeping kids in school and starting a school mediation program. Tuesday afternoon I had coffee with a young lawyer
who spent the last couple of years working on death penalty cases
in Alabama but who now wants to do restorative justice work in
Maine. We talked about engaging other lawyers in the restorative
justice movement. Yesterday was a snow day. I think we had about
ten inches. This morning I met with a dozen people at the Episcopal church in Thomaston. It was the third all-day meeting for the
group in three months as part of their involvement in a multi-session
workshop. The question of the day was "How do you engage others
in restorative justice?"

The highlight of the week was this afternoon. I arrived late but was still welcomed into the weekly Circle at Anthony House here at the farm. Every Thursday, beginning at 3:00, students, teachers, and staff meet to talk about what it means to live in community. I arrived in time to listen to discussions about sharing the laundry facility, keeping the refrigerator organized, and maintaining a clean kitchen. A talking piece is used to ensure that everyone has a say. Equal weight is given to the opinions of students and staff. There is plenty of disagreement, but these teens, who have struggled in traditional school settings, demonstrate a remarkable maturity. This is a family, and each member brings strengths and struggles to the running of the household.

A major concern this evening was the dirty dishes left in the sink. Some of the students are clean freaks and others are quite comfortable with some disorder. I learned some new terms as the talking piece made the rounds—"Tetris-izing," for attempting to fit everything into the refrigerator; "dish orphans," for stray cups and bowls left where last used; and the notion that dishes don't just get done by the "dish fairy." Joseph, the director of residential programs, told the kids just before the dinner break that the discussion is relevant to the larger issues of life.

These are smart, creative kids who have been given a chance to succeed in an environment that doesn't label or pigeonhole. They are involved in internships in the morning—working with horses, preschoolers, the elderly, and at the local airport and in a school library. In the afternoon they study creative writing, science, the environment—looking at the world through a social justice lens. There is an educational model here that has much to teach us about young people and how to excite them about the world.

Making a Bad Situation Worse

I drove to Wolfe's Neck Woods State Park this morning to snowshoe. The park, twenty miles from Wayfinder School, is a slender, wooded peninsula that separates the Harraseeket River from Casco Bay. With ten inches of new snow since Thursday, the deep forest trails were a blessing for legs still weary from a week of back-road driving. After two hours on the Harraseeket Trail, I visited with two conservation officers who had set up shop in the parking lot, outfitting visitors with cross-country skis, free for the day. One of the officers, "Doc," oversees Vaughn Woods, the John Paul Jones Historic Site, and the Fort McClary Historic Site, all south of Portland. But today he traveled north to help with the free ski day. Next Saturday he'll be at Sanford Lake teaching kids to ice fish. Doc told me that he retired once, a few years back, after twenty years in the New York state park system and another ten years managing a state park in Connecticut. He retired to Maine to take it easy, but taking it easy got boring pretty quick and he took a ranger position with the Department of Conservation. It didn't take long for Doc to work his way up to management. Doc saw my Iowa plates and wanted to know what brought me to Maine. I told him I had retired a few years ago but that taking it easy got boring. I then told him about the Restorative Justice Institute and its efforts to educate the people of Maine about a different way to respond to wrongdoing. Doc told me he had heard of restorative justice and it makes sense to him. He said that when he was younger and working the New York parks he had a tough-guy approach. Over the years he has come to see that being a tough guy doesn't work most of the time.

In between stretches of our conversation Doc helped adults and their kids get fitted with ski boots, skis, and poles. He's a gentle man. I couldn't help but wonder what brought him to looking at humanity in a different way. Doc told me he adopted a boy who was a good athlete and a good kid, but who had a temper. He said his son always stuck up for his buddies. As a result, he was suspended from school so many times he didn't finish. Doc's son struggled for a while but finally got a job, fell in love, got married, and had a child. But Doc wonders if things might have gone better for his son if the folks at the high school had tried to understand him, if they had taken the time to work with his anger problem. Then Doc told me about his experience working with inmates assigned to the parks to do community service. He gets to know many of them, and they are oftentimes like his son. He wonders what would have happened to them if they had been helped when they were younger and in school.

Doc said we lock too many people up, give them records, label them, and, in the process, we make a bad situation worse. Doc said a lot of people he knows are looking at things differently these days, and maybe this restorative justice thing needs to be given a chance. Doc is an alderman and he wants me to come and visit him. He wants me to meet a friend of his in law enforcement and another friend who is a judge.

I could have spent all morning with Doc, but a little kid tugged at his sleeve, asking for help. Doc stooped down to the level of the little boy's eyes and helped him with his bindings.

Does It Have a Heart?

When I'm in Maine I attend Sunday service at First Parish Church in Portland. It's a Unitarian Universalist church, a non-creedal faith community. It's a welcoming place—you know this when you first walk in and see the faith symbols of the major traditions displayed on the wall behind what I would have called the altar when I was a kid. You know it is welcoming when people introduce themselves to you because they want to. You know it is welcoming when Christian stories walk hand in hand with Buddhist practices, like they did yesterday.

Pastor Christina Sillari gave a sermon on the heart. She read the Heart Sutra and spoke about our physical, emotional, and spiritual hearts. She talked about the Western tendency to live in the brain and not in the heart, and the problems that have arisen because of that. She shared how her father had triple bypass surgery fifteen years ago and how he now lives in his emotional heart. She engaged us in a heart rhythm meditation, helping us to listen to and be calmed by our own heartbeats. She talked about how indigenous peoples used the beat of a drum to remind them of the beat of the heart of their Mother Earth. She brought out a drum and did the same. Christina concluded with a quote from Carlos Castaneda's *The Teachings of Don Juan*: "A path is only a path, and there is no affront, to oneself or to others, in dropping it if that is what your heart tells you to do. . . . Look at every path closely and deliberately. Try it as many times as you think necessary." She said that we should ask ourselves, alone, one question: "This question is one that only a very old man asks. . . . Does this path have a heart? If it does, the path is good; if it doesn't, it is of no use."

I had a conversation last evening with a colleague of mine. The conversation centered on practices labeled "restorative." We talked about the ongoing debate about these practices and the disagreements over which practices are the most restorative. We agreed that, while debate can be a good thing, it can be counterproductive, it can cause us to lose sight of the imperative that restorative justice offer a clear vision in sharp contrast to the predominant retributive approach to wrongdoing.

Early this morning, in the dark, I practiced the heart rhythm meditation I learned yesterday. It occurred to me that what restorative justice really offers is "heart." It offers a sharp contrast to the "head" approach of the Western justice system that has concluded that "to spare the rod is to spoil the child"; that we must "hit them hard and hit them early"; that we must be "tough on crime." Nearly everyone I know who is moved by the promise of restorative justice has been drawn to that promise by their hearts. They don't suggest that we abandon logic, but they have come to see, oftentimes late in life, that what really matters is relationships. They know in their hearts that restorative justice offers the promise of the healing of broken relationships, whether between friends, colleagues, or family members, or between strangers who have come into relationship because of a crime and its consequences. We in the restorative justice community must continually remind ourselves that restorative practices are merely that: They are practices. We practice them. They are paths. And if a practice is wanting, if it is lacking heart, there is no affront, to ourselves or others, in dropping it. The question must always be: Does this practice have a heart? If it does it is good, if it doesn't it is of no use.

We Must Train Thousands of Listeners

The morning after my last exam at Saint Louis University I walked to the on-ramp at South Grand and I-64 and stuck out my thumb. It was 1974 and I was twenty. In my backpack I had a sleeping bag, a small tent, clothes for three days, a camp stove, a bowl, a cup, eating utensils, and probably a toothbrush. I don't remember much about that first morning, but I do recall thinking, "I have to create a history for myself." I was gone for sixteen months. I traveled by freight train, ferry, freighter, and even once by single-engine plane. But mostly I hitchhiked. I worked occasionally—thinning apples, picking cherries, in a hotel, on a floating crab cannery, in a dog food factory, at a Florida resort, on a yacht bound for Boston.

I remember all of those times, but what I most remember are the conversations. Through the night across Wyoming or Utah or British Columbia. The rides of an hour or two in nearly every state and province. Sometimes high up in a semi or in an old school bus or VW van. But mostly just in a car, a driver and me. I remember that I didn't say much during those hundreds of rides. And I wasn't asked many questions. Mostly people wanted to talk. They wanted to tell their stories. I was fine with that. It felt good. From time to time I would think that listening was my payment for the ride.

After many months I began to see that it was more than that. It was a therapy. I was raised Catholic and spent many childhood hours in dark confessionals, knowing the priest was there but never seeing him. Sometimes I made things up just to get out of there, but other times I told him about real stuff. Hitchhiking was like that. There was the bravado, the yarn, the hyperbole. But most of the time there was the real stuff. It was easy to tell the difference. When the real stuff came out there was a silence, oftentimes interlaced with an ache, a sadness, a loss, a vulnerability. I came to realize that it wasn't so much that I was the passenger but that there was a passenger. There was someone to receive the story—the story being told, being heard, being accepted unconditionally. That made all the difference.

I think the great service restorative justice offers those who have been hurt is a place where their story can be told. I have seen it many times over the years, observing or facilitating victim–offender meetings. I have seen the early minutes of anger, or defensiveness, or posturing, or making demands. But almost every time the real stuff comes out. The ache, the sadness, the loss, the vulnerability—interlaced with silence. It would be wrong to call this therapy—to do so would probably get us restorative justice practitioners in trouble. But it is right to say that if there is any humanity in how we process thousands upon thousands of criminal cases—every year, in every state, and in every county—it is when we provide a safe place for both victims and offenders to tell their stories. The stories may be told with just a facilitator present as midwife, or they may be told in a Circle with others present as witnesses and with stories of their own.

What is important is knowing that if we are ever to have healing communities, we must have storytelling. We must allow for it, provide space for it, provide appropriate processes to hold it. We must insist that justice professionals make room for it in the course of the day-to-day doing of their business. We must train listeners, thousands of them, to serve as midwives for the truth that these stories teach us.

Different Is Good

I walked down the hill in New Gloucester, Maine, this evening to the Village Store, hoping for a bowl of their incredible haddock chowder. It wasn't an easy walk. We're in the middle of a blizzard, a fierce one even by Maine standards. Winds of 35 mph. Driving snow. A woman in the store said it's a nor'easter. The store was nearly full. The soup was bubbling. I asked if they might close early. I was politely told it wasn't likely.

Folks are a little different here—for example, the toll attendants. Whenever I drive from New Gloucester to Portland and back I pay two tolls each way. I always apologize for requesting a receipt. They always say it's not a problem, they need the job. The attendants are generally men, older, and with that accent. Their eyes have a twinkle. They are genuinely nice. You'd take any one of them as your grandfather. There is a cop here who is a little different too. At least different from any I know back home. Actually Jonathan Shapiro is not a cop. He's a sergeant with the Maine State Police—Troop A. He has a master's in leadership studies. He's developed a program to improve police response to juveniles in crisis.

Sergeant Shapiro cares about kids. He knows that the usual tools for dealing with kids, tools using some form of negative discipline, generally don't work well with them. That's probably why Sergeant Shapiro is a champion of restorative justice. He travels all over the state making a case for it. I've yet to meet a local involved in restorative justice at any level who doesn't know him. He's passionate about restorative justice. He thinks that someday Maine will be a restorative justice state.

Sergeant Shapiro emailed me today. He says he wants to be a mediator and that once he gets a grasp "on the mediation thing" he wants to talk about how it might work for police in general. He said he wants to get a better handle on my mediation style. He asked if it's my own "invention" or if there is some written material out there on how to do it. He wanted to know if I think he could really learn it. He finished by saying, "I want the troopers to be able to mediate issues themselves, but I need a high-speed, low-drag style for practicality and to fit their personalities." Sergeant Shapiro is a little different. Here in Maine different is good.

The Untidily Unplanned Life

I went snowshoeing again today. The thick carpet laid down by the blizzard called for a visitor. Halfway down Gloucester Hill is Lower Gloucester Cemetery. Like many New England graveyards, it tells of loss two centuries and more ago. I entered from the road, skirted the rows of black stones, and dropped down into a wooded gully. At the bottom and meandering nearly parallel to the cemetery is a stream, alive but nearly hidden by three inches of ice and the white cover. I fully expected to be greeted by deer or a moose or the fox the man at the Village Store told me about. But none appeared. I suppose I wasn't quiet enough.

When I returned I read some Thomas Merton. He wrote sixty years ago today about Conrad, a twelfth-century Cistercian monk turned hermit. Merton says that Conrad was an embarrassment to the entire Cistercian Order, that he "apparently" got nowhere "as if his life was a series of incomprehensible accidents, ending in midair." Merton, also Cistercian, says that when he was in the novitiate he didn't care for Conrad or for many of the Cistercian hermits. Merton thought their lives were inconclusive, that "they seemed to have died before finding out what they were supposed to achieve." But Merton's attitude toward Conrad changed. He came to see that there was something important about the "very incompleteness" of Conrad. Merton saw that Conrad's "untidily unplanned life," his life without order, allowed him to travel a path unavailable to most others.

I'm wondering if Conrad's life might be seen as a metaphor for restorative justice. Not the restorative justice embodied in programs, or the restorative justice systematized and seen as an alternative to the system, or even the restorative justice that informs the practices that best manifest its spirit. A few years ago I took a class at Eastern Mennonite University. Howard Zehr had us blog weekly. In an exchange I had with Howard he commented that he has always seen restorative justice as a spark, as something more ephemeral and less concrete. I took this to mean that restorative justice as we know it is not the end-all. That one of its strengths is that it can't be easily defined. If we imagine restorative justice as a spark and not a prescription, perhaps it will lead us to reflect more deeply on its possible applications in the world around us.

I think it's a good thing that there is an incompleteness about restorative justice, that there is something untidy about it, that it's not easily reduced to statistics, flow charts, data, or outcome measures, that it lacks symmetry or appears to be without order. I think its very untidiness suggests its humanity. What restorative justice *isn't* suggests what it *can be* in the individual lives touched by it.

I would like to have known Conrad. If he were alive today he would not be a leader in the restorative justice movement in the traditional sense, but his incompleteness would be a source of healing for those who came in contact with him.

Do Away with Desks

What is it about sitting in a circle? Why is it that when we gather in a circle a door opens and we are allowed entry into the lives of those gathered with us? You have to wonder if the inventor of the school desk did us a disservice. How did the classrooms of our youth shape us to be in the world? What neural pathways were created by sitting in little wooden enclosures and facing forward all those years? It's not difficult to imagine our ancestors in a circle around the communal fire, nothing separating them but the magical centerpiece of heat and flame. Socrates met with his students circled around him. It's interesting to consider the extent to which that simple arrangement,

What seeds of justice were planted in you?

When did you first recognize that there is

something called "justice"? When did you first

recognize that there is also injustice?

a peer to the left and a peer to the right, contributed to the birth of democracy. Jesus gathered his followers "around" him. An ethic of love and respect was the result. King Arthur met with his knights at a round table, and all present were considered equal.

A few years ago I rented a bike in the Peruvian village of Ollantaytambo. I bicycled up into the Andes until I came to a much smaller village and the road's end. There was no town square, no courthouse or buildings of commerce. There was, however, a communal green. About twenty women were gathered that morning—in a circle. There didn't appear to be a manager or supervisor or anyone directing what was to be done. Each woman was working on her craft of choice. The conversation was gentle. At the same time their hands were amazingly industrious. What I witnessed was a circle of good will.

Last week I had the good fortune of meeting in a Circle with thirty AmeriCorps volunteers. They had come to Opportunity Farm for a three-day retreat. I was asked to introduce them on the second morning to restorative justice. I have found that when you have three or four hours, a good way to introduce restorative justice is to say nothing about it the first hour or so. It seemed the right approach for these young people. After a brief introduction to the Circle process and the use of the talking piece, I asked them to introduce themselves and then reflect on three simple questions: What seeds of justice were planted in you? When did you first recognize that there is something called "justice"? When did you first recognize that there is also injustice?

I passed the stone to the left: "A boy picked on me in kindergarten." "My brother beat me in Parcheesi by cheating." "I was bullied a lot in middle school." "I learned about injustice by hearing my parents talk about unfairness in their jobs." "I went to Haiti when I was a freshman. I was overwhelmed by the poverty and the inequality." "I made mistakes when I was younger. My record has followed me." "In third grade a girl pushed me into a pricker bush. The teachers didn't believe me." "In second grade a girl from Colombia joined our class. The kids treated her different." "I grew up in the south and saw racism every day. Kids were taught to hate." "The U.S. response to 9/11. We killed so many noncombatants." "I was seven and saw the news about the 'death of an angel'—JonBenet Ramsey. A black girl was shot. They didn't call her an angel." "I grew up poor. I was bullied because of the clothes I wore." "In seventh grade I reported the really smart kid for cheating. The teacher said I was lying." "Realizing that some friends, because of money, didn't have the opportunities I had."

The stone had made it halfway around the Circle. By the time everyone had held it we were ready to talk about restorative justice and its response to wrongdoing.

A Much-Needed Conversation

A friend wrote me over the weekend. It was to comment on my January blog post "Responding to the Real Needs of Victims." Dale is a retired professor and has a deep interest in justice. He knows more about it than anyone I have ever met. When we get together for coffee he usually has a list of books I should read. Recently, knowing that I probably won't read the book itself, he sent me his own review of a new favorite. I greatly appreciate Dale's erudition and insight. It means a lot to me that he embraces restorative justice, both in principle and in practice.

I suppose it was not a coincidence that Dale's email came just a few hours after I had a conversation with a woman from New Gloucester. She wanted to tell me about her mother and an incident that occurred a few years ago. She said her mother was driving through a residential area when, suddenly, her windshield shattered and a large stone landed on the front seat of her car. Miraculously, there was no accident and no injuries. It didn't take long for a teenage boy to be arrested and charged. As soon as the elderly woman found out about the boy and the arrest, she went to the police station. She told the arresting officer she didn't think any good would be served by the boy being prosecuted and put through the system. She said what she really wanted was to meet the boy and work out an agreement on how he could take responsibility for the damage done to her car. The officer told her that wasn't possible, that the boy had to be prosecuted and had to face the judge. She responded that if she couldn't meet with him to discuss how he could make things right she at least wanted to have a conversation with him. She wanted to find out about his circumstances. She wanted to know what was going on in his life. And she wanted the boy to know how fortunate they both were that nothing more serious had happened.

There was never a conversation. And the elderly woman never understood why. She told her daughter that kids make mistakes. They do stupid things and when such things happen, when a window is broken, it's the repair and the apology that are important, not the punishment.

It's easy to blame the officer for the direction this case took—both for the boy and the woman. But perhaps he would have liked to have done something different but didn't think he had the authority to do so. Maybe the culture of the police department pressured him to take a hard line. Or it could be it was the environment he grew up in, the culture of punishment that dictated how he exercised his discretion. Whatever the reason, whatever the genesis for the attitude the officer carries with him as he patrols the streets of his community, it is incumbent on that community to have a conversation with him about the real needs of victims.

Some Stories Contain a Mystery

If I had it to do over again, I would want to study the mind. What I wish I had been is often informed by what I hear, read, or experience in the present. Sometimes I imagine myself a psychologist, at other times a neuroscientist. And sometimes I imagine studying the mind through the stories it offers up.

This morning I was up just before sunrise. I was reminded of a sunrise a woman told about several years ago. I was with the woman in a small room, seated to her right at a small round table. To her left was a man who, over many years, had become skilled in helping people with difficult conversations. To his left was a young man and then the young man's lawyer. The woman, in her mid-forties, was telling us about a phone call. It was after midnight, maybe 1:00 or 1:30. A police officer told her that there had been an accident. Her mother had been critically injured. The woman dressed and was on the road within minutes. It was a four-hour drive from Minneapolis to Des Moines. It was early summer and the roads were clear. Her life with her mother was laid out before her in the dark. For nearly three and a half hours the images and memories of childhood held her together.

As she approached Des Moines, the sun broke the horizon to her left and she had a vision. She saw her mother as she had seen her the week before—tall, graceful, silver hair. She saw her mother walk from her car. The Toyota was a crumpled heap, but her mother walked with no sign of injury or limitation. She entered a second car, the car that had caused the accident. There was a young man behind the wheel. He had been injured but was conscious. They spoke. As the daughter recounted her vision, the young man across from her began to cry. The facilitator held all of this. He offered the young man a tissue, touching his arm lightly.

After the daughter finished her story there was silence for a few moments. The young man then asked if he could say something. The daughter said yes, by all means. The young man spoke of the accident, of falling asleep for just an instant, of the unexpected collision. He told about the ambulance ride, the emergency room, of recovering from the surgery. He told about the police officer entering his room and taking a seat beside his bed. He told the officer everything and then he asked for the name of the woman who had come into his car. He said he wanted to thank her. The officer asked what he meant. The young man said that when he woke from the collision there was a woman in his car. She was holding his hand. She stroked it, told him that he must have hope and that everything would be all right. The young man asked again for the name of the woman. The officer said the woman in the other car was killed. "Her name was Hope."

Some stories are meant to teach us. Others call us to action. And some contain a mystery for which there is nothing to do but honor it.

It Takes One

Over the years I have seen that it takes one. In the beginning, in a community, it takes one person to say "this doesn't make sense," "this isn't working," "the system is broken," "there has to be a better way," "aha, there is a better way." Sometimes it's a sheriff or a police chief. Sometimes it's a minister, a rabbi, or a priest. Sometimes a prosecutor or a judge. Sometimes a community leader or an activist. It is less important what their role is in the structure of things and more important where their heart is. What they have seen is also important. It is critical. They have to have a vantage point. They have to be able to look back. Sad to say, they have to have seen damage done. They have to ache from the knowledge that lives have been lost and that the system has been complicit in that loss. That system can be the family, the school, the justice system. If you have the right vantage point, you see that these systems are all interconnected and that the failure of the family system often leads to school failure and then justice failure—unless something is done. That something must be dramatic. It cannot be a Band-Aid.

In York County, Maine, there is the town of Biddeford. It has more than its share of today's problems—high unemployment, substandard housing, poverty, alcohol and drug abuse, broken families, children and teenagers in great need. And it has systems that struggle to respond to these problems. In part they struggle because of the weight of the problems. They also struggle because of their own inadequacies. Systems are like industries in many ways. If they don't retool, if they fail to reimagine, they will die. Biddeford has not died, but it is ill, like thousands of communities, big and small. Biddeford's school and justice systems have staff and administrators who are competent and who care to do a good job. They care about those in their charge and those they have been hired to serve. But in many ways their job descriptions and their vision have been defined by the systems within which they operate and that are now proving to be inadequate.

And then there is Heidi O'Leary. Heidi is the director of special education for the Biddeford School District. Heidi has a vantage point. She has seen a lot. She can tell you about the problems and the failures. She will tell you that her own system has been complicit in these. Heidi is not one to recognize the problems, ache over them, and then do nothing about them. She has been reading lately about restorative justice. More than reading, she has been studying it. She now knows about its power to change systems—within law enforcement, within the justice system, and within schools. She refuses to sit on what she knows. Heidi is an activist. She is a change maker.

I first met Heidi two weeks ago. She was aching over the number of Biddeford kids sent to Long Creek, one of two "youth development" centers serving the entire state of Maine. Heidi told me that on a recent day Biddeford kids made up 35 percent of the Long Creek population. Almost none of the kids were there for serious offenses. They were there because of small offenses that had added up. She said that the traditional system responses had failed these kids. She was convinced that had restorative justice responses been in place, the Biddeford kids might still be in school, in the community, at home. Heidi wanted to know what the Restorative Justice Institute might offer. We talked about an in-school mediation program, one in which trained volunteers would be at the school one day every week helping kids in trouble or in conflict learn to talk and learn to listen. We talked about how this model has worked elsewhere. How suspensions and arrests have been reduced dramatically. We brainstormed about how it could work in Biddeford.

Heidi O'Leary doesn't sit still. A week later we met in the same room, only this time the school superintendent was there, and so was the high school principal, and so were police and juvenile court officers and members of the Biddeford community. Heidi chaired the meeting and made sure everyone had a say. It was clear that everyone present wanted to save the children of Biddeford and they knew the various systems would have to respond in a different way.

Heidi and I met again two days ago. Elizabeth Chapman was there too. She heads up a group of restorative justice practitioners from Portland who are willing to help Biddeford High School get going. Elizabeth is another of those "it takes one" people. We brainstormed about the logistics—the staffing needs, the scheduling, the structure, the concrete things that must be put in place so that restorative practices can flourish. And we set a time for another large-group meeting so everyone's voice could be heard.

In Biddeford it is Heidi O'Leary. In Waterville it may be the high school principal, and in Oxford it may be the Spanish teacher. In every community it is and will be the one who has the skills and the vision and the patience—and the vantage point—to inform and excite and to bring along the many.

It's About Knowing the Rules

I met Thomas at a recent racial profiling clinic in Des Moines. Handsome, married, two kids, employed full-time, part-time college student. Thomas spoke with ease about his encounters with the police. Like other victims of racial profiling I've interviewed, Thomas was neither angry nor bitter. To the contrary, he was matter-of-fact about a phenomenon he experiences on a regular basis. Thomas had several incidents he could have shared, but we limited the formal part of the interview to the two most recent stops, one in Pleasant Hill and one in West Des Moines, both suburbs of Des Moines. He said they were characteristic of the others. He said that almost without exception the first question he has been asked is "Why are you here?" It was the same for these two stops. And the end result was the same, too—no hassle and no ticket.

Thomas has learned to play the game. Sometimes he didn't play the game well when he was younger. When he was a teenager his father taught him to always be polite and always put both hands on the steering wheel. But Thomas let his anger show a few times, and he always paid for it. Now he knows better. He spelled out the rules for me: "You can't look at them when they're in their car. That's a red flag. If they stop you, you've got to pull over right away. You don't move, you don't reach for anything—or you'll be gone. You can't wear a hat, you can't have music high. You can't slump down. You can't look like a gang banger. Posture is so important." And the absolutes: "No drugs, no warrants, no passengers."

Thomas said that in Des Moines driving on the west side at night is a no-no. The "west side" is anything from Second Avenue north. The river to 31st is the worst for racial profiling, particularly University, MLK, and Forest Avenue—they are "hot streets." But Thomas says it's not just the cops. You can't go into a store without being followed. According to Thomas, the malls are the worst, except for Merle Hay Mall. It's a "black mall." They leave you alone there.

Thomas has had some troubles in the past but says he was raised right. He's trying to do the same for his kids, and he knows that "If you don't stay on top of it you're going to lose them." He worries most for his son. Twelve years old and in seventh grade, he's an A student and a star basketball player at 6'2". The suburban schools are already recruiting him. Thomas tries to teach him everything his father taught him, and more. He knows his son can't have a record of any kind. It will follow him: "One thing on your record and they have all they need not to hire you."

Thomas is certain that it's all about teaching your kids about values and character, and about "knowing the rules."

The Long, Liberating Road to Reconciliation

A November 3 trial date has been set for Dzhokhar Tsarnaev, the "Boston Bomber." Attorney General Eric Holder has announced that the federal government will seek the death penalty. Prosecutors predict the trial will last twelve weeks and if Tsarnaev is convicted, the death penalty phase could take another six weeks. In his statement announcing the government's position, Holder said: "The nature of the conduct at issue and the resultant harm compel this decision." Holder failed to articulate how the execution of Tsarnaev would remedy the "resultant harm."

The reality is that by imposing the death penalty, the beginning of the healing process for the victims' families is likely to be delayed because of the years that will pass before the execution takes place. And even then, will there be healing? In response to Holder's statement, the Conference of Major Superiors of Men, made up of the leaders of Catholic men's religious orders in the United States, issued a statement last week calling for a restorative justice response rather than the death penalty. The CMSM recognized that many were tragically involved in the harm and that "Dzhokhar both significantly contributed to the harm yet also experienced harm." The statement went on to say that "[the] political leadership continues to deepen the harm and wounds by advancing the use of the death penalty," but that restorative justice offers ways to "[achieve] authentic accountability, . . . care for the victims and the meeting of all parties' human needs, cultivate deeper understanding and empathy, lower recidivism rates, and assist communities with more sustainable commitments to human dignity."

There is little doubt that Dzhokhar will be convicted. But if given the death sentence, will he have an opportunity to be accountable for what he did? Will victims and surviving family members who want to meet with him be allowed to do so? Will they be given the opportunity to tell him, face-to-face, how his actions changed their lives forever? Will they be allowed to express anger and grief in the presence of the one person who should most know of it? Will they have the chance to ask questions only he can provide the answers to?

The death penalty process, with its appeals and delays, takes the focus away from victims and puts it on the offender. It would seem that justice would be best served, and the needs of victims better met, if Dzhokhar were to be allowed to plead guilty and given a sentence of life in prison without parole. Then it might be possible for the healing process to begin. The death penalty fails to humanize our lives. Conversely, restorative justice offers a path to humanization and dignity. Restorative justice allows us, as the CMSM stated, to "travel the long, difficult, but liberating road to reconciliation."

A Mother's Love

Deng called this morning. He is from Sudan and for years has helped refugees who have fled their war-torn country. I don't know what Deng studied at the university, but here he is a social worker, teacher, peacemaker, financial adviser, family counselor, and always an advocate for his people. I once helped Deng run a free legal clinic at the Sudanese Center. If he had his license, he could practice law.

Deng called to see if I would meet with a woman. Her son is in jail and she needs help getting him out. I met her this afternoon in a small conference room adjacent to Deng's cramped office. She doesn't speak or understand English, but she was accompanied by another son whose English is perfect. Deng described the situation. The boy in jail is seventeen but has been charged with robbery as an adult. The authorities say he is one of six boys who used a BB gun to rob a man. The other five boys have bonded out. The woman has to decide whether to give a bondsperson $5,000 and never get a penny of it back. She has nine children. Her adult children have received their tax refunds and the $5,000 has been collected.

Deng spoke about the boy's father, a good man who died in 2011. He had returned to Sudan to visit his mother. Blind and critically ill, she wanted to touch her only son before she died. While there, he drank bad water and passed away before she did.

I asked about the boy's siblings. Had they been in trouble? The boy's brother responded. Not a one—except Daniel, the one in jail. I asked why Daniel and not the others. He said Daniel was the smallest of the family. When he was seven or eight some of his classmates started picking on him. They taunted him for being small and black, and for being different. Daniel repeatedly asked for help but never received any. When Daniel was ten an acquaintance told him he should smoke marijuana, that it would help him be strong and brave, and would also help drive the fears out of his brain. Daniel started smoking marijuana and it worked. When he was high, the fears went away. That helped him become a tough guy. He started hanging out with other tough kids. Even though he was always the smallest, he gained their respect. His brother said he would see Daniel with other kids, and he was tough. But when Daniel was at home he still had the fears. I asked if Daniel would be in jail today if he had never been bullied. He said he was sure he wouldn't be.

Through the brother I asked the mother some questions. Did she understand that if she gave the bondsperson $5,000 she would never get any of it back? Did she know that Daniel is charged with robbery? Did she know that if convicted he would receive a mandatory prison sentence of twenty-five years? Did she understand that if she gives the bondsperson the $5,000, Daniel would be at home only until the end of his trial, unless he is found not guilty or unless he is convicted of some other crime and not sent to prison?

Daniel's mother said yes, she understands all of these things. She said Daniel is her son. She wants him home, even if only for a few months. It's worth $5,000 to have that.

Things Will Never Change

I'm watching the Academy Awards tonight and pulling for *12 Years a Slave*—for best movie, best actor, best supporting actress. I saw the film in November and have yet to get it out of my mind. I'm thinking of how far we've come. And I'm thinking of yesterday morning.

I was in the basement of a Des Moines church with a dozen distinguished men. It was the weekly meeting of the Men's Club at one of the established African American churches. I was told that twenty-five to thirty usually show up, but the bitter cold and coming storm had limited the attendance. Harvey Harrison, like me a "recovering" lawyer, and I had been asked to talk about the ACLU/ AMOS/NAACP racial profiling project. There was support for the project, and skepticism: "What good will it do?" "What good will come from telling our stories, from telling how we've been treated?" "Nothing has really changed." I was surprised, and I felt naive and a little ashamed. These men had seen and endured so much. Most were over sixty. The man seated next to me was ninety-three. He spoke about how he has known it all his life—racism comes with being black. He recalled an early memory of being prohibited from walking with white girls. A man with a PhD in statistics said his biggest fear is "being beaten by the cops." A therapist told how he dismissed a patient from his office because the man called him a "nigger." He then had to defend himself against a professional misconduct complaint.

Everyone acknowledged being a victim of racial profiling—by police, by store employees, by the system. One man asked if we couldn't just "pull the lawsuits that have been filed." He said there are enough names to "prove what they do." There was talk about when only one black firefighter was on the Des Moines fire department, thirty years ago. A lawsuit was filed and won, and within a couple of years the department had thirty-six black firefighters. The number has dwindled to fifteen.

A lawyer spoke. He introduced his granddaughter, a recent University of Iowa graduate. He said we can't rely on what's gone before. That it's important to still tell the stories. And it's equally important that data be collected because the elected officials and policy makers can't ignore the numbers. There was more conversation, and then an explanation was given of the racial profiling interview process. An offer was made to meet with anyone interested at a time and place of their choosing. A pad with a pen went around the table for sign-ups. As the meeting drew to a close, Pastor Gaddy reminded those leaving that "we can never give up, we have to keep trying." I noticed that Chauncey, the man next to me who wasn't allowed to walk with white girls, hadn't signed up to be interviewed. I asked him why. He shook my hand, looked me in the eye, and quietly said "things will never change."

I Would Vote for Ray Jasper

Ray Jasper is in a Texas prison because of the death of a white man in 1998. Ray, nineteen years old at the time, was present. He was an active participant in the robbery of the man but didn't commit the murder. Another man did. That young man later entered a plea of guilty to capital murder. He's now serving a life sentence. A second young man, an accomplice, also pleaded guilty and received the same sentence. Ray was charged as an accomplice too. Rather than plead guilty, he went to trial. In January 2000 he was convicted of capital murder. On February 4, 2000, he was sentenced to death. Ray is now thirty-three. He has an eighth-grade education. He is black. Two weeks from tomorrow, unless something happens, Ray will be dead.

I have read the appellate court's opinion sustaining the trial verdict. There is no doubt that a gruesome crime was committed and little doubt that Ray Jasper was involved. The question, of course, is the imposition of the death penalty and the role that race played in the decision of the jury. On February 15, 2014, Ray wrote a letter from his death row cell in response to a request from Hamilton Nolan of Gawker that he share his story. He writes, "Looking through the eyes of empathy & honesty . . . It's my only perspective." He writes eloquently about the death penalty, "a very Southern practice from that old lynching mentality."

When Ray writes about race you have to take notice:

> I understand that it's not popular to talk about race issues these days, but I speak on the subject of race because I hold a burden in my heart for all the young blacks who are locked up or who see the street life as the only means to make something of themselves. When I walked into prison at 19 years old, I said to myself "Damn, I have never seen so many black dudes in my life." I mean, it looked like I went to Africa. I couldn't believe it. The lyrics of 2Pac echoed in my head, "The penitentiary is packed / and its filled with blacks."

It's really an epidemic, the number of blacks locked up in this country. That's why I look, not only at my own situation, but why all of us young blacks are in prison. I've come to see, it's largely due to an identity crisis. We don't know our history. We don't know how to really identify with white people. We are really of a different culture, but by being slaves, we lost ourselves.

Ray doesn't write as a victim or as a martyr. Neither does he write with anger or cast blame on others. But he does speak a truth that can't be ignored:

People point their fingers at young blacks, call them thugs and say they need to pull up their pants. That's fine, but you're not feeding them any knowledge. You're not giving them a vision. All you're saying is be a square like me. They're not going to listen to you because you have guys like Jay-Z and Rick Ross who are millionaires and sag their pants. Changing the way they dress isn't changing the way they think. As the Bible says, "Where there's no vision the people perish." Young blacks need to learn their identity so they can have more respect for the blacks that suffered for their liberties than they have for someone talking about selling drugs over a rap beat who really isn't selling drugs.

If a miracle happens, if Ray's life is somehow spared at the last moment, if his message could be disseminated and heard, he would make a difference.

Just as there is little doubt that Ray Jasper was an accomplice to a killing in 1998, there is little doubt that his is a life worth saving. He has a wisdom men twice his age will never have:

Before Martin Luther King was killed he drafted a bill called "The Bill for the Disadvantaged." It was for

blacks and poor whites. King understood that in order
to have a successful life, you have to decrease the odds
of failure. You have to change the playing field. I'm not
saying there's no personal responsibility for success, that
goes without saying, but there's also a corporate responsibility. As the saying goes, when you see someone who
has failed, you see someone who was failed.

If Ray Jasper were a candidate for public office in my hometown,
in my state, I would vote for him. It would be an honor.

Outside the Boxes with Restorative Justice

Sarah Mattox wrote today. Sarah is the court diversion coordinator for the Restorative Justice Project of the Midcoast. She wanted
to know if I had done my homework. She didn't quite say it that
way, but I knew that's what she meant. Sarah included her draft of a
"Restorative Services Menu" and gently suggested that "if [I] haven't
yet turned [my] attention to this project" I might want to spend a
little time on it before looking at what she had produced.

Before doing what she does now, Sarah worked for years in the
Boundary Waters area of Minnesota with at-risk youth. A couple
of years ago she was ready for another challenge, so she and her
husband canoed from Minnesota back home to Maine. When that
journey ended she started another.

A few weeks ago Sarah and I met to brainstorm. She wanted to
get her arms around the options available for restorative responses
to misbehavior, wrongdoing, and crime. We talked about healing
circles and restorative circles, about restorative mediation and restorative community conferencing. And we talked about the variations
of these. We considered whether or not each fits within a spectrum
along with the others or whether it's even appropriate to talk about
a spectrum. We considered whether or not it's the number of participants that determines the process to be used, or whether it's the
nature of the offense or conflict. We also considered the role the

referral source plays in determining the appropriate venue for bringing people together. We made some headway but acknowledged that
further reflection was needed.

As usual, I've procrastinated.

There are some ways of working restoratively with youth that
don't fit easily within the usual boxes. I was thinking today about a
program I was involved in a few years ago when I was still a prosecutor. It was with ninth graders who were failing. They had been
moved from "day school" to "night school." This meant they attended
class four afternoons a week, from 2:30 to 5:30. If ever there were a
prescription for failure, this was it. And the school district knew it.
I was asked to put together a restorative response. These kids weren't
in conflict, and they hadn't misbehaved. But the usual ways in which
teachers and administrators approached them weren't working. So
the school identified the twenty students most at risk. The approach
we adopted was simple: have a "restorative meeting" at least once
a month with each of the students. The meetings were held every
Friday. The conversations were not about deficiencies but what each
student was good at and needed to succeed.

I remember one boy, Tony. He was a big, likable kid, but he didn't
like school. And his parents weren't good at getting him there. The
previous school year he was absent at least fifty times. At the rate he
was going, he wouldn't have enough credits to graduate. At the first
meeting in September, I learned that Tony liked horses. He lived on
a small acreage with his parents and two sisters, spending most of
his free time caring for the family's horses. I also learned that Tony
wanted to be a comedian. I asked him what he was doing to get
there. He said he told jokes to his friends and that he's pretty funny.
I said if he wanted to be a comedian someday he would have to get
on a stage to tell his jokes. Tony knew that, but he didn't know how
to get there. The conversation turned to the possibility of Tony getting involved with the theater department. Tony liked the idea but
didn't know what to do. Needless to say, Tony got involved in theater
and he blossomed. As a result, he came to school almost every day.
We continued to meet with Tony one Friday a month throughout

the school year. His absenteeism went down and his grades went up. By November he had already returned to "day school." By the end of the year he was caught up on his credits. The results were the same for almost every one of the other "night school" kids. The program was not a miracle program, but it worked because—with the help of a facilitator—school officials, Tony, and Tony's family took the time to have a conversation once a month without fail.

I'm not sure where the process Tony was involved in fits within a restorative services menu, but I'm sure it must. I need to get back to Sarah with my proposed menu. I'm not very good with boxes but I'll figure it out.

Justice Delayed

A man wrote to me recently from the Fort Madison Penitentiary, where he is serving a life sentence without the possibility of parole. Below his signature he printed in a delicate script, "Justice Delayed Is Justice Denied." Of course I know the expression. And I've witnessed the consequences of delayed justice many times over the years. Yesterday I had a conversation with my son about the detrimental effects of high bonds and pretrial detention. Phil has been in practice since September and already he sees the difference between a person released from jail pending trial and another person awaiting trial in a jail cell.

Justice can be delayed in other ways. Several months ago I was asked to facilitate a victim–offender dialogue. I sat in a small room with a seventeen-year-old boy and his neighbor. The boy lived with his mother. The neighbor, about forty and a bachelor, lived alone. He was a mechanic and had a repair shop. The boy, when he was sixteen, purchased a car with his own money and frequently talked with his neighbor about maintaining the car and about cars in general. On two occasions when the boy's car needed repair, he took it to the neighbor's shop, where it was fixed at no charge except for the cost of the parts. One day the boy skipped school and broke into the man's house. An alert neighbor saw him enter through the back door and

called the police. The boy was arrested, charged with felony burglary, and entered a program that would allow him to plead guilty
to a misdemeanor.

The boy did well. He completed his treatment, offender classes,
and community service. After nearly a year he was told there was
going to be a meeting. It would be with his neighbor. They would
talk about restitution and the effect the boy's crime had on his neighbor. At the meeting the man was angry. He was also hurt that the
boy had not cared enough to apologize and make amends. The boy

The problem is not in recognizing

the need for speedy justice.

The problem is our definition of justice.

tried to explain that he had wanted to apologize right away but that
his probation officer had told him that he couldn't have contact with
the man until he completed all of the program requirements. It took
a while for the boy and the man to work through this, but once they
did they were able to move on and talk about why the boy had committed the burglary.

The boy explained that his parents, even though divorced, continued to fight. To deal with his anxiety and depression he started
using marijuana, more than he could afford. He broken into his
neighbor's house because there were several jars filled with quarters
and half dollars, and he didn't think the man would notice any missing if he took coins equally from each jar. The man spoke about how
he felt betrayed and that the betrayal hurt more than the loss of the
coins. The man accepted the boy's account and his apology. Both
were teary during the exchange.

The two agreed on an amount of restitution and agreed that the
boy would work at the man's shop in order to pay back the money.
In exchange, the man would continue to teach the boy about cars.

I wondered after the meeting why it had taken so long for the conversation to take place. Why did the system dictate a prescription for justice contrary to what the two most affected by the crime needed? It seemed that real justice took place in the meeting. The system's need for the boy to complete a program in order to earn a "good deal" should have been secondary to the real needs. The research is clear that victims and offenders report a higher degree of satisfaction with the criminal justice system after they have met in a facilitated dialogue and been given the opportunity to tell their story, discuss harm, and reach agreement on repair. The problem is not in recognizing the need for speedy justice. The problem is our definition of justice.

In a Circle There Is Always Another Chance to Do Right

To attend a Kay Pranis "Peacemaking Circle Training" is to begin to understand the possibility of community. Earlier this week twenty-one of us, with Kay as our facilitator, met at Plymouth Church in Des Moines—teachers, ministers, social workers, justice workers, community activists, retired folks. We had come together seeking a different way to work with troubled youth in need of healing. Common to each of us was a belief that restorative justice offers a needed vision for how communities might respond when young people make mistakes and come to the attention of the authorities. Everyone in attendance had seen enough to know that our punishment-driven system is ineffective at the least and is often damaging. Over three days we immersed ourselves in the wisdom of the Circle through exercises, discussion, and the sharing of stories. We experienced that individuality is not lost in the Circle process; that the voice of each is important but that no voice is more important than another; that in a Circle, where everyone has a voice, the group won't allow one person to take over. Kay says, "If people don't have a voice, they tend to resist."

I first met Kay Pranis in 1994. At the time she was the restorative justice planner for the Minnesota Department of Corrections. One of her responsibilities was to put on a statewide restorative justice conference. She needed a restorative justice prosecutor. At the time there weren't any in Minnesota, so I was the closest. I met up with Kay a few years later when the Department of Justice sent a team of restorative justice practitioners to travel around the country putting on community symposiums. I think each of us thought that restorative justice was making inroads into the public consciousness. We were premature in our thinking. I lost track of Kay until a few years ago, when I attended her Circle training at Eastern Mennonite University. She had left her position in Minnesota to bring peacemaking circles to communities in the United States and abroad. I had been doing a form of the Circle process in schools and had completed the training offered by the International Institute of Restorative Practices. But it wasn't until taking Kay's training that I really began to get it.

When you train with Kay you go on a journey. But like a Circle, the journey is not linear. There's a meander to it, with resting places along the way. There is simplicity to it as well, at least on the surface. But internally, within the process and within each participant as the training moves on, there is a wisdom that transcends logic, at least Western logic. This is to be expected once you learn that the peacemaking Circle practice taught by Kay draws on Native American traditions and the use of the talking piece. There is a Navajo saying that "if someone does wrong there is something out of balance in the community." Kay says when the community meets with an offender in a Circle "we need the person for whom the Circle is formed just as much as that person needs us." And she says when meeting in a Circle "there is always another chance to do right, to make amends."

Thirty Years Is Enough of a Failed War

I was at a meeting this evening at First Parish Church in Portland, Maine. We had a conversation about what justice looks like in the community. The definition of community was enlarged to include the entire state of Maine. The conversation took place in a Circle, where all such conversations should take place. And a talking piece was used, ensuring that each voice would be heard and respected.

The conversation turned to the governor of Maine, Paul LePage, one of the most unpopular governors in the country with only a 41 percent voter approval rating. LePage has announced that he wants to up the ante in the war on drugs, the war that almost everyone else acknowledges has been lost. In a poor state struggling to pay its bills, the Republican governor is proposing to spend $2 million to hire fourteen drug agents, four prosecutors, and four new judges to sit in drug courts around the state. But LePage isn't saying where the money would come from or how much would be needed to pay for related jail and court costs or for treatment requirements. LePage says the state's county jails have plenty of space to take on more prisoners and that a strain on jail resources is no reason not to move ahead.

But Mark Dion, a Democrat and a former sheriff, says county jails are underfunded and overcrowded and the courts face a similar predicament. Dion believes that a balanced approached is needed, one that looks at the problem as a public health issue as much as a criminal one.

But the issue is no longer divided along party lines. One need only go to www.rightoncrime.com to see what leading conservatives are saying about criminal justice reform—things they never used to say. It's clear that Governor LePage is soon to be in the minority, even in his own party, when the Manhattan Institute, never known for being a bastion of liberal thinking, weighs in on the issue:

> What, over the last thirty years, has the "system" produced? An endless temptation to spend money. The image of a system induces us to try to create a fiscal balance between the parts. More police mean more criminals arrested, more arrestees mean more prosecutors and judges to convict, more convicts mean more prisons and more parole and probation offices. But perhaps that idea is wrong. Perhaps instead of spreading resources evenly over a system to process criminals, we need to concentrate them on the agencies that prevent crime. Perhaps, to put it bluntly, we need fewer prisons and

far more cops—not cops who will feed the system, but cops who will starve it by helping communities protect themselves.

It would seem that before Governor LePage wastes any more taxpayer money he would be wise to sit down in a Circle with a cross section of Maine voters and truly listen to the voices of each as they hold the talking piece. He may find they have also come to realize that thirty years is enough of a failed war and it's time to bring the troops home and send in the physicians, the counselors, the therapists—the healers.

Giving People Permission to Think Differently

Driving to Yarmouth, Maine, this afternoon I struggled with a question—several actually. Why are some communities in Maine ready for restorative justice and others are not? Why do forty people show up at Oxford Hills High School to learn about restorative justice? Why do another twenty-five brave a February morning to fill a conference room in Waterville for the same reason? Why has Biddeford High School hosted two gatherings in the last month to see what restorative justice might offer the school and the community? Why do high schools in Hiram and Gorham want to have similar conversations? Why these schools and communities and not others? Why do high schools that are more urban and with more students appear disinterested? Do the answers lie in community—both where they exist and where they do not? Although modest in size, does Portland consider itself a community? Does it ache when one of its own is lost, whether by expulsion or arrest or imprisonment? Does it sense that something is missing when a child falls through the cracks and there is no net to catch him? Does it even know the child has fallen?

These are merely questions. I can't answer them for Portland. But in Biddeford they are being answered. At the high school yesterday morning the conversation continued. The school superintendent set the tone: "This is not just a school problem, it's a community problem, and it's important that we talk with the kids." He asked: "How do we break from being reactionary?" A police officer responded: "All of us must act together. Shouldn't we look at an approach that's district-wide?" And then a state trooper: "We don't talk to each other enough." The superintendent again: "It's the community piece. What's out there in the community? What resources are available?" A juvenile court officer said he knows what the resources are but "I may not know about the ten-year-old who is at risk but not on the radar." The director of special ed said: "The crimes that happen on the street happen in the school." The district attorney spoke up: "What we're doing now isn't necessarily working. I'd love to see meaningful interventions for kids who have crossed the line." A school counselor who uses a Circle process with fifth graders said: "It starts with a commitment—the will to commit to a restorative approach." According to the superintendent: "Only 15 percent of families take suspensions and detentions seriously. We need to look at these problems differently." A high school English teacher said she uses a restorative approach in her classroom: "When someone is disruptive, we stop everything and get into a Circle. We start to talk about what's going on in the classroom, and students begin to manage each other. They begin to take responsibility for their learning environment." The superintendent continued to advocate for change: "We need a cultural change. We need to give people permission to think differently." Another police officer: "What we handled in the school 10 to 15 years ago now results in a charge."

The conversation continued. Not all of the questions were answered, but everyone agreed the dialogue should continue. Others from the community should be included, and restorative responses should be part of the solution.

Another meeting has been scheduled. More people will be included and asked to contribute. There is a growing sense of urgency in Biddeford. The health of the community is at risk and everyone needs to know that. The superintendent understands this as well as anyone: "For us as a community, to open up and talk about this is a very big deal."

The difference between Biddeford and Portland, it seems, is that Biddeford sees itself as a community and understands that its continued viability is dependent on its children, every one of them.

The Importance of Patience

Circle keepers who are true to the vocation approach each Circle with the belief that every person in the Circle already knows the principles of restorative justice. They may not be able to enumerate them, they may not know anything about them, but they "know" them. Some might argue that the principles are etched in our DNA and are as necessary for survival as the codes for fight, flight, and nurture. Indigenous cultures certainly knew the principles, since the continued existence of the community was dependent on them. For our ancestors, each individual was indispensable and each voice was important, including the voice of the young person and the dissident, who often would bring forth the new idea or insight that would allow the community to respond to unforeseen challenges. Circle keepers also understand that it's the nature of the space created within the Circle that is critical. It does not exist to determine right or wrong, good or bad. By its very nature, the questions inherent within the Circle are, What's going on with each person? What is the experience of each?

Twice I've participated in peacemaking Circle training. Each time, the trainer used the "driftwood exercise" to draw us into the power of the Circle. It's a simple exercise, done in silence. There is a table, low to the ground, in the middle of the Circle. And there is a bag of driftwood. The instructions are simple: take driftwood from the bag and do anything you want. The movement is from left to right. Each person starts where the previous person finished. The exercise ends when no one wants to continue. It's a fascinating exercise. Some take one or two pieces from the bag. Others take several. Patterns and structures emerge. They are added to, subtracted from, modified, destroyed, rebuilt. Some people prefer simplicity, others complexity. Some symmetry, others disproportion. Some refuse to disturb an existing work, others revel in that. Round and round it goes.

The exercise can last an hour or two. Some get frustrated. You can see it in their faces, in their twitching. But insights arise. Every moment is change. An outrageous action may move the whole group. Patience is important. Questions arise. What was the meaning of my turn? What was the meaning in the actions of another? What was my reaction to their actions? When the action is done and the silence is broken there is processing. The reflections run the gamut and personality traits are revealed along with likes, dislikes, propensities, and fears. These are all placed in the container of the Circle and, like the alchemist's cauldron, they are transformed into a collective wisdom.

Following a recent exercise, our trainer shared with us how others have acted and responded. She said occasionally it does not go as peacefully as ours did. Some people get angry. Some won't participate after the first or second round. Some take all of the pieces off the table and put them in the bag, only to have the exercise start over. Most of the time the group wants resolution, not necessarily a consensus as to form, but a consensus that it's the right time to end and move on. Our trainer then told us about one particularly powerful ending. The exercise had gone like many others. Some people were impatient. Others continued to add to and subtract from the collective work.

There was a police officer in the group. When it came to his turn, after the sixth or seventh round, he put all of the pieces in the bag and left the room. Everyone followed. He left the building, got into his patrol car, and drove off. He returned an hour later, bag in hand. He said nothing but walked to a wall where there was open space. He took from the bag a Polaroid photograph and then another. He taped the first to the wall. It was a photo of the bag on the floor of a jail cell. He taped the second below it. It was a photo of the bag leaning up against a tombstone. Below the photos he taped a white sheet of paper on which he had written in large, black letters: "This Is What Happens To Young People When We Aren't Patient."

A Passion for Justice

A dear friend wrote yesterday. Johanshir is an environmental engineer. He has a PhD. Two of his children are physicians and a third has a PhD in mathematics. His wife, Olya, is a computer scientist. She says there are at least twenty-two physicians in her family, not counting the children. Johanshir's life spans sixty years plus. His history goes back another seven thousand. Johanshir's passport says he is Iranian. His blood says he is Persian. He is a descendant of kings, statesmen, diplomats, and businessmen. His family has been doing business in India for nearly three hundred years. I hope to write a book about Johanshir someday, in part because of his history but, more importantly, because he is a man of compassion with a keen sense of justice. He has seen both sides of it. As a student he was taken by the authorities, held, and tortured. After his release his family found a way to get him to the United States, where he finished his undergraduate and graduate work. I know of no one more thankful for the gifts this country has given him.

And yet for over forty years he has been the victim of bias and prejudice, both intentional and unintentional. When he was a university professor a realistic fake bomb was strapped to the lectern in his classroom. Soon after, he received threats that his infant daughter would be kidnapped. There was a time when he feared going to the university recreation center because he had been assaulted there. He has been harassed by police and city officials. Johanshir and his family have lived in the same house for more than twenty years. They have been loyal to their community and have given much more than they've taken. But they've had the misfortune of having neighbors who would prefer they return to Iran.

Three years ago I had yet to meet Johanshir. I was in his city doing Circle work with the local police department; some of the staff were having difficulty getting along. During a break I took a call from a colleague with the Attorney General's Office. He wanted to know if I could meet with a friend who had been falsely accused of two simple misdemeanor offenses. I said of course and met over the lunch hour with Johanshir, Olya, and their daughter who had just graduated from medical school. They were in pain—all three, as well as the two children not present. They didn't know what to do. There lives had been turned upside down by the accusations. I suggested mediation. They said yes, that's exactly what's needed. They thought that if they could come to an understanding with their neighbor, their relationship could be mended.

In the days that followed I learned more about the conflict as well as the background of their well-connected neighbor. I was given permission to approach the prosecutor. I made the call and was informed, rather bluntly, "We don't do that kind of thing here. This case is going to trial." The prosecutor was a man of his word. Two months later we were in court. For two days testimony was taken and arguments made. The jury deliberated. In less than two hours Johanshir was acquitted. Despite it all, Johanshir is not a bitter man. His passion for justice continues. A dream of his is to start and fund an international justice center. He frequently emails me accounts of justice work being done around the country and in other countries as well. Johanshir is following closely what is going on Maine. He wrote yesterday offering an assessment:

> Urban areas and cities are like an ocean where everything is washed into them, good and bad. Smaller towns are like headwaters, they are pure. New ideas such as restorative justice are like pure rain drops that pour into the headwaters. To spread pure good ideas into the ocean they must start from headwaters. To spread pure good ideas into the cities, they must start from the towns. In Maine they are starting to clean up the ocean and starting it from the headwaters. The way to Portland and the big cities is through the small towns. Things are looking good. . . . Things are good indeed. Restorative justice will make its way into Portland. There is no other way. . . . It will get there! It takes time to fill up an ocean. . . . We just need more rain, more headwaters and more small towns in order to do it. Once you have seeded the clouds, the rain will pour.

It seems the rains have started. The future looks hopeful for restorative justice.

I'm thinking I should suggest to Johanshir and Olya that they move to Maine. Johanshir could start his justice center here. I know he would be well received.

Not Too Old to Learn

I'm not too old to learn. Thank goodness. I used to think that people got to restorative justice only because of direct involvement with the existing criminal or juvenile justice systems: Maybe as a victim they met an offender in a facilitated dialogue, told their story to the person who had harmed them, and as a result, obtained some closure. Or maybe as a police officer they came to see, after years of doing things by the book, that being tough and uncompromising didn't work a lot of the time. Or maybe as a judge they had an epiphany, a realization that each individual sentencing contributed to the phenomenon of mass incarceration. Or maybe as a prosecutor, like me, they came to see that how we respond to wrongdoing is just as important as proving guilt and seeking punishment.

People do continue to get to restorative justice as a result of bumping up against the system. But that's not the only point of entry. I'm beginning to see that. Just this week I've been reminded that sensitivity to justice is acquired not just by being pulled into the system as the result of a crime or because of years as a justice system professional. Some get to restorative justice because of an injustice unrelated to the formal system. It could be something that happened when they were in school, as early as kindergarten, or because they were the victim of bias or discrimination. For others, their life in the community brings them to awareness that things are not as they should be.

Tuesday afternoon in South Paris, Maine, a group met at the high school, in a Circle—teachers, ministers, social workers, mental health workers, a victim advocate, a mediator, two students. Throughout, it became apparent that there is a collective need to do things differently. The concept of restorative justice kept coming up. Questions were posed. How would it look? What processes would be used? Where would it start? Who should be added to the Circle? What is community?

After the meeting I drove to St. George. I spent the evening with Susan and Richard Bates, engineers by training and profession. They are leaders in the effort to spread restorative justice throughout Maine. Susan and Richard moved to the peninsula a few years back. They know the importance of community. They discovered the work of the Restorative Justice Project of the Midcoast and got involved. They saw how bringing victims, offenders, and communities together can make a difference. In collaboration with others,

For a long time I held the belief that those who have been blessed with good fortune, good upbringing, and a fair measure of success do not understand the inequities of a justice system that favors the wealthy and punishes the poor and the powerless. I was wrong.

they helped create the Restorative Justice Institute of Maine. They believe that what is good for the Belfast area of Maine is good for the whole state.

Yesterday morning I had breakfast in Rockland with Bill Walsh, who shares the vision. A retired businessman from Boston, Bill has known great success in his life. For the past six months he has served as the interim director for the Restorative Justice Project of the Midcoast—for free. Bill thinks big, like Richard and Susan Bates. Having helped raise millions of dollars over the years for worthy causes, he says he's never felt more connected to his work. Bill understands that both vision and creativity are required to move Maine forward into a new age of justice.

After meeting with Bill I stayed in Rockland and had lunch with Dick Snyder at Café Miranda. Dick is a retired professor, having taught theology for years in New York City. He's been around since the beginning, helping found the Midcoast Project nearly a decade ago and the Institute two years ago. Dick has no doubt that his adopted state is in great need of restorative justice. Having worked with inmates at Sing Sing prison, he knows firsthand what a retributive justice system can produce.

This morning I met Peter Jenks at the Highlands Coffee House in Thomaston. Peter is a transplant from Minnesota and an Episcopal priest. He's seen a lot since coming to Maine and has a keen understanding of the struggles of many in his community. We talked for two hours. Early in our conversation Peter was cautious about the possibility that people in Maine might change the way justice is done. By the end he was planning a meeting and listing the people he wanted to bring together to talk about first steps.

I'm not too old to learn, and I'm not afraid to admit my mistakes. For a long time I held the belief that those who have been blessed with good fortune, good upbringing, and a fair measure of success do not understand the inequities of a justice system that favors the wealthy and punishes the poor and the powerless. I was wrong.

What If

I woke this morning thinking of Bob Scott. Bobby was a classmate of mine. He was the Huckleberry Finn of our sixth grade class. If there had been frogs close by, he would have been the kid to hide one in Sister Claire's satchel. Bobby had a lot of energy, but he rarely channeled it into schoolwork. He was an explorer and a showman, finding the spotlight more than his share of the time. Looking back, I wonder how much attention he received at home.

One day in April, when we all knew that winter was over, Bobby brought a knife to school. It was a pocketknife with three or four blades. A group of Bobby's admirers, including me, huddled around him in the back of the classroom before morning prayer. He displayed each blade, one by one, and described how they might be used. Without warning Sister Claire was in our midst, just as Bobby was holding the longest blade up to Tony's nose. Sister Claire was quick, and within seconds Bobby was gone. We didn't see him the next day or the next. Bobby didn't finish the year with us. We had theories, but it wasn't until summer that we found out for sure that Bobby had been expelled and enrolled in a public school a few miles away.

What happened to Bobby really bothered me. It was years later before I knew about due process and years more before I learned about restorative justice. But something told me that Bobby hadn't been treated right and we hadn't been treated right either. As far as any of us knew there weren't any rules about bringing knives to school. Those would come later. And there was no acknowledgment the next morning about what had happened. Sister Claire never said anything about Bobby. It was as if he never existed.

It's easy now to imagine how things might have been handled differently. If Bobby brought his pocketknife to school in 2014, and if our school had volunteer mediators, there would be a dialogue with Bobby, his parents, Sister Claire, and maybe the principal. In addition to the incident with the knife, there would be a conversation about how Bobby was doing in school and at home, about his needs and what could be done to help him succeed. The conversation would end with an accountability agreement. Limitations placed on Bobby's behavior would be supported by positive measures designed to help Bobby do better. Within a few days of the facilitated dialogue, a Healing Circle would be held in the classroom. A volunteer Circle Keeper might be brought in, or perhaps Sister Claire would facilitate—having previously been trained as a Circle Keeper. A talking piece would be used, and after introductions and sharing about school life, the conversation would turn to Bobby, his knife, what happened, and what could have happened with a knife in the classroom. Even before meeting in Circle, Sister Claire might have taught us about the use of peacemaking circles by indigenous cultures, how there have been communities in which every person is seen as valuable and where each individual is indispensable to the well-being of the group.

Not long ago I ran into Larry, a classmate with Bobby and me. Larry said things hadn't gone well with Bobby after the move. His experience with school went from bad to worse. He dropped out when he turned sixteen. Life has been tough for Bobby ever since. Larry and I talked about how things might have been different.

The Circle as Building Block

Seven of us met last evening at First Parish in downtown Portland to talk about justice. It was the third such meeting in as many weeks, but with a different group each time. We met in Circle as is the practice. After introductions we each provided a brief background— youth, work, family—and then talked about what had moved us to come together for an evening of conversation and storytelling. There was an experienced disability lawyer, a political science professor, a restorative justice volunteer from the church, a lawyer with a long history of working with at-risk kids, and a social worker turned restorative justice organizer. And there was John, a native of the Congo.

John is new to Maine. He's an asylum seeker. He lived in Rwanda for many years, where he facilitated healing and reconciliation workshops for victims of the Tutsi genocide. He also facilitated victim–offender dialogues for truth telling and apology. I first met John yesterday afternoon outside his apartment near the waterfront. John spoke of his history and his long journey through the war and its aftermath. We talked about our mutual interest in restorative justice. His favorite book is Howard Zehr's *The Little Book of Restorative Justice*. His second favorite is Howard's *Changing Lenses*. John's dream is to meet Howard one day and study conflict transformation at Eastern Mennonite University. He wants to improve his skills as a peacemaker so he can empower the people of the African Great Lakes region who, he says, are hungry for peace.

John's work has been informed by restorative justice. It's his experience that the punishment of offenders doesn't contribute to the long-term task of rebuilding community. He says restorative justice is an essential tool for real peace and security in Africa. When John held the talking piece he spoke passionately about the healing and transformation possible when victims and offenders come together. He's witnessed crimes most of us can't imagine. And yet he is optimistic. John has seen firsthand the capacity of humans to heal one another, and themselves, when coming together in restorative processes, which he considers sacred.

Others in the Circle spoke about injustices they witnessed growing up or as young adults. Others spoke of their professional work, the inequities of wealth and power, and of systems that grind people down. When the talking piece was passed for the final round, each reflected on whether or not there is hope for the future. To a person, there was optimism—not so much for a leveling of the inequalities, or the evolution of a justice system that ceases to harm those caught in its net, but instead, the shared optimism was similar to John's. After two hours of sitting in Circle, there was a heightened sense of the value of relationship and community and of the potential created by coming together for conversation and storytelling: anything is possible.

Restorative justice processes such as peacemaking Circles are essential building blocks for relationships and for communities.

Three Questions

The towns are becoming familiar, their names and the sounds of them. Biddeford, Alfred, Old Orchard Beach, Westbrook, Gray, Falmouth, Cumberland, Freeport, Brunswick, Topsham, Auburn, Lewiston, Oxford, South Paris, Augusta, Waterville, Newcastle, Waldoboro, Thomaston, St. George, Tenants Harbor.

Last week there was the drive up to Boothbay Harbor. Actually, as much out as up. You follow the coastline from Portland, from southwest to northeast, skirting Casco Bay. Boothbay Harbor is out there. Its name is cumbersome at first. Two words but it sounds like three. But there is a poetry to it. The alliteration. I'm not quite sure how we got there, Chris and I.

Chris wears two hats—four if you count being a husband and a father. He is a facilitator with the Restorative Justice Project of the Midcoast and a community coordinator for the Restorative Justice Institute of Maine. A week earlier he asked me to accompany him to a meeting at the high school in Boothbay Harbor. I wished I had a map, but Chris didn't need one. With Chris at the wheel we passed through Wiscasset, North Edgecomb, and then Edgecomb, dropping south to Boothbay Harbor, midpoint to Newagen at the tip of the peninsula.

We were greeted at the front door of the school by a Boothbay police officer who carried himself with a wisdom that comes with having responded to thousands of calls. He's the peace officer you want when there's a problem at home with a teenager and what you need is advice and not an arrest. We met in a small conference room, a dozen of us around an oval table. The police officer started with introductions, but the actual conversation had started several months earlier, shortly after a local student was arrested for a serious offense. Everyone agreed at the time that he was a good kid who had made a bad mistake. But what do you do when tradition and practice allow for only one response? At least one person, perhaps more, said: "Slow down. Stop the train."

There were questions. What will the consequences be if we go forward with this in the usual way? Can we do something different? What would that look like? Whom do we call? That's when Chris got involved—Chris the facilitator. He helped those most concerned craft a restorative response that included the convening of a Circle. The result was expected by those familiar with restorative justice. For those not familiar, it was life-changing. The young man, his family, and the community are on the mend. And now people in Boothbay Harbor want to know how restorative justice can be the customary response for many, if not most, young people who make a bad mistake. It was fascinating, and an honor, to sit at that table and be present to a birthing process. To witness a police officer, a lawyer, a coach, a counselor, committed volunteers, local business people, and the young offender turned committee member, talk about the kind of justice they want in their community and begin to articulate steps necessary to get there.

There will be more meetings. The oval table won't be large enough. Others will be recruited to contribute, including more young people. There is little doubt that Boothbay Harbor has within its town limits the right problem solvers and process makers. And it's likely that something else will be added to the mix: compassion. The man to my left, a big bear of a guy and a longtime worker with at-risk kids, said it loud and clear: "I believe in a strict correctional attitude, but sometimes these kids just need a big hug."

Afterward I spoke with Doug, owner of the local bait shop and a man the police officer said really knows kids. Doug talked about how he raised his own. He told me whenever one of them did something wrong, hurt someone, he always asked three questions:

1. What were you thinking at the time?
2. How did your actions impact others?
3. What are you going to do about it?

Sounds like restorative justice to me.

A Prosecutor Who Gets It

Twenty-three years ago this June I opened a letter from Bob Cook, a Presbyterian minister. A few years earlier Bob and I had worked together. I was a Legal Aid attorney in Des Moines spending much of my time in court representing clients threatened with eviction. Bob was part of a small but vocal group advocating for the rights of the homeless. We joined forces and some good things happened, including the creation of Anawim Housing, which, over the years, created hundreds of housing units for families in need of transitional shelter.

When Bob wrote in 1991, it wasn't to talk about housing. It was to talk about justice. Bob was a passionate man. He still is. When he "retired" at the age of sixty he moved to El Salvador and worked with the poor for several years. If my dates are correct, Bob is currently on a walk across the United States with several others to raise awareness about global warming.

Bob isn't one for introductions or formalities. Blunt and to the point, and with white hair and white beard, he speaks like a prophet. In his 1991 letter he stated simply: "Fred, you've got to find out about this thing called restorative justice!" Enclosed was an article from a justice official reporting on restorative justice efforts taking place in Canada. I was a prosecutor and had never heard of such a thing. But I started reading what I could find about restorative justice and was soon convinced that it offered a process desperately needed by a justice system indifferent to the real needs of victims and offenders. Des Moines was fortunate to have the Neighborhood Mediation Center (which later became the Polk County Attorney's Restorative Justice Center). Within months, training in victim–offender mediation was provided to about twenty of the mediators. The rest is history.

It was slowgoing at first, but within a few years capacity was built to provide facilitated dialogues to every victim with the need to sit across the table from the person who had caused them harm. Elected officials recognized the importance of the process to their constituency. Taxpayer dollars paid for the staff necessary to integrate restorative justice into the existing system. Money was allocated to compensate mediators on a case-by-case basis. Few offenses were off-limits. The primary question was, Are the parties ready? The offenses ranged from theft, property damage, and assault to burglary, robbery, and rape. Even family members of loved ones who had been murdered found healing in a process that recognizes as sacred the telling of the story in the aftermath of wrongdoing, no matter how serious.

Fast-forward to Maine in April 2014. A meeting was held recently in Augusta, convened by Maeghan Maloney, the district attorney for Kennebec and Somerset Counties. Maeghan gets it. She understands the needs of victims. She has an intuitive sense that when an offender hears how his or her conduct has affected the lives of others, a transformation is possible. Carie James, the chief juvenile prosecutor, accompanied Maeghan. Carie gets it too. She says that restorative justice is needed in her jurisdiction. Also at the table were five juvenile probation officers, the people who work in the trenches. They understand that victims oftentimes would like to meet with an offender and get an answer to the simple question "Why?" There was a spirited conversation for nearly two hours. By the time we finished, May 29 was selected for the three first victim–offender dialogues. The juvenile probation officers accepted responsibility for reserving a room, scheduling meetings, and inviting victims and offenders to the table. The Restorative Justice Institute of Maine will provide the facilitators.

It will be slowgoing at first, but if history is a predictor, Maeghan Maloney, her staff, and the juvenile court in Kennebec County will create a model for other prosecutors and courts to follow. These are exciting times in Maine. People are waking to the challenge of defining justice for their communities. Other innovative models are being envisioned. It will be interesting to observe the collaborative efforts that emerge. Communities and justice system professionals are recognizing the need to partner. Neither can go it alone.

Gaining a Competency About Justice

When I was a young prosecutor, Dusty Rhoades was a frequent visitor to the courthouse. I don't know if Dusty was his real name, but it suited him well. He was in his seventies when we first met. Despite his age, Dusty had the look of a cowpoke—short and wiry, with a quiet intensity. I imagined his early years were spent in a saddle in Oklahoma or Texas. What brought him to the courthouse and made him a celebrity of sorts was his interest in justice. Dusty loved to observe trials. He had a keen mind, and even veteran lawyers sought him out for his insight and observations. At the time, I thought there was no one like Dusty. I still think of him with admiration, but he is no longer alone.

There are more court watchers now. Most of them are retired, like Dusty. But there are some differences. Today's court watchers have completed a training. They've learned how a case gets into the system and how it works its way through it. They've learned the lexicon of the juvenile justice system as well as the roles of the various system players. They've learned something about the research around delinquency, detention, and the unintended and adverse consequences of putting a young person deep into the system when they don't belong there. And they've learned that children of color are disproportionately represented among all children who appear before our juvenile judges.

Like Dusty, today's court watchers are interested in justice. Most often, they observe hearings with a partner while sitting in the back of the courtroom. They use a court watch form to record the specifics of each hearing and their observations and opinions about the fairness of the proceeding. They record the race and gender of everyone involved in the hearing, including the young person before the court. Everything they record is entered at a later date into a database. In the last fifteen months, six training sessions have been held and over a hundred people have earned a court watcher badge. Last July a dozen African American ministers completed the training. A few months earlier twenty-five undergraduate honor students did as well.

Everyone I've talked with who has completed the training and spent time in one of the six Polk County juvenile courtrooms has said they are much better off for the experience. Their eyes have been opened to a system that does work well sometimes but oftentimes appears to be broken. They wonder why they see black and brown juveniles more than white ones. They wonder why young people are brought into courtrooms wearing handcuffs and shackles when they have been accused of relatively minor offenses. They wonder why these same young people enter guilty pleas fifteen to twenty minutes after meeting their court-appointed attorneys for the first time.

This afternoon I had coffee with Jeanne, who is recently retired and wants to court watch. Jeanne has worked in schools and in the office of the local prosecutor, and she has concerns. She wants to gain a competency about justice and form her own opinions about what justice should look like for juveniles. Like many others, Jeanne is concerned that if we don't figure out how better to respond to wrongdoing by juveniles, we will one day regret it. Jeanne doesn't expect to accomplish much on her own. But she believes there is value in sitting quietly in courtrooms with other trained observers. And she is hopeful that those who run the system will see that the community is interested in justice too.

The Winds of Change

I had a conversation with an astrologer recently. I've never been an adherent to astrology, which many consider a pseudoscience; I've supported the Carl Sagan position that astrology is unscientific. Recently, however, I've shifted a bit and come to realize, thanks to the late psychologist Rollo May, that astrology has an entirely different basis. May taught that astrology is a myth, that it requires the language of myth, and that like all myth, it contains within it a truth. Anyway, this astrologer told me that what we are now witnessing has not been seen since the '60s: Our traditional institutions and systems are weakening, and those who are servants to those institutions are holding fast to the old way of doing things. Fear of change is human, and those who have the most to lose are the most fearful. According to the astrologer, change is in the air, and the winds of change are at the backs of the change makers. But, he warned, the door will not be open long. It may be open less than a decade, since those who cling to the old ways will do their best to slam the door shut.

I had breakfast yesterday with a friend, the CEO of a large non-profit that serves children and families that have more than their share of challenges. We talked about the local justice system and its apparent blindness to the reality that we all live in the same community. My friend spoke passionately about restorative justice and how the way it balances the interests of victims, offenders, and the community offers her hope. I saw my friend again this morning at Plymouth Church. We sat together with several others to continue discussions about a fall conference. It's to be modeled after the TED Talks and will introduce to many the restorative justice paradigm for the first time. It will also attempt to educate professionals and community members on the realities of the developing brains of juveniles and the growing body of research that demonstrates that

the traditional punitive model of accountability is counterproductive and can actually increase the risk factors for future problematic
behavior.

Those at the table—health care and business executives, county
officials, nonprofit leaders like my friend, and justice advocates—
believe it's time to have a community conversation about the implications of our present approach to juvenile accountability. As the
head of a major hospital foundation put it, "Our community is ready
to dive in deeper." A business leader said, "We are not inventing
something new here; the information is out there," adding that our
challenge is "to create a story, to create a reason for change." Those
who met this morning were not just the usual suspects, not just the
liberals who decry the tough-on-crime approach. There is a growing
number of new voices demanding to be heard. They believe in the
efficacy of the restorative justice approach. They also believe that the
findings of scientists and economists must be included in the conversation. They know that the restorative justice message resonates with
many but that traditionalists need more than that if they are to be
convinced of the need for reimagining the way we do justice.

The winds of change are behind the change makers. The number
of change makers calling for justice reform is increasing. The question is: Will the door remain open long enough?

The Road Less Traveled

I tell people my kids raised me. Each has taught me lessons I couldn't
have learned elsewhere. My daughter Sarah texted the other day.
She's finishing her first year of medical school. Usually she wants me
to know how a test went or about an interesting lecture. Sometimes
she wants to talk about an ethics question that came up in a small
group discussion. She's beginning to look deeper into the system that
will soon define much of her life.

Our text exchange the other day was about the big picture:

Sarah: Hey Dad, I think I'm getting to be more like you.
  Me: Really, how so?

Sarah: I just feel more and more that I'm supposed to do something different and important with me life. And that I'm not meant to have the life of a normal doctor.

Me: How could you? You have a soul that is different from most others.

Sarah: I feel like it will get me into a lot of trouble.

Me: But it will be a great journey. You always liked amusement park rides.

Sarah: Ha ha, indeed. It's just weird because I have always been well liked and I can already tell a lot of people will dislike me if I speak out and stand up for myself.

Me: You know, when I was a prosecutor and tried to change the juvenile justice system I was vilified by some.

Sarah: I remember that. It's hard for me to get past caring what my superiors think of me because it could affect my career.

Sarah gave a presentation a couple of weeks ago at a sexual assault conference. She spoke for an hour to students, physicians, other health care professionals, and to victims. She spoke openly about being a survivor and the challenges of being a medical student dealing with post-traumatic stress disorder. Sarah stood before two hundred people and told about the night last June when five men broke down the door of her room at the hostel in remote Nicaragua; how they each had a weapon, either a gun or a machete; how she was raped and how she fought, knowing she might not survive.

Sarah lives in a different world now. For months she was convinced she had AIDS. And for months she had nightmares; she still does from time to time. But she is a survivor. Sitting in large lecture halls, she panics because her attention span isn't what it used to be. But she's figured it out. She goes back to her apartment and watches the lectures online, doubling the speed and forcing herself to pay attention.

We finished our text conversation:

Sarah: I can't buy into the system anymore.
Me: Do you remember what Robert Frost said?

> Two roads diverged in a yellow wood,
> And sorry I could not travel both
> And be one traveler, long I stood
> And looked down one as far as I could
> To where it bent in the undergrowth;
>
> Then took the other, as just as fair,
> And having perhaps the better claim,
> Because it was grassy and wanted wear;
> Though as for that the passing there
> Had worn them really about the same,
>
> And both that morning equally lay
> In leaves no step had trodden black.
> Oh, I kept the first for another day!
> Yet knowing how way leads on to way,
> I doubted if I should ever come back.
>
> I shall be telling this with a sigh
> Somewhere ages and ages hence:
> Two roads diverged in a wood, and I—
> I took the one less traveled by,
> And that has made all the difference.

Sarah: That's awesome. I love that. I find it to be very
soothing.

Sarah has started down the road less traveled. She's decided she also wants to get a master's degree in public health. She wants to work with AIDS patients and with victims of sexual assault. She wants to help victims become survivors.

Joseph Campbell taught that although our lives and the stories of our lives are personal, they contain elements of the universal. People in this country and around the world have come to restorative justice for many reasons, most of them personal. They have chosen a road less traveled, having diverged from what, at one time, they thought was the only road. They are learning from victims and from offenders. They are teaching each other. They are gaining in number and in strength because they can't buy into the system any longer. They have chosen the road less traveled, and it is making all the difference.

The Restorative Process as Container

I've spent most of the week in the Twin Cities. Three of my daughters attend the University of Minnesota. If I don't make the trip, I rarely see them. I give them rides, take them to lunch, and watch *Alias* with them. After the fourth or fifth day they begin to inquire about my flight plans.

When I'm here I like to walk along the Mississippi and hang out at the nearby coffee shops. And if she's available, I meet with a friend who is a practicing Jungian analyst. Jean has explained to me that the aim of Jungian psychology is not the cure of a disease, in a medical sense, but to assist the analysand toward a more meaningful life. In doing this, she says, she doesn't give advice. Instead, she helps those who come to her ask questions about what the deepest part of the self really wants. Because the primary focus of her practice is personality development, during the second half of life I find our conversations helpful.

Over coffee we talked about the analytic process. Jean said she thinks of the process as a vessel or a container. It's a safe place that becomes a repository for all kinds of "stuff." The analysand brings the stuff and the analyst is witness to it without judgment. Jean says it's critical that the analyst not bring to the process his or her own agenda. She says when there is a witnessing without an attempt to fix, the analysand is "seen" in a way rarely, if ever, experienced in other relationships.

As Jean spoke it struck me that a restorative process has similar elements. It is not analysis, but if facilitated properly, it does provide a place of safety to which all manner of "stuff" can be brought. The skilled facilitator does not have an agenda or pass judgment on what the parties bring, either to the table or to the Circle. There is no rush to apology or to agreement. The facilitator is the keeper of a process and has faith that the process can be a locus of healing. Like the analyst, the facilitator does not offer advice. The real parties to the dialogue provide the answers or solutions. The facilitator does not offer wisdom. Instead, wisdom is discovered from within by those in conflict with each other or by the victim and offender who have come into relationship as the result of wrongdoing.

I shared all of this with Jean. She acknowledged knowing little about restorative justice but immediately saw the similarities between her analytic practice and the best of what restorative practitioners have to offer.

We continued our conversation. I asked her what the next stage of her life looks like since she has taken the first steps toward winding down her practice. She wants to move from the privacy of her office and into the community. She would like to learn more about victim–offender dialogue. She can see how it might be a vessel for healing. And she can imagine herself as a Circle Keeper, holding a talking piece and passing it on. I imagine the transition for Jean will be an easy one.

To Plan, Or Not: A Theory

Sometimes it's good to have a plan—probably most of the time. Like this week when twenty restorative justice advocates and professionals gathered at a farm near Hallowell, Maine, to learn how to take what they know best and teach it more effectively to others. It was one of those train-the-trainers trainings. But this one was different. Two talented men from Vermont engaged us for four days, convincing us that what we do intuitively isn't always best. This is particularly true when working with adults. Peter and Jon, from Global Learning Partners, aren't so much teachers of content as they are teachers of method and process. Through subtlety and humor, and some cajoling, they help you discover that a learner-centered approach is more effective than a teacher-centered one and that using a methodology that requires patience and planning is necessary for making the change. This is difficult for me. As with most lawyers, flying by the seat of my pants has been the quickest way to get somewhere. But I'm a convert now, a true believer. I get it that learner-centered "dialogue education" works and that you have to follow a plan to get there.

Most of the time it's good to have a plan, but not always. I was reminded of that this week. A couple of days ago I received an email from Janelle Myers-Benner. Janelle is at Eastern Mennonite University and coordinates the Graduate Program in Conflict Transformation, which is housed in the Center for Justice and Peacebuilding. She wanted to know if I'd written my "graduation paragraph." I didn't want to admit it, but I'd spaced it. Not wanting to disappoint Janelle—she's been really good to me—I sat down last night to remember how I got to where I am.

Five years ago I was a prosecutor, a little more than a year from retirement and wondering what to do with my life. I was one of those soon-to-be-retired-and-without-a-plan people. While sitting in a lecture with a hundred other prosecutors at a conference that had nothing to do with what my heart wanted, the question came: Am I too old to go back to school? A friend had told me about Eastern Mennonite University and the incredible experience she had at the Summer Peacebuilding Institute. During a break at the conference I got online, read about Eastern Mennonite, the people who come from all over the world, the course offerings that open doors to work that is more than work, the stories of newly discovered meaning, the transformation that is possible no matter who you are and what conflict you are in. During the lunch hour I dialed the number for the Center and spoke to Janelle for the first time. I think she answered yes to every question I asked. The following January I arrived in Harrisonburg for an intense one-week training called "Strategies for Trauma Awareness and Resilience." By the end of the week my life had changed. My practice as a mediator would change as well.

Other courses followed. One on Circle Keeping. Two weeks after completing it I facilitated a Peacemaking Circle at a maximum-security prison. One on conflict analysis allowed me to work over a six-month period with a Catholic Worker community in conflict. A third, on advanced issues in restorative justice, introduced me to blogging, restorative justice practitioners from around the world, and the possibility that restorative justice might someday become a social movement.

While I still didn't have a retirement plan, the courses and the people at Eastern Mennonite nudged me in a particular direction. I worked for a year and a half as the director of mediation services at a nonprofit in Des Moines. That led to helping start the Center for Restorative Justice at First Parish Church, which led to becoming a community organizer for several Des Moines area churches. After a while I accepted the position of Justice Coordinator with the Restorative Justice Institute of Maine.

I don't think that five years ago I could have come up with a plan that would have ended with where I am today. There are times when our limited consciousness is incapable of such things. But sitting here at Logan Airport, waiting for my flight to Minneapolis, I am reminded of the psychologist James Hillman and his acorn theory. Hillman suggests that our psyche contains a "superior factor" that aids us in the discovery of our individual nature and our life's calling. I think that means there is a planner in each of us that oftentimes doesn't care a whole lot about what we think we want. More important is what we are meant to be.

Thoughts on Kindness

Holy Week takes me to a place that has little to do with my present belief system. Jesus' arrival in Jerusalem thrusts me back to a time before the onset of skepticism and teenage logic. The world slows down, and I find myself serving Mass again at the Basilica of St. John in Des Moines. For the three years before high school I was an altar boy. Wearing a black cassock with a white surplice over it,

I entered a realm beyond the drab and the mundane. Latin was the language there, and mystery was its waters.

I'm reminded of the nuns who also wore black and white. They lived in community, across the street from the church and a block from the school. In school I was occasionally sent to deliver something there, or to retrieve something one of the sisters needed for the day's instruction. Every time I entered their home I was greeted by one of the retired nuns. They treated me like a guest and always gave me a cookie or piece of candy. I was never rushed out the door or told I had to get back to school, and I was always treated with kindness. Back in the classroom, I had two recurrent thoughts: How do they go to the bathroom under all of that? and There really are people in this world who do things out of kindness and not for personal gain.

* * *

On the drive from St. Paul, Minnesota, this morning I asked Sarah and Mary if they wanted to stop for breakfast. Sarah said she wasn't hungry; she'd been up in the middle of the night and had eaten a slice of pizza. I asked if it was a leftover. She said it was, from a pizza she purchased the day before for herself and a homeless man. I asked how that came about. She said she doesn't have time to volunteer at a shelter so she often looks for an opportunity to purchase a meal for a street person. She will see someone and ask if they are hungry. The initial response is usually "No, but thank you." Sarah is persistent, though, and will reply that she's going to buy herself something and would like to share it. Almost always she then has a companion for lunch.

* * *

This evening at Good Friday service Mr. Sheaff sat in front of us. For years he's been the theater director at the local Catholic high school. He has seven kids. One of them, Bridget, is a longtime classmate of Mary's. I coached Bridget in basketball beginning in the second grade. That entire season Bridget never made a basket, either in practice or in a game. The same was true the next season. As a fourth grader she started to understand layups and made a few in practice. For the season, though, she went scoreless. At the beginning of fifth grade Bridget told me it would be her last season. She said she wasn't cut out for basketball. I told Bridget if she came early to practice we could work on her game. She oftentimes did, and her layups improved. Eventually, the last game arrived. Bridget had yet to score that season. It was a back-and-forth game, but with a minute to go we held a four-point lead. Bridget still had yet to score. With fifteen seconds left, I called a time-out. We all agreed that Bridget had to score. I drew up a play. Rose would set a screen. Bridget would be free in the middle of the lane, ten feet from the basket. Mary would inbound, fake to Emmy, and feed Bridget. The play worked to perfection. Bridget swished it from eight feet. The girls went wild and hugged Bridget until she cried for help. After the game, as Mary and I walked through the parking lot, we saw Bridget and her father in their car and approached. Mr. Sheaff had never spoken a word to me in four seasons. We congratulated Bridget on her game. Her father stuck out his hand and shook both Mary's and mine. He said, "Thank you." I said Bridget had a great game. His eyes welled up with tears. He said, "I really mean it. Thank you." Mary has never forgotten that, nor have I.

* * *

There is a story about a Buddhist monk who was meeting with a famous old lama for the last time. The master beckoned the student to approach. He did, believing he would receive the master's most secret instruction. The master whispered his final teaching: "Be kind."

Time to Speak Up

This afternoon I met a woman for coffee in Ankeny, Iowa, about halfway between her home and mine. Recently turned sixty, she is a community organizer. But not in the traditional sense—she doesn't organize around issues. Instead, she organizes around hope. For the past eighteen years she's worked in her community with those without a voice—the poor and the mentally ill. She helps them create and maintain their own community. They meet weekly, in a Circle, and share their struggles. She has found, as they have, that by using a talking piece they are empowered to speak their truth in a way previously denied them. From time to time they have conflicts. As a result, she has learned how to help them manage conflict. She has trained as a mediator and uses her skills, and her ability to listen, to help those in conflict find common ground.

She shared some of her life with me. Born and raised middle class, she was always the quiet one. She suffered with depression, although she didn't know what to call it. It was years before she discovered she had celiac disease, which causes her to have significant mood swings. To be with others made her uneasy, so she kept to herself. She was particularly averse to conflict and avoided it at all cost. But now she advocates for people who have yet to find their own voice and mediates with people who have yet to learn the skills of compromise and reconciliation. She is also a conflict coach, meeting privately with individuals to help them discover their own strengths so they can dialogue with people they have disagreements with. She is presently working with an individual with Asperger's syndrome. They practice the art of conversation, the give and take of it, so the awkwardness of social interaction is lessened.

Our conversation turned to restorative justice. She says it meets her need for inclusiveness. Having worked with the marginalized for so many years, she has come to realize the extent to which there is community is the extent to which each individual is recognized as indispensable. She is particularly sensitive now to the way the justice system works, how it ostracizes. She sees the poor, the mentally ill, and people of color increasingly filling our jails and prisons. She is ready to enlarge the scope of her community organizing efforts. She wants to join with others, those who organize and those who are silent, to engage in dialogue about what justice is and what it could be. Having been silent for so many years, she says it's time to speak up.

Communities of Resistance

Thich Nhat Hanh and Daniel Berrigan met in Paris in 1975. U.S. military involvement in Vietnam had ended two years earlier. The two great peace activists, one a Buddhist monk, the other a Jesuit priest, talked about the war, its destruction, the aftermath, and the many levels of casualties. Relevant for today was their conversation about "communities of resistance." They didn't limit their conversation to resistance against war. In fact, they broadened the definition of war beyond that of a military conflict engaged in by combatants. For both men, resistance must extend to all things that are like war. There must be resistance to anything in modern society that makes it difficult for the individual to retain integrity and wholeness.

I have a friend who is a community organizer. The son of a minister, he learned about organizing from his father, who didn't just preach economic and social equality from the pulpit, but fought for it in his rural Nebraska community, which was in danger of dying at the hands of big banking. My friend says community organizing must have two qualities: It must be against the forces in a community that diminish people, and it must be in favor of community institutions, churches included, that provide a buffer between the people and the dominant culture that deadens.

I thought of Daniel Berrigan, Thich Nhat Hahn, and my friend earlier this week while facilitating a Circle at a church in Des Moines. Ministers and staff met for six hours to celebrate the work the church does in its neighborhood. And they met in the hope of improving relationships within the church so the good work can continue. Despite the best of intentions, time had taken a toll. Slights, even minor ones, had led to withdrawal and distrust. Friendships had been damaged, and others suffered as a result. The first two hours were spent getting to know one another and learning about the values and joys of each person. Only by taking the time to relate was it possible to move on to issues that threatened the viability of the church's mission. People began to open up, sharing what brought meaning to their work and what saddened them about the present difficulties. The sharing allowed for a discussion about communication—the lack of it and how it can be improved. Honesty and vulnerability went hand in hand:

> "Triangulation is an issue for me."
>
> "If I have a problem with someone, I should take time with them."
>
> "I see generational problems here and I need to help bridge the divide."
>
> "Different levels of communication lead to difficulties."
>
> "Face-to-face communication is best."
>
> "I need to be able to speak with others without getting emotional."
>
> "It takes effort to learn what others are doing."
>
> "It takes intention to know who someone is."
>
> "A lot of grace is needed everywhere."

The Circle process has an internal clock. While not every issue was resolved, the group knew when it was time to end for the day. Resolutions were made to continue the conversation. Difficult work had been accomplished. Trust was possible again. What Daniel Berrigan and Thich Nhat Hahn termed "communities of resistance" might also be called "communities of restoration" or "communities of trust." Those who seek to be healers must heal themselves first. If the world is to be healed, those working alone will need to start working together. It will take communities working within larger communities.

Restorative Justice Musings

For years I've wondered what a restorative justice system would look like. As far back as the mid-1990s I would attend restorative justice conferences and corner experts who had researched and written about program design, best practices, effective processes, and success stories. When I could get one of them alone I would ask the question that begged for an answer: "But what would a restorative justice system look like?" Without exception, the question would be followed by a silence of one length or another, and then, "I don't really know."

At first it seems preposterous that the many fine minds that have thought deeply about restorative justice for decades have not come up with a schematic of a restorative justice system rivaling the present system, which so effectively grinds out justice. Even more than a schematic, why hasn't a team of experts identified the ideal city, descended upon it, and made the commitment to move it from a retributive city to a restorative one? Perhaps the answer lies in the fact that the present system is so complicated and convoluted that few people, experts included, can tell how it works down to the minute details. Without understanding the machine as it is, how can even the experts come up with a machine to replace it?

But where would you start? What would be the ideal incubator or laboratory for a grand restorative justice experiment? We are often told that politics is local. When you consider where most of our justice is meted out, it can be said that justice is also local. Where most people experience justice—and injustice—is in their own communities. That's where the schools are, the police, the lawyers, the judges, and the courthouse. It's where the crime is. Nearly all the makings of a justice system can be found in communities of ten thousand or more. In Iowa, there are ninety-nine counties, each with a county courthouse. (Lee County has two courthouses.) Most county seat towns in Iowa have a population between five and fifteen thousand people. Each has its own justice system. Why not start there? Why not pull a few good minds together, maybe even a design engineer from BMW or Mercedes, and start at square one? Chances are, square one would be the town square. That's where you find the locals. You would want to sit with them. Invite them one or two at a time to have coffee. Find out what their attitudes are about justice, what experience they've had with their justice system, and what they think of it.

My guess is that before those wonderful German engineers start designing and building a new model, they sit down with a lot of folks and find out what they like and don't like with the cars they are already driving. They ask a lot of questions and make few assumptions. When it's all said and done, they design and construct a product that works for the people.

There's No Substitute for Experience

Eight of us met last evening in an upstairs room at First Parish Church. The director of the Portland Center for Restorative Justice and I engaged six newcomers in a lengthy role-play. The volunteers took turns playing a part—the adult victim of a burglary, the teenage offender, the mediator. Lecture all you want, talk about philosophy and principles, but it takes role-playing to get people to a point where they actually feel the process.

I'm always fascinated by the transition from problem solver and fixer to listener and mediator. A few take to it quickly. For many it's a struggle. And for some, try as they might, it never happens. One of the naturals arrived a little late. During a break, she apologized. She had been at her seventeen-year-old son's baseball game. I asked how it went. She said he had a hit, his first in four years. After the game he was ecstatic and declared that by the end of the season he would be hitting home runs. Then she told me that despite his modest success, he plays for the love of the game.

I'm reminded of a case I prosecuted a few years ago. It involved another high school senior. School had let out, and on his walk home he was jumped. Three boys took him to the ground. He was hit and kicked, and somewhere in the struggle a knife came out. A single thrust lacerated his spleen, and he was left in a pool of blood. An elderly woman walking her dog saw everything and called the police. An eight-hour surgery followed. The boy's parents were told afterward that the width of a quarter had been the difference between life and death. It didn't take long for the three boys to be identified, arrested, and charged. Kids talk. All three were nearly sixteen. Had they been a few months older, they would have been charged as adults. Even at fifteen that was still a possibility. If convicted in the adult system, a lengthy prison sentence would follow.

Early on, that's what the parents of the injured boy wanted. They had nearly lost their son and, as punishment, they wanted the perpetrators to lose their youth. But an attorney for one of the boys called to see if there might be a different way to hold the boys accountable.

It is a challenge sometimes to explain to the uninitiated what restorative justice offers that our retributive system can't. Like love and compassion, it must be experienced.

The attorney was a longtime advocate for juveniles caught up in the system. He had seen how restorative justice could help make sense out of a senseless act. We talked at length about the need for the victim and his parents to be included in the discussions. Conversations were held. The pros and cons were explored. The parents finally agreed that they and their son needed to meet the three boys and tell them how their lives had been changed by their acts of brutality.

I will never forget the evening when everyone came together. The parents were nervous, as was their son. The three boys feared for their lives. One of our best mediators would facilitate the dialogue. He was skilled in managing the complexities of anger, fear, and shame. The injured boy's mother spoke first and then his father. They told of receiving the call, of rushing to the hospital, of waiting helplessly through the night. They described the tense days that followed, when survival was not assured. They told of their concern for their other son, his identical twin, and how they later kept both boys home for fear of retaliation.

The offenders sat motionless. Not one of them appeared moved by what had been said. Then the young victim spoke. He told of his love for baseball. How every year he looked forward to the coming of spring. How this was to be his last season and how, having grown three inches and gained twenty pounds over the winter, he hoped to hit his first home run. He described what it was like to sit on the bench the entire season, keeping score while his teammates went on to win the championship. He looked at the boys across from him and started to cry, sharing how it felt to have baseball stolen from him. The three started to cry as well. Nothing was said for several minutes. And then the injured boy looked at the three again and told them he forgave them.

It is a challenge sometimes to explain to the uninitiated what restorative justice offers that our retributive system can't. Like love and compassion, it must be experienced.

A Fire in the Center

I had a dream last night. It was about justice. I'm sure it was prompted by the ACLU of Maine Justice annual award dinner, which I attended earlier in the evening. There were stories told of justice, the struggle and the fight for it on behalf of individuals and of groups. On the drive home I felt proud to be a lawyer. I woke from my dream in search of a metaphor—not for justice as we know it, but for restorative justice, that toddler trying so hard to find its legs.

In the shower I thought of the elephant and the blind men, and how each man believed that what he touched was the whole truth. The story became a daydream, and I saw one man holding tight to the tail. He proclaimed that he had found it, that school conferencing was restorative justice and that Bethlehem, Pennsylvania, is its holy city. A second man grabbed a leg, asserting that victim–offender dialogue is restorative justice. A third man clutched another leg, shouting out that youth court is restorative justice. Then a fourth man said it's community restorative boards, and a fifth said it's restorative circles. A sixth man, riding on top of the great beast, said that restorative conferencing is what restorative justice is all about.

I finished my shower, but I wasn't satisfied because the elephant story was incomplete. It spoke of processes but was lacking in some way. I remembered the passage from the Book of John: "In my Father's house are many rooms." Perhaps restorative justice is like a house where place is as important as process. In my mind's eye I could see a mansion with long hallways and rooms of various sizes and uses throughout. I opened one door after another. There were schools, churches, workplaces, neighborhoods, justice systems, jails, and prisons—each one a place in need of healing and an opportunity for restorative justice. I liked this image, but I'm not sure that Jesus had such a dwelling in mind. It's too Western and too segregated. Maybe a Mediterranean house provides a better image, with its doors opening to a common courtyard. Or perhaps better yet is the image of a traditional Kenyan or Navajo village with thatched huts or teepees opening to the communal fire. In the village everyone participates in the life of the community, whether to celebrate a wedding, honor the passing of an elder, or meet in a Circle to weigh the effects of a harm inflicted by one on another.

And then the young Perceval and the search for the Holy Grail came to mind. It could be that the Grail myth is an appropriate metaphor for restorative justice, unattainable and yet worth pursuing. The Grail was thought to be a container for what is most precious. For the Celts it was a symbol of plenty, and for early Christians it symbolized eternal life. Psychologically it's a symbol for wholeness never to be completely realized.

A few years ago I took a course on advanced issues in restorative justice. There was great discussion about what restorative justice is, is not, and could be. Near the end of one class, Howard Zehr commented that he had long thought of restorative justice as a flame or spark, that it informs our work without defining it. Maybe that's why the image of an indigenous village resonates—the communal circle around a fire in the center.

The Circle Process in the Service of Truth

My son is a young trial attorney. To further his education, I recently gave him my well-worn copy of Francis Wellman's *The Art of Cross-Examination*. It's a classic, recommended by my trial advocacy professor when I was in law school. Wellman cites numerous examples from famous and not so famous trials, giving credence to John Henry

Wigmore's assertion that cross-examination is the great engine of truth.

As a young criminal defense attorney I witnessed its power. My client, an eighteen-year-old boy, was charged with first-degree murder in the death of his girlfriend. He swore it was an accident following a night of drinking at the neighborhood bar. The prosecutor saw it otherwise and was seeking life in prison without parole. The State's key witness was the coroner, who testified on direct examination that an intentional blow caused the girl's death. I was convinced the coroner had botched the autopsy, but he stuck to his opinion. It was only through cross-examination that the truth came out. The jury returned a verdict of involuntary manslaughter, and the young man was given a five-year sentence.

Trial by jury is a foundation of our democracy. It's designed to reveal the truth to a panel of the defendant's peers. But it's not perfect. Overreaching prosecutors or incompetent defense attorneys can lead to a result that fails to reflect what actually happened. Complicit, oftentimes, is cross-examination, that great engine of truth, which can be lethal when employed by experienced win-at-all-cost lawyers or by novices. Even when the playing field is level, the real truth may never come out.

I thought of this during a phone conversation this morning with Frank Cordaro, the former priest who cofounded the Des Moines Catholic Worker community in the late '70s. Frank has seen more than his share of trials. For more than thirty years he has exercised his conscience and has been charged on numerous occasions with criminal offenses resulting from his protest activities. Like many of this country's great dissenters, Frank has served jail and prison time in cells throughout the country. Unlike others who break the law, dissenters want to get caught. They stage their actions before reporters and cameras, hoping the brief news coverage will somehow influence public opinion.

I once prosecuted Frank. He and other Catholic Worker protestors had crossed a protest line at the Iowa Air National Guard, where fighter jets were being deployed to the Middle East. Twenty were arrested, but by the day of the trial, Frank and all of the other protesters had entered guilty pleas except one, Michael. He told the story of the international law violations that occurred as the result of the no-fly zone operations over Iraq that were conducted by our government. The jury trial lasted five days. Constitutional law experts testified, as did National Guard attorneys and other personnel. The jury returned a verdict of trespass and the judge imposed a small fine. A judge, a prosecutor, a defense attorney, expert witnesses, a court reporter, a court attendant, and six jurors had been employed in order to obtain the result.

This past St. Patrick's Day another Catholic Worker action was held at the Air National Guard, now a drone site. Seven were arrested, and the trial is set for late June. I've been asked to assist in the defense. A few weeks ago Frank told me he was considering another way for the truth to be told. The reason for his call this morning was to continue that conversation. He wondered about mediation. I said I didn't think there was anything to mediate and that a compromise wasn't possible.We then talked about the use of a peace-making Circle. What if the seven defendants and an equal number of guard personnel sat in a Circle with a Circle Keeper present to facilitate the conversation? What if, like a trial, the process was open to the public? Anyone could attend, sit outside the Circle, and listen to everything said. There would be truth telling—by the defendants and by the National Guard. There would be no attempt to reach consensus. It wouldn't be possible. The protestors abhor the use of drones. The Guard personnel, while perhaps sympathetic to the protestors, have chosen to join the Guard and have a job to do. Each side has a truth. Each side is unwavering. But unlike cross-examination, with its potential for abuse, the Circle process is a sacred one—one that honors each person's truth no matter the chasm between. And wouldn't the sharing of these truths in the presence of the community at large render a great service?

Justice Is Local

It's interesting to think of justice as local but it's easy to forget. We're more likely to think of justice as top-down, with Congress, the Supreme Court, state legislatures, and state courts grabbing the headlines. Each has a role, making the rules and interpreting them. Without them, there would be no "Rule of Law." Without the Rule of Law, there would be chaos. Civilization as we know it would cease to exist. Travel to any number of foreign countries and you will know this. But laws do not necessarily equal justice, unless justice is defined narrowly as the consequence imposed as the result of a violation. But there are times when temperance is required, times when the laws applied to a particular situation don't really fit, times when the consequences outweigh the seriousness of the conduct.

Last week I listened to a lawyer with fifty years of practice under his belt speak about the need for rewriting the Maine criminal code. He said it was last done in the '70s, and it's time again. Many of the laws on the books are antiquated and irrelevant. Times change, and our laws need to change with them.

Last night I was at a pub in downtown Portland. Five guys were making great music with their fiddles and acoustic guitars. During a break I spoke with the lead, a man in his sixties who makes violins during the day. He told me it's against the law in Maine to have two stages with live music within a hundred feet of one another. He pointed across the street at a bar that also hosts musicians. Because the two establishments are less than a hundred feet apart, they can't have music playing at the same time. Then he told me there's another silly law that says a musician can't stand up and have a beer in his hand. If he's sitting down, it's ok. He said recently a local Cajun band was playing at the same pub, near the window that looked out on the street. A police officer saw one of the band members standing up with a drink in his hand. The band lost its gig and the proprietor was fined a thousand dollars.

These examples might seem petty, but the point is that even with the best of laws, there must be temperance. There must be the exercise of reasonable discretion. This is particularly true when it comes to kids.

Sixteen-year-olds may be as tall as adults, may weigh as much or more, but they don't have the brain of an adult. The neuroscientists are teaching us this. The risks teenagers take, the decisions they make—these are not thought through with the aid of a mature brain. Compound that with what we know about early childhood trauma and we find ourselves with a canon of laws and a justice system not suited to respond to the misbehavior of our youth. That's why there must be reasonable discretion. Sometimes law enforcement exercises it and sometimes it does not. The same is true of juvenile corrections officers and juvenile prosecutors.

It's easy to get frustrated with and angry at kids who commit offenses that, if they were eighteen, would be considered crimes. But we can't ignore the science, and we must be cognizant of the unintended consequences that can result when our schools and our justice systems label youth because of misbehavior.

Here in Maine there is something to be encouraged about. Communities are taking greater notice of kids caught up in our systems. Individuals are coming together to address the inequities and unfavorable outcomes. One thing being considered is the use of community review boards. Once in place, police officers will have the discretion to refer a teenager to a board of community members and professionals rather than to the formal system. The teenager, his or her parents, and members of the board will meet collaboratively, placing equal emphasis on the needs of the teenager and the community's need for accountability.

Justice is local. And because it's local, it's best served when the community realizes it has a stake in its administration and in its outcomes. This is particularly true when the lives of our kids are at stake.

Grandma's Story

It's Mother's Day. What they say is true: the loss is felt long after the burial. My mother died a week before Christmas seven years ago. Time doesn't make it easier. I've been thinking of my mother's story, how her life was forever changed by an indifferent and uncaring system and how she eventually overcame the blows the system inflicted upon her. My mother's story is similar to many people I have met, although the end is unique, as it is for all of us.

Lately I've been considering a different approach to my writing and bringing an end to the *Justice Diary* blog in its present form. A year ago, with one class left in my graduate studies at Eastern Mennonite University, I made a promise to Howard Zehr that I would blog for a year. In exchange, he said, I would earn three hours of credit. It sounded like a good deal, and I have to say I've enjoyed it for the most part. Howard told me last week that, as far as he's concerned, I've blogged enough. And the folks at EMU say I get to graduate. But to some extent I've not done what I set out to do.

I was talking recently with a friend, a fellow introvert. We were discussing why it is that introverts often have a need to write. We considered various reasons. Then it struck me. We write to finish our sentences. Extroverts, wonderful people that they are, don't understand this. They rarely have trouble getting in the last word. But as an introvert, I can attest to the innumerable times when I didn't start a sentence, knowing there was little chance of a successful conclusion. I think that's why what I'd hoped to do with blogging didn't happen. What I wanted to do was to explore justice through the stories of others. I wanted to learn about justice as James Baldwin exhorted, to go to the unprotected and listen to their testimony.

I haven't done that—I suppose because I had some things to say. I had some sentences I needed to finish. But now I'm ready to learn from others. I'm not sure what a new project will look like. I need time to think about it. I know there are questions I want to ask of the unprotected. I know it's their testimony that's more important than my own. Perhaps I'll take one city, Portland perhaps, and scratch below the surface, dig deeper and give voice to those not normally heard.

In the meantime, I'll catch up on some reading. I'll mow the lawn and take my grandson on bike rides. And I'll give serious thought to those who need the law's protection most.

With Mother's Day nearly over, I'm thinking of my mother's story. She knew some things about justice and injustice. Quite a bit actually. At her funeral service I attempted to tell her story for the benefit of her grandchildren. What I shared with them is some of what they know as "Grandma's Story":

It's customary at services like these for people to pay tribute to a loved one. My mom wasn't one for tributes. She thought they were boring, and she would have said she didn't deserve one. Instead, I think my mom would have wanted someone to tell her story. She would have wanted those she cared about to understand her for her accomplishments and her failures. She would have wanted her story told to her grandchildren, whom she loved more than anything in the world. To the extent anyone can tell another's story, I want to do that for my children so when they are asked someday by their children what their grandmother was like, they will have something to add to what they already know from their own experience. So this story is for you, her twenty grandchildren.

More than anything, your grandma was a complicated woman. Her mother and her father studied at Iowa State University. Her father was an electrical engineer and her mother an accountant. Her grandfather, the Dutch one, was a lawyer, and for a while was the city attorney for Des Moines. Her German grandfather helped run the family brewery in Dubuque. Your grandma also had a sister, the obedient one.

Your grandma grew up in a home with a lot of rules and very little love. Because of that, she became a rebel of sorts. Your grandma was also very smart—smart enough to skip two grades at Visitation Elementary School. When it came time to attend high school she was offered a full scholarship to the Academy, the all-girls Catholic high school on the other side of town. She refused to go. She couldn't understand why anyone would want to go to a school with no boys. She went to East High School instead and, by all accounts, was the one you'd want to have at your party. She was funny, witty, and knew everyone. Your grandma was also a good athlete and loved to swim. She won a lot of races until she was stricken with polio. When it came time to go to college your grandma again was offered scholarships. But she refused to go. She said she was going to marry her high school sweetheart, the wrestling star who was also the life of the party. Your grandma did what she said she would do, perhaps out of love and perhaps to spite her parents.

Like most girls, your grandma wasn't ready to be married at eighteen. She also wasn't ready to be a mom at nineteen, at twenty-one, at twenty-three, at twenty-five, and at twenty-eight. She was a strong woman, but not strong enough to be the mother of five children at such a young age. Your grandma had been strong enough to overcome the disease of polio. She was not strong enough to overcome another disease—depression, which crippled her more than polio ever did. And when she divorced your grandpa at the age of thirty, the disease paralyzed her. Your grandma was smart, but she didn't have the skills to take care of herself and her five children. She had never known poverty, but she found herself having to navigate the welfare system, waiting for the monthly check, waiting for the food stamps to come, waiting in long lines to get government peanut butter and cheese, waiting to see if she could get help so she and her kids wouldn't get evicted. Ultimately, your grandma's disease left her unable to parent. When the authorities came and took her five children away, she had to be taken away too.

At that time, the disease of depression was not well understood. People thought the best way to fix your grandma was with hospitals and electrical shock treatments. They were wrong. The best way would have been to give her the love and support she needed so badly. That never happened, and your grandma never got her children back—except one.

For a long time, your grandma was bitter at the system that never came to her aid. But she was smart, and she was also courageous. She woke up one day and said she was going to fix herself. She started taking college classes while working as a store clerk. She quit that job when Judge Harrison hired her to work at the county substance abuse center.

It turns out your grandma had a gift for helping people who had been laid low by life. It also turned out that your grandma's bitterness against a system that never came to her aid blossomed into a compassion for those caught up in that same system. Your grandma's compassion enabled her to get up in the middle of many nights when the calls would come from an alcoholic or a heroin addict or a crackhead. She would always respond. It didn't take long for the authorities to say that your grandma should be in charge of the county programs for helping people with substance abuse problems. She was the best person for the job, and she did it well. Then the authorities called. They said she was the best person to run the county's General Relief Program—the program that helped moms and kids who were getting evicted, who had run out of food stamps, or who were having their electricity turned off. Your grandma took that job and helped a lot of people there too.

Your grandma wasn't perfect. She sometimes got in trouble for breaking the rules. She couldn't understand why there would be a rule that said a mom couldn't get help just because she had gotten help nine months before. But they couldn't fire your grandma because she helped too many people, and she was the best person for the job.

The authorities called your grandma again. They said she was the best person to run the county programs that helped old people. She didn't want to stop helping moms and families, but she decided to take the new job—perhaps she was thinking of the day when she would be old. You know this part of your grandma's story. She helped a lot of old people. She helped get them meals when they couldn't get out of the house. She got them fans when the temperature in their apartments was 95 degrees. She helped them get money for rent when their landlords wanted to evict them. And when she had to, she broke the rules.

When I was going through some of your grandma's papers yesterday, I found a job evaluation her boss had written when she was running the programs for the elderly. The evaluation said your grandma was very good at all she did. It ended with the statement, "If one can tolerate individuality in an employee, then Mary is an asset."

Your grandma had to stop working just before she turned sixty. Her mind was still sharp, but her health was poor—and she was still haunted by depression. Without the work that meant so much to her, she was oftentimes hard to deal with. But she always loved her grandchildren. As you know, two years ago we took your grandma to Kavanagh House. They said she had two weeks to live. She had ideas of her own. Eight months later they said she had to leave because she hadn't died soon enough. With the help of hospice nurses, she stayed with us for the next six months. It was oftentimes challenging, but also a blessing. We finally had to put your grandma in a nursing home because the hospice nurses said they couldn't come any more. They said your grandma wasn't going to die anytime soon. We thought she wouldn't last long in the nursing home, but we were wrong. She met Willa there.

Willa was your grandma's roommate. She was ninety-nine years old, the daughter of a slave, and the loving mother your grandma never had. There were times when I would visit your grandma late at night. She and Willa would be holding hands. Your grandma was oftentimes in a lot of pain, and Willa would get out of bed to comfort her. Many people cared for your grandma, loving her, each in their own way. But Willa was the first person in your grandma's life who loved her unconditionally. Willa brought out the best in her. The last few months of your grandma's life were times of both pain and peace. Near the end, she shared her love uncon-ditionally with those around her. When your grandma was moved to a second nursing home, it broke her heart to be separated from Willa. But she didn't give in.

A week ago yesterday she was taken by ambulance to the hospital in Des Moines. It looked like she didn't have long to live. When she was lying on the gurney in the emergency room she pulled me close and said: "I could have died tonight but I decided not to. Is that alright?" Your grandma didn't die that night, and they took her back to the nursing home. Two days later we took her a small Christmas tree. When she saw us she was an expression of pure joy. Shortly after that she went to sleep and never woke up.

Your grandma's story is one of promise, rebellion, despair, courage, accomplishment, suffering, and, ultimately, redemption. But your grandma was more than her story. As I said earlier, your grandma was a complicated woman. She loved politics, and she loved the Democratic Party, with all of its faults. Your grandma was always asking about the courthouse and what boneheaded thing the Board of Supervisors had done. She loved John Kennedy and hated Richard Nixon. She loved Bill Clinton and hated George Bush, both of them. Your grandma loved ideas, controversy, and debate, and she loved Larry King. Your grandma loved to travel, when she finally had the resources to do so. But she didn't go to Paris and Rome like others. Instead, she went to Russia—four times. She loved to talk to people there about their struggles. Your grandma hated the Nazis and was fascinated by the Holocaust. The last trip she took was to Poland—she had to visit Auschwitz. And finally, your grandma loved her church, particularly Jesus' mother, and all the Marys of the New Testament.

If your grandma were here today, she would tell you to engage in the struggles of the world and debate the burning issues of our time. She would tell you to never stop learning. She would tell you to lift up those who have fallen and always be kind to strangers. She would tell you to hug those who are close to you and never forget to tell them you love them. And finally, she would tell you to never, never become a Republican.

Epilogue

In the early '90s, when I was first getting my feet wet with restorative justice, I would frequently telephone crime victims. The reason for the calls was to offer victims the opportunity to meet with offenders in what we then called "victim–offender mediations." But before I would ask the ultimate question, I would first let them talk. I would encourage them to tell their stories of victimization, the how and the when of the offense, and the journeys they had traveled since the day their lives were changed. I would then ask, "What should justice look like?" Most often, my question was greeted with silence. If, instead, I asked, "What should the punishment be?" most victims were quick to respond. However, an inquiry into justice in relation to what had happened created a dilemma. Justice was not part of their vernacular when it came to what should be done to the offender. But a justice inquiry was what was needed to open the door to a conversation about restorative justice and, ultimately, how a victim's real needs might be met by participating in a restorative process.

As time went on, and as the Polk County Restorative Justice Center developed the capacity to offer victim–offender mediation to a greater number of victims, staff was trained in the language of restorative justice. They became skilled in asking the questions necessary to open the door to conversations about how the victims had been hurt, what their needs were, and how their needs could be met. As a result, an increasing number of victims in our community experienced real justice through dialoguing with those who had hurt them. Offenders were also healed when given the opportunity to answer victims' questions, tell their own stories, and express feelings of remorse for their actions.

When I set out two years ago on my first *Justice Diary* road trip the question that drove me was: What does justice look like to the millions of people in this country who, in one way or another, encounter our criminal justice system? Many of the entries in this book offer individual answers to that question. But the more I traveled and the more I reflected, the more I returned to that earlier question, What should justice look like? and its companion question, How do we get there? It's clear that the community needs to be more involved in the local justice system. Advocacy groups need to be initiated, developed, and maintained. There must be a community entity that serves as a watchdog on the system.

What justice looks like now is being written about and talked about—in the *New York Times* and the *Des Moines Register*, on CNN and the *Daily Show*, on street corners and in coffee shops everywhere. That question can no longer be ignored, and the answers are forthcoming. We are learning all too much about police brutality, dishonest prosecutors, and indifferent judges. The questions must continue to be asked. We have to know the truth. But the truth isn't enough. We have to go further. We have to discern the true nature of justice and then begin the long, slow journey of constructing a justice system, and a just society, that looks at wrongdoing through a restorative lens rather than a punishment lens.

I have reason for optimism. Just recently, twenty Drake University students went through court watching training as a requirement for their restorative justice class. Their awareness about the system, and how individuals are treated within it, increased dramatically between the time they were trained in September and the time they reported on their experiences in early December.

Trainings have also been held for volunteers who are concerned about the school-to-prison pipeline, who believe that by getting upstream and serving as peacemakers within schools they can dramatically reduce the number of suspensions and arrests, thereby increasing the chances that our children will complete their educations. The "Let's Talk" program was created and volunteer mediators now serve in six middle schools in Des Moines. It is hoped that the program will expand to local high schools in the near future.

The AMOS racial profiling project created eighteen months ago in Des Moines is continuing. Organizers are now interviewing victims of racial profiling at African American barbershops. There is healing in the telling of their stories, and hopefully systemic change will result. The project has the attention of the Des Moines Police Department, resulting in the creation of a racial profiling task force. In recent weeks the DMPD has agreed to work with AMOS, Iowa Mediation Service, and the Des Moines Pastoral Counseling Center to create a "second chance" mediation program to keep juveniles out of the formal system. The DMPD has also agreed to participate in a series of community justice Circles, in which street officers sit with youth of color to share experiences and concerns.

I continue to spend significant time in Maine serving as the restorative practices coordinator for the Portland Center for Restorative Justice. The Center has trained a committed group of volunteers to facilitate victim–offender dialogues. In recent months we have conducted restorative justice trainings at a county jail and at a state prison. We are also involved in an ongoing restorative justice program with at-risk youth at a local high school.

If I have learned anything these last two years, it is that, like so many things in life, we get what we asked for. It has taken decades for us to make our criminal justice system what it is today—broken and in need of significant repair. The community—all of us—must share in the responsibility for causing the system to become an often destructive machine. For the most part, the community has left the system alone, and we are now paying the price. If we choose to do nothing, the brokenness will continue, resulting in broken lives and broken communities. However, if we take notice, become educated, and join with others in demanding justice, there is hope. It's a significant challenge and a difficult process. We have to get our hands dirty. We need more sermons and letters to our newspapers. We need an army of mediators. We need local justice centers to push back. We need ordinary citizens to take an interest and get involved in how we recruit and train police officers, prosecutors, and judges. It's a daunting task, but the alternative is a future that we do not want for our children and our grandchildren.

List of Entries

Notes

vii   **two metaphors for the knowledge-seeker**—Svend Brinkmann and Steinar Kvale, *InterViews: Learning the Craft of Qualitative Research Interviewing*, 3rd ed. (2015), 57–58.

5   **"Atonement"**—A version of this post was published in the *Des Moines Register* on April 22, 2012, under the title "Growing Past Hate— 'Restorative Justice' Helps Heal Pain from Teens' Vandalism."

12   **"We Need to Repair, Not Throw Away"**—A version of this post was published in the *Des Moines Register* on July 22, 2012.

12   **In less than thirty years**—Michelle Alexander, *The New Jim Crow: Mass Incarceration in the Age of Colorblindness* (2010), 6.

13   **children's diminished culpability**—*Miller v. Alabama* (2012), Justia: U.S. Supreme Court, https://supreme.justia.com/cases/federal/us/ 567/10-9646/opinion3.html.

14   **According to the Des Moines Police Department**—Personal communication with the Des Moines Police Department and the Polk County clerk.

15   **The criminals we incarcerate**—William J. Stuntz, *The Collapse of American Criminal Justice* (2011), 312.

16   **"Keeping an Eye on Justice"**—A version of this post was published in the *Des Moines Register* on January 5, 2013, under the title "Iowa Court Watchers Help Keep Eye on Justice."

34   **needed to examine all these circumstances**—*Miller v. Alabama* (2012), Justia: U.S. Supreme Court.

35   **I'd see the bus pass every day**—Rosa Parks, quoted on the Henry Ford Museum website, thehenryford.org: https://www.thehenryford .org/exhibits/rosaparks/story.asp.

36   **Many times I had problems with bus drivers**—Rosa Parks, quoted in "Remembering Rosa Parks on Her 100th Birthday," NPR, February 4, 2013, http://www.npr.org/2013/02/04/171079150/ remembering-rosa-parks-on-her-100th-birthday.

36   **I just sat in there for a moment**—Barack Obama, quoted in "President Obama Sits in Rosa Parks Bus," NPR, April 19, 2012, http://www.npr.org/blogs/thetwo-way/2012/04/19/150970124/ photo-president-obama-sits-in-rosa-parks-bus.

36   **if Martin Luther King Jr. is right**—Alexander, *The New Jim Crow*, 260.

44   **Iowa Board of Parole's 2011 report**—Iowa Board of Parole 2011 Annual Report, http://www.bop.state.ia.us/Document/67.

47   **There are more people who go to jail in hard times**—Clarence Darrow, "Address to the Prisoners in the Chicago Jail," http://www .bopsecrets.org/CF/darrow.htm.

49   **When I looked at Rutilio lying there dead**—Oscar Romero, quoted in "The Obama Diary," March 22, 2011, http://theobamadiary.com/ tag/romero/.

72   **These are the times that try men's souls**—Thomas Paine, "The Crisis" (1776), in *The Writings of Thomas Paine, Volume 1*, Project Gutenberg (2010), http://www.gutenberg.org/files/3741/3741-h/3741-h.htm.

79   **"the NYPD is laying 'siege'"**—Robert Gearty and Corky Siemaszko, "Controversial NYPD Stop and Frisk Tactic Goes on Trial after New Yorkers Claim It Violates Constitution," *New York Daily News*, March 18, 2013, http://www.nydailynews.com/new-york/nypd-stop-frisk -trial-article-1.1291774.

86   **We need to "go out"**—Pope Francis, quoted in *Independent Catholic News*, March 28, 2013, http://www.indcatholicnews.com/news .php?viewStory=22251.

98   **"Wealth Inequality in America"**—The video is available here at
      http://www.youtube.com/watch?v=QPKKQnijnsM.

99   **CCA manages more than sixty facilities**—"CCA Announces 2012
      Fourth Quarter Financial Results," Yahoo Finance, February 13,
      2013, http://finance.yahoo.com/news/cca-announces-2012-fourth
      -quarter-213000117.html.

99   **[John Baldwin] received a salary of $151,252**—Find the Best, Iowa
      State Employees, http://iowa-employees.findthebest.com/l/1835/
      John-R-Baldwin.

99   **Iowa football coach Kirk Ferentz**—Jason Clayworth, "Iowa Football
      Coach Kirk Ferentz Tops Highest Paid State Employee List," *Des
      Moines Register*, November 1, 2012, http://blogs.desmoinesregister
      .com/dmr/index.php/2012/11/01/new-iowa-state-worker-3-billion
      -salary-database-released/article.

100   **opens the door to the humanity of wrong-doing**—Molly Rowan
      Leach, "American Justice—For Profit Prisons or Truth?" *Huffington
      Post*, February 21, 2013, http://www.huffingtonpost.com/molly
      -rowan-leach/american-justice-for-prof_b_2735980.html.

106   **The entire legal profession**—Warren E. Burger, "The State of
      Justice," *ABA Journal*, April 1984, pages 62 and 66.

107   **Discourage litigation**—Abraham Lincoln Online, http://www
      .abrahamlincolnonline.org/lincoln/speeches/lawlect.htm.

108   **Lawyers are almost four times more likely**—Joseph G. Allegretti,
      The Lawyer's Calling: Christian Faith and Legal Practice (1996), 2–3.

108   **map without a meaning**—Steven Keeva, *Transforming Practices:
      Finding Joy and Satisfaction in the Legal Life* (2009).

108   **The competition started**—J. Kim Wright, *Lawyers as Peacemakers:
      Practicing Holistic, Problem-Solving Law* (2010), 8.

108   **too many lawyers hide**—Quoted in John W. Allen, "Lawyers as
      Healers: Feel Better About Yourself and the Law through Six Simple
      Suggestions," *Michigan Bar Journal* (October 2001), 43.

112   **There are very few**—Barack Obama, "Remarks by the President on
      Trayvon Martin," Office of the Press Secretary, White House, July
      19, 2013, http://www.whitehouse.gov/the-press-office/2013/07/19/
      remarks-president-trayvon-martin.

125   **The evidence is clear**—David A. Harris, testimony, "Ending
      Racial Profiling in America," hearing of the Subcommittee on the
      Constitution, Civil Rights and Human Rights of the U.S. Senate
      Judiciary Committee, April 17, 2012, emphasis original. http://www
      .aila.org/File/Related/12041748B.pdf.

129   **Whether because of public choice problems**—Neil Gorsuch, quoted
      in Vikrant P. Reddy, "Judge Neil Gorsuch on Overcriminalization,"
      RightOnCrime.com, November 18, 2013, http://www.rightoncrime
      .com/2013/11/judge-neil-gorsuch-on-overcriminalization/.

131   **Thrown into solitude**—Alexis de Tocqueville, quoted on the Eastern
      State Penitentiary home page, http://www.easternstate.org/learn/
      research-library/history.

132   **It was during those long and lonely years**—Nelson Mandela,
      "Nelson Mandela Reflects on Working Toward Peace," Santa Clara
      University Architects of Peace Project, www.scu.edu. http://www.scu
      .edu/ethics/architects-of-peace/Mandela/essay.html.

136   **Who are these so-called dissidents?**—Vaclav Havel, "The Power of
      the Powerless," in *Living in Truth* (1986), 36.

139   **Right now more than two million children**—Lauren E. Glaze and
      Laura M. Maruschak, "Parents in Prison and Their Minor Children,"
      U.S. Department of Justice, March 30, 2010, http://www.bjs.gov/
      content/pub/pdf/pptmc.pdf.

142   **Today, a vicious cycle of poverty**—Eric Holder, "Attorney General
      Eric Holder Delivers Remarks at the Annual Meeting of the
      American Bar Association's House of Delegates," U.S. Department
      of Justice, August 12, 2013, http://www.justice.gov/opa/speech/
      attorney-general-eric-holder-delivers-remarks-annual-meeting
      -american-bar-associations.

142   **There is an urgent need**—Newt Gingrich, quoted in "What
      Conservatives Are Saying," RightOnCrime.com, http://www
      .rightoncrime.com/the-conservative-case-for-reform/what
      -conservatives-are-saying/.

143   **Today's criminal justice system is big government**—Grover
      Norquist, quoted in "What Conservatives Are Saying,"
      RightOnCrime.com, http://www.rightoncrime.com/the-conservative
      -case-for-reform/what-conservatives-are-saying/.

143   **Conservatives are known for being tough on crime**—William
        Bennett, quoted in "What Conservatives Are Saying," RightOnCrime
        .com, http://www.rightoncrime.com/the-conservative-case-for-
        reform/what-conservatives-are-saying/.

146   **outrageously long drug sentences**—Editorial, "A Small Step Toward
        More Mercy," *New York Times*, December 22, 2013.

149   **What'd you do for Christmas?**—Transcript for "Fr. Greg Boyle—The
        Calling of Delight: Gangs, Service, and Kinship," NPR, *On Being
        with Krista Tippett*, February 26, 2013, http://www.onbeing.org/
        program/father-greg-boyle-on-the-calling-of-delight/transcript/5059.

154   **Whether the mask is labeled Fascism**—Simone Weil, quoted
        in "Sunbeams," *The Sun*, June 2014, http://thesunmagazine.org/
        issues/462/sunbeams.

156   **Will there never be any peace**—Thomas Merton, *A Year with Thomas
        Merton: Daily Meditations from His Journals* (2009), Kindle edition.

158   **One of the great liabilities of history**—Martin Luther King
        Jr., "MLK: Remaining Awake through a Revolution," quoted
        on the Invisible Children website, http://invisiblechildren.com/
        blog/2013/01/21/mlk-remaining-awake-through-a-revolution/.

158   **I would not accept the award**—Al Levie, quoted in Allen Clifton,
        "MLK Day Flashback: Teacher Refused Award from Paul Ryan,
        Called Him a 'Lackey for the 1%,'" Forward Progressives, January 20,
        2014, http://www.forwardprogressives.com/mlk-day-flashback
        -teacher-refused-award-from-paul-ryan-called-him-a-lackey-for-the
        -1-watch/.

160   **We cannot do everything**—Bishop Ken Untener of Saginaw,
        "Archbishop Oscar Romero Prayer: A Step Along the Way" (1979),
        United States Conference of Catholic Bishops, http://www.usccb
        .org/prayer-and-worship/prayers-and-devotions/prayers/archbishop_
        romero_prayer.cfm.

168   **1. Change the mission of the system**—David Link, quoted in Maura
        Poston Zagrans, *Camerado, I Give You My Hand: How a Powerful
        Lawyer-Turned-Priest Is Changing the Lives of Men Behind Bars* (2013),
        230–31.

171   **If I don't make it to sixty-five**—Thomas Merton, *A Year with Thomas
        Merton: Daily Meditations from His Journals* (2009), Kindle edition.

176 **A path is only a path**—Carlos Castaneda, *The Teachings of Don Juan: A Yaqui Way of Knowledge* (1985), 74–75.

180 **as if his life was a series of incomprehensible accidents**—Thomas Merton, *A Year with Thomas Merton: Daily Meditations from His Journals* (2009), Kindle edition.

189 **The nature of the conduct**—Eric Holder, quoted in Adam Goldman and Sari Horwitz, "U.S. to Seek Death Penalty in Boston Bombing Case," *Washington Post*, January 30, 2014, http://www.washington post.com/world/national-security/us-to-seek-death-penalty-in-boston -bombing-case/2014/01/30/c15465d8-8785-11e3-833c-33098f9e5267 _story.html.

189 **Dzhokhar both significantly contributed**—The Conference of Major Superiors of Men, quoted in Navar Watson, "Restorative Justice, Not Death Penalty, Urged for Accused Bomber," *National Catholic Reporter*, February 21, 2014, http://ncronline.org/news/peace-justice/ restorative-justice-not-death-penalty-urged-accused-bomber.

193 **Ray wrote a letter from his death row cell**—Ray Jasper, "A Letter from Ray Jasper, Who Is About to Be Executed," Gawker.com, March 4, 2014, http://gawker.com/a-letter-from-ray-jasper-who-is -about-to-be-executed-1536073598.

201 **What, over the last thirty years**—Paul LePage, quoted in "What Conservatives Are Saying," RightOnCrime.com, http://www .rightoncrime.com/the-conservative-case-for-reform/what -conservatives-are-saying/.

222 **Two roads diverged in a yellow wood**—Robert Frost, "The Road Not Taken," in *Mountain Interval* (1916).

CPSIA information can be obtained at www.ICGtesting.com
Printed in the USA
LVOW12s1452170515

438812LV00008B/8/P

9 780996 267908